It's Not the End of the World
It's Just the End of You

Spengler

channeled by
DAVID P. GOLDMAN

It's Not the End of the World
It's Just the End of You

THE GREAT EXTINCTION
OF THE NATIONS

RVP Publishers
New York

RVP Publishers Inc.

95 Morton Street, Ground Floor

New York, NY 10014

© 2011 David Goldman / RVP Publishers Inc.

First edition: September 2011

Photo cover: Yves Marchand & Romain Meffre

Library of Congress Control Number: 2011937241

ISBN 978-1-61412-202-9

www.rvpp.com

Contents

Introduction

Not since the 1930s has the leadership of the West seemed so dispirited and confused. In the darkest days of the Cold War, the West had at least a unified purpose and the appearance of solid alliance. Even when the United States seemed in decline, after Vietnam and Watergate and a decade of stagflation, and a handful of cynics forecast its decline, it came roaring back under the Reagan administration. America went on to lead the world into a quarter-century of unprecedented prosperity founded on the freeing of markets, and total victory over communism. Exactly thirty years after the fall of communism, though, America has lost its self-confidence, the European Community is at risk of disintegration, and vast areas of the developing world face intractable instability. America remains stuck in an economic slump for which no leader offers a credible cure, and its leaders no longer speak to an enervated electorate about a grand mission to bring democracy to the world.

How did it come to this? Conservatives have complained for

a generation that for all our economic and political victories, including control of the White House during five of the last eight administrations, we have lost the cultural war. But economics and politics ultimately are a function of culture, as we are learning to our dismay. In recent years, fiscal crises have dominated most of the capitals of the world's nations, not to mention most American statehouses. And the lingering effects of the American housing collapse of 2007 and 2008 continue to suppress economic activity in the world's largest economy. Yet all of these crises are manifestly of cultural origin: the industrial world failed to raise a new generation in adequate numbers, and the entitlements due to its retiring elderly threaten to swamp the capacity of governments to raise revenue. The problems range from barely soluble in the case of the United States, the only large industrial nation whose working-age population will continue to grow during the next forty years, to entirely insoluble, in the case of the southern European lands who barely raise one child per family and whose future workforce cannot sustain the needs of future retirees.

It is not only the industrial nations that threaten to founder on cultural failures. The so-called Arab Spring was not a leap into democracy but a swoon into societal failure. What prompted the popular uprisings across the Mediterranean coast from Tunisia to Syria was not a spontaneous desire to change political circumstances but rather the terrible realization that the backward, sclerotic, and tyrannical social system dominating most of the Arab world no longer could provide for the most basic needs of its people. The Arabs had grumbled in private against their overlords for more than half a century, but they revolted when the world market priced basic foodstuffs out of their reach. The great enemy of the Arab world, it turned out, was neither Israel nor America, but emerging Asia. The newly rich people of Asia can pay an arbitrarily large amount for grain, and Chinese pigs would eat before Arab peasants.

All of the foreign policy models are broken. Many of the essays included in the present volume were composed when the received wisdom in Washington held that America's democratic model could be exported, like a prefabricated sewage treatment plant. Since then the so-called Color Revolutions, without exception, have melted down and disappeared into the cracks. The Orange Revolution in Ukraine has ended with the Russian party in control, along with the Tulip Revolution in Kyrgyzstan, and the Cedar Revolution in Lebanon has ended with the Iranian party in control, along with the Purple Revolution in Iraq. In the first week of August 2011 an Egyptian mob chased the "Internet-savvy" democracy activists out of Tahrir Square, blaming them for the collapse of the Egyptian economy. Wael Ghonim, the Google employee who became the poster-boy for the Egyptian revolution, toured the United States accepting book deals and public service awards while Egypt plunged into deep economic distress. The *punditeska* barely had weeks to drool over these Nile apparitions of Western coolness before mourning their disappearance.

Turkey, the supposed exemplar of Muslim democracy, is turning by degrees into a repressive Islamist state that detains thousands of opponents for years without trial. Rather than emerging as the bridge between the West and the Muslim world, Turkey appears headed to become another basket case at Europe's periphery. The Bush administration's "Freedom Agenda" has not a single success to show for all of its efforts.

Virtually all the assumptions on which Western foreign policy was founded during the past decade have been refuted. Instead of emerging democratic states, America is looking at a sea of chaos from Libya to the Persian Gulf. But where is the self-critique, the questioning of assumptions, the sense of wonder and anguish at the failure of an entire generation's efforts to move from the victory in the Cold War to a calmer and better world? The policy elite of the United States is too busy guarding its reputations and renewing (when it can) its foundation grants from the dwindling pool of philanthropy to question its manner of thinking.

The economic doldrums in the West and the societal disaster in the Muslim world have a common origin. Modernity exchanged the calm tyranny of traditional society for the anomie of the atomized individual, who was free, that is, free to wander alone in the universe and ask for an indication of his significance from an unhearing and indifferent cosmos. The attenuation of faith in the West took three hundred years, until its last redoubt became the evangelical Christians and ethnic Catholics of the United States. With the end of faith came also the end of fertility. Parts of the Muslim world are repeating the Western experience in a single generation, with startling consequences. Today's average Iranian woman was raised in a family of seven children but will bear one or at most two children, such that Iran's population will age faster than the population of any country in recorded history.

During the too-brief run of the print edition of the *Asia Times* in the 1990s, the newspaper asked me to write a humor column, and I chose the name Spengler, as a joke—a columnist for an Asian daily using the name of the author of *The Decline of the West*. Barely a dozen "Spengler" items appeared before the print edition went down in the 1997 Asian financial crisis. A malicious thought crossed my mind in 1999, though, as the Internet euphoria engulfed world markets: Was it really possible for a medium whose premise was the rise of a homogeneous global youth culture to drive world economic growth? Youth culture, I argued, was an oxymoron, for culture itself was a bridge across generations, a means of cheating mortality. The old and angry cultures of the world, fighting for room to breathe against the onset of globalization, would not go quietly into the homogenizer. Many of them would fight to survive, but fight in vain, for the tide of modernity could not be rolled back.

As in the great extinction of the tribes in late antiquity, individuals might save themselves from the incurable necrosis of their own ethnicity through adoption into the eternal people—that is, Israel. The great German Jewish theologian and student of the existential angst of dying nations, Franz Rosenzweig, had commanded my undivided attention during the 1990s, and I had published a pair of essays about him for the Jewish–Christian Relations website. Rosenzweig's theology, or, better put, his sociology of religion, had broader applications. The end of the old ethnicities, I believed, would dominate the cultural and strategic agenda of the next several decades. Great countries were failing in their will to live, and it was easy to imagine a world in which Japanese, German, Italian, and Russian would turn into dying languages only a century hence. Modernity taxed the Muslim world even more severely, although the results sometimes were less obvious.

The three hundred or so essays that I have published under the name Spengler since 1999 all proceeded from the theme formulated by Rosenzweig: the mortality of nations and its causes, Western secularism, Asian anomie, and inadaptable Islam. Why raise these issues under a pseudonym? There is a simple answer, and a less simple one. To inform a culture that it is going to die does not necessarily win friends, and what I needed to say would be hurtful to many readers. I needed to tell the Europeans that their postnational, secular dystopia was a death trap whence no one would get out alive. I needed to tell the Muslims that nothing would alleviate the unbearable sense of humiliation and loss that globalization inflicted on a civilization that once had pretensions to world dominance. I needed to tell Asians that materialism leads only to despair.

And I needed to tell the Americans that their smugness would be their undoing. In this world of accelerated mortality, in which the prospect of national extinction hung visibly over most of the peoples of the world, Jew-hatred was stripped of its mask and revealed as the jealousy of the merely undead toward living Israel. And it was not hard to show that the remnants of the tribal world lurking under the cover of Islam were not living but only undead, incapable of withstanding the onslaught of modernity, throwing a tantrum against their inevitable end. I have been an equal-opportunity offender, with no natural constituency. My academic training, strewn over two doctoral programs, was in music theory and German as well as economics. I have published a number of peer-reviewed papers on Renaissance-era philosophy, music, and mathematics. But I came to believe that there are things even more important than the high art of the West and its most characteristic endeavor, classical music, the passion and consolation of my youth. Western classical music expresses goal-oriented motion, a teleology, as it were—but where did humankind learn of teleology? I no longer quite belonged with my friends and colleagues, the artists.

As a young man I wandered in the fever swamps of fringe politics. I found my way thanks to the first Reagan administration. The righting of America after it nearly capsized during the dark years of Jimmy Carter was a defining experience for me. I owe much to several mentors, starting with Norman A. Bailey, special assistant to President

Reagan and director of plans at the National Security Council from 1981 to 1984. My political education began in his lair at the old Executive Office Building in 1981, when he explained to me that the United States would destroy the Soviet Empire by the end of the 1980s. I thought him a dangerous lunatic, and, like Tertullian, immediately signed on. I worked for Bailey's consulting firm after he left government, simultaneously pursuing a doctorate (never quite finished) in music theory. I owe most of all to the music theorists (in the school of Heinrich Schenker) with whom I studied in the doctoral program at City University.

Another mentor was Robert Mundell, the creator of supply-side economics, among his other contributions. As an economist for the supply-side consulting firm Polyconomics in the late 1980s and early 1990s, I had dozens of conversations with Mundell, who won the Nobel Prize in 1999. I can't claim to be a Mundell student, but he graciously allowed me to acknowledge his help in an article I published in 1994 in the *Journal of Applied Corporate Finance*. What I gleaned from Mundell allowed me to begin a successful career on Wall Street at an age when most of its denizens already are thinking about retirement. I no longer quite belonged with my old friends the economists. I had left economics for music, and left music for finance, eventually working in senior research positions at Bear Stearns, Credit Suisse, and Bank of America. At Bank of America, I created from scratch a highly rated fixed-income research department from 2002 to 2005, with 120 professionals and a mid-nine-figure compensation budget.

By 2005, it was no longer clear how the financial industry would play a helpful role in fostering prosperity, and what might be called "philosophical differences" prompted me to take my leave. By the late 1990s, I no longer believed that solving problems of economic stability and growth was sufficient to resolve problems that manifested themselves in economic form. Working in the inside of the financial world, ultimately as a member of the executive committee for fixed income of America's largest bank, I saw how easy it was to prejudice the efficiency of markets and to introduce distortions that eventually would have awful consequences. Exile among the fleshpots of Wall Street had its benefits, but I had other ambitions.

My commitment to Judaism came relatively late in life, in my mid-thirties, but was all the more passionate for its tardiness. The things I had been raised to love were disappearing from the world, or changing beyond recognition. The language of Goethe and Heine would die out, along with the languages of Dante and Pushkin. Europe's high culture and its capacity to train universal minds had deteriorated beyond repair; one of the last truly universal European minds belongs to the octogenarian Pope Benedict XVI. In 1996, the then Cardinal Joseph Ratzinger had said in an interview published as *Das Salz der Erde* (The salt of the earth), "Perhaps we have to abandon the idea of the popular Church. Possibly, we stand before a new epoch of Church history with quite different conditions, in which Christianity will stand under the sign of the mustard seed, in small and apparently insignificant groups, which nonetheless oppose evil intensively and bring the Good into the world."

The best mind in the Catholic Church squarely considered the possibility that Christianity itself might shrink into "seeming insignificance." Renewal could not come from music, or literature, or the social sciences. The wells of culture had run dry, because they derived from faith to begin with. I was raised in the Enlightenment pseudoreligion of art and beauty. Initially I looked at faith instrumentally, as a means of regenerating the high culture of the West. But art doesn't exist for art's sake.

The high culture of the West had its own Achilles' heel. Even its greatest cultivators often suffered from the sin of pride and worshiped their own powers rather than the source of their powers. Painfully and slowly, I began to learn the classic Jewish sources. My first guide back to Judaism was the great German Jewish theologian Franz Rosenzweig, and my first essay on these subjects was published by the Jewish–Christian Relations website in 1999 under the title "Has Franz Rosenzweig's Time Come?" In recent years I have been learning my Judaism from the writings of Joseph Dov Soloveitchik and Michael Wyschogrod. The intersection point in the Venn diagram of my background had shrunk to the point of vanishing.

As a returning religious Jew, I had less and less to discuss with the secular Zionists who shared my passion and partisanship for Israel but could not see a divine dimension in Jewish nationhood. So-called cultural Judaism repelled me; most of what passes for Jewish culture comes down to the mud that stuck to our boots as we fled one country after another. The Hebrew Bible and its commentaries over the centuries are the core of Jewish culture, with a handful of odd adjuncts, such as the novels of S. Y. Agnon or the last, devotional poems of Heine. I was in, but not of, the world of rabbinical Judaism, of classical music, of cultural history, of conservative economics, of practical finance—I belonged everywhere and nowhere. I could address each of these spheres only ironically and aphoristically, and anonymity allowed me to be in but not of all of them. The essays I wrote over the course of a decade for *Asia Times Online* and *First Things* provided the basis for this book. That material does not appear here quite as it did originally but is redacted in an updated manner that better reflects an organization of my thoughts. To a great extent, these essays anticipated the crises we are currently witnessing. We have the misfortune to live in one of those periods where the long-term irrupts into the headlines. And that is why it sometimes is beneficial to turn off the news feeds and take stock of ourselves.

Most of this volume seeks to get under the hood of the culture and examine the engine that drives it. We are, first and foremost, the person we are in our moments of leisure, the object of the things that move, inspire, or horrify us. It may seem fanciful to examine the music of Richard Wagner, horror movies, modern art, and the novels of J. R. R. Tolkien in a book whose subject is the global strategic crisis. But the imagination of our hearts more than the ratiocination of our frontal lobe is what determines the outcome of great events.

Part One

It's Not the End of the World

It's Just the End of You

CHAPTER 1

Why Nations Die

Irrational belief threatens world peace, in the strident view of enlightened secular opinion. Humankind seemed to have deserted the national, religious, and ideological passions that drove the great wars of the past. Civilizational war no longer seemed possible because civilization had ceased to be the source of impassioned loyalties. After the Second World War, enlightened young people of the world saw in the melding of civilizations a guarantee that humankind would find no more reason to fight. In the great salad bowl of the civilizations, religious conflict seems like a specter haunting dusty corners of old universities rather than a threat to the modern world. Not only traditional religion, such as the Christianity that gave rise to the Spanish Inquisition, but the worship of race in Nazi Germany, the personality cult in Soviet Russia, emperor worship in Japan, and other forms of fanaticism spawned the slaughter of the past century. Humanity's hope therefore lies in the restoration of rationality. In that case enlightened people can devise solutions for all the world's problems, as in Immanuel Kant's claim that he could devise a constitution "for a race of devils, if only they be rational."

Enlightened opinion contrasts two stances toward the world, the religious versus the rational. One might think of them like the two young men locked in the lunatic asylum in the Barber's Tale that begins the second book of Cervantes' *Don Quixote*. One claims to be a sane man committed to the asylum by evil relatives seeking to steal his inheritance, and a committee of notables has come to examine him. In the adjacent cell another young man, obviously mad, raves that he is the god Neptune and threatens to start an earthquake. The notables examine the first prisoner and conclude that he is quite sane. As they undo his restraints, one comments on the condition of "Neptune" in the next cell. "Don't worry about him," says the liberated young man, "for I am really the god Jupiter, and, if he starts an earthquake, I'll hit him with a lightning bolt." In Cervantes' lunatic asylum, the inmate who works hardest to convince us of his sanity is madder than all the rest. Educated Europeans look with distain on the boorishness and bumptiousness of the United States, which continues to maintain a military that actually can fight wars. The prevalence of religious faith in America fills Europeans with revulsion, especially the enthusiastic devotion of the evangelicals, who constitute almost 30 percent of America's population. Faith in a personal God is prima facie proof of mental defect to most educated Europeans, and so America by definition is a giant madhouse. Yet the countries that have abandoned nationalism, religion, and ideology in favor of the milquetoast administration of daily affairs—for example, the Europeans—suffer from the most dreadful psychic symptom of all. They fail to have children. The triumph of secularism in Europe recalls the proverbial operation that was a success except for the death of the patient.

There is one problem with the enlightened view: In the absence of faith, human beings show little interest in living. Humankind cannot bear the burden of mortality without the promise of immortality. We know of countries destroyed by war or plague but of not a single nation that simply willed itself out of existence. Today the majority of the industrial nations are heading toward demographic death, and some have passed the point of no return. For the first and only time in recorded history—leaving aside fragmentary evidence from late antiquity—prosperous, secure, and peaceful societies facing no external threat have elected to pass out of existence.

Formerly Catholic Spain, formerly fascist Germany, formerly communist Russia, and formerly imperial Japan have in common a birth rate so low that it is hard to imagine what their national existence might look like half a century hence. Ethnologists warn that, over the next century, somewhere between half and nine-tenths of all the languages now spoken will go silent forever; in two or three centuries, Japanese and German may pass out of the world. Rather than pave the way for universal peace, loss of faith has turned important parts of the world into a nursing home, and then a cemetery. Rather than the utopia sketched by Kant in his tract *Universal Peace* (1792) and preached by enlightened opinion, the weakening of religion has produced a wave of what for lack of a better term we call ethno-suicide. Europe in a sense has less in common with the relatively fecund United States than it does with the endangered peoples of the New Guinea highlands and the disappearing languages of the Siberian taiga. Why have so many branches of the human family lost the will to live? And what does the despair of Stone Age peoples in New Guinea have in common with the despair of modern peoples who choose not to reproduce?

For the casual consumer of world news, almost daily suicide

bombings by Muslims draw constant attention to the phenomenon of ethno-suicide. Never before in history has a culture produced so many individuals willing to commit suicide simply in order to inspire horror and terror among a hostile population. Japan's kamikaze pilots tried to sink American ships; today's suicide bombers murder ordinary folk in mosques and marketplaces. In several modern wars, armies fought with resolve but no hope of victory—for example, the American Confederate Army after Gettysburg and Vicksburg, the American Indian "Ghost Dancers" after Little Big Horn, and the Serbs during the First World War. This might be termed "suicidal" in a loose way. But it is very different from the regular deployment of suicide bombers as a routine instrument of terrorism against civilian populations. Never in history do we observe a comparable contempt for human life, one's own as well as the enemy's.

Reason itself appears to betray us in this investigation, for precisely the parts of the world that succeed in extirpating faith through the installation of the cult of reason seem most committed to demographic extinction. The countries of Eastern Europe were among the first to impose atheism as an official ideology. Their total working-age population by midcentury likely will decline from 200 million today to barely more than 100 million in 2050. The formerly Christian countries of Western Europe are following in various degrees of infecundity, while Japan clearly has passed a demographic point of no return. No suprarational faith contends with reason in old Europe, Eastern Europe, or Japan. In the most reasonable fashion they will pass into oblivion during the next century or sooner. One has the peculiar sense of conducting a logical discourse with a man who is determined to commit suicide. He may have some good arguments or, rather, arguments that would have been good if they had been present in the mind of someone who was not planning to commit suicide. Enlightened, secular opinion is thus a self-liquidating problem, for it is infertile not only in the mind but in the womb. The more evidence mounts that secular societies fail of their will to life, the more vociferously the professional atheists, the Richard Dawkinses and Christopher Hitchenses, rail against faith, in vain.

The horror of religious wars of the past weighs heavily on enlightened opinion today. The most horrible of the religious wars, to be sure, had nothing to do with religion. Most of the killing in the Thirty Years' War occurred during its second half, in which the Catholic–Protestant issues were long superseded by a Franco–Spanish proxy war on German soil. The black legend of bloody religious fanaticism dominates liberal thinking. Avoiding a new religious war—that is, achieving a global accommodation with Islam—has become the fixed idea of liberal foreign policy for the twenty-first century, so much so that on June 4, 2009, the president of the United States for the first time in history addressed the adherents of a religion rather than the citizens of a country.

To make sense of today's world is to account for two phenomena that have no precedent in the history books: the willful disappearance of declining peoples through infertility, and the proliferation of suicide as an instrument of warfare. What if the infertile Italian is the alter ego of the fanatical Iranian, the fraternal twins of existential despair?

Faith has forced its way back into the policy sphere, but policymakers are ill equipped to understand it. To the extent they take religion into account at all, they include it as one more doctrine, like positivism or communism. Religion, though, cannot be reduced to doctrine. It is a life—specifically, a life organized around the hope of immortality. God is not a concept to be parsed by philosophers but rather the dialogue partner of a congregation who prays to God as "thou." God exists in the second person, not in the third, as the party whom the congregation addresses in the second person, as Martin Buber argued—a "Thou," not an "It." What makes God a reality to the person of faith is not a doctrine but the congregational act of prayer itself. Religion is a set of human institutions and practices instituted in response to an experience of communion with the Transcendent, a mode of ordering life on this earth so that life will continue past this earth. The formal study of theology offers small benefit to the political analyst who seeks to make sense of the new and unwelcome force of religion in world events. In the case of Islam, as the Vatican Islamologist Fr. Samir Khalil Samir observes, both a violent and intolerant as well as a peaceful and tolerant reading of Islam are supported by the classic sources, and there is no Islamic theology that can validate one or the other.

Sentience of morality distinguishes us from lower animals. "From the fear of death," Franz Rosenzweig began his treatise *The Star of Redemption* (*Der Stern der Erlösung*, 1921), "arises our understanding of the All." In response to the sentience of mortality we build culture, the capacity to order our behavior consciously rather than by instinct. Unlike animals, human beings require more than progeny: We require progeny who remember us. To overcome mortality we create culture, a dialogue among generations that links the dead to the yet unborn. Even the Neanderthals buried their dead with grave-gifts, a witness of belief of life beyond the grave. Whether or not we pray to a personal God or confess a particular religion, we cannot evade the existential question. Without the hope of immortality we cannot bear mortality. Cultures that have lost the hope of immortality also lose the will to live. With sad frequency, ethnic groups will die rather than abandon their way of life, or will fight to the death out of despair. Historic tragedy occurs on the grand scale when economic or strategic circumstances undercut the material conditions of life of a people, which nonetheless cannot accept assimilation into another culture. That is when entire peoples fight to the death.

The type of man we encounter in the dying nations, not only in the remote rivulets of the human current but on the Baltic, the Black Sea, and the Sea of Japan, is a stranger to modern social science. He is not Freud's man, driven by libido, nor economic man, maximizing utility. He is not Hobbes' man, averse not to life's hardships and dangers; he is averse to life itself, for he rejects life precisely at a moment when hardship and danger have begun to fade. He suffers from the restless heart that St. Augustine ascribes to those who are far from God.

Today's intellectual elite feel something like the mad Englishman in a lunatic asylum whom Karl Marx sketched in *The Eighteenth Brumaire of Louis Napoleon*. He imagines that his warders are barbarian mercenaries who speak in a welter of unintelligible tongues, and he mutters to himself, "And all this is happening to me—a freeborn Englishman!" So felt France on the return of the Napoleonic dynasty, and so feels the intelligentsia on the return of religion to world politics. To such perplexed secularists, I recommend Franz Rosenzweig's *The Star of Redemption*, but with a caveat: It might cure them of secularism. That the English translation is miserably inadequate is another matter; it is probably no worse than its prospective readers. In fact, there is no idea in *The Star of Redemption* that one cannot find close to hand in the mainstream of Christian and Jewish teaching. Rosenzweig's act of genius was to show that Christianity and Judaism are not ideas, not mere religions (his dismissive characterization of Islam), but rather lives.

From death—from the fear of death—arises the perception of the transcendent. So his book begins. And in the face of the fear of

19

death, one proceeds—to life, as he avers in the book's last sentence. But the path to life requires a life outside of time—that is, the hope of immortality. Man cannot abide his mortal existence, cannot tolerate the fear of death, without the prospect of life eternal. Faith can be neither proven nor defended but only lived, Rosenzweig taught. It is not a system of beliefs but an existential choice, not a proof but an affirmation. Critics call *The Star of Redemption* a difficult book, and that it is, not because Rosenzweig's conclusion is difficult but rather because modern readers will resist his conclusion to the bitter end. Sadly, it is easier for today's readers to consume Homer in the original than to read Rosenzweig. First, he cannot easily be translated into English, for there are few scholars active today with a command of language commensurate with one of the sublime masters of German letters. Second, even if well translated, Rosenzweig no longer can be understood, as his 1920 volume refers to a cultural realm long since annihilated. Third, even if Rosenzweig were understood, he is rather unwelcome.

A tragedy of twentieth-century history is that Leo Strauss, who began as Rosenzweig's student, transferred his intellectual loyalty to the odious Martin Heidegger. Strauss' disciple Irving Kristol, the "godfather of neoconservatism," once wrote me that he had intended to learn German in order to read Rosenzweig. It is a pity he did not. But one still can hope that Rosenzweig's star will ascend. One does not read Rosenzweig for inspiration, the way Christians read C. S. Lewis. "Rosenzweig isn't an inspiration—he's a graduate course," a prominent Orthodox Jewish rabbi says. A secular German Jew trained in Hegelian philosophy, Rosenzweig was ready to convert to Christianity in 1913 when his attendance at Day of Atonement services brought him back to Judaism. He was not, or ever could be, a traditional Jew, but remained the outsider looking in with the critical eye of a trained skeptic. There is a circle of liberal Jewish theologians who embrace Rosenzweig as a nonsectarian exponent of their faith. There are better books on Judaism than *The Star* (Joseph Dov Soloveitchik's *From There Shall You Seek*, for example, and Michael Wyschogrod's *The Body of Faith*), which Rosenzweig wrote just as he was returning to Judaism. But it was not merely a Jew who wrote *The Star* but also a German soldier, making notes on army postcards at an antiaircraft battery in Serbia. *The Star* is a German book as much as it is a Jewish one, for it is the record of a German philosopher's return to faith—that is, a philosopher's critique of philosophy, and a European's critique of modern civilization. As Rosenzweig observed in "The New Thinking," his précis of *The Star*, he offered first and foremost a sociology of religion: an account of the experience of religion through the eyes of the believer, in the quotidian setting of ordinary life.

"The history of the world is the history of Israel," Rosenzweig asserted. That is not an utterance of ethnic megalomania but rather a statement that human history is a quest to overcome mortality. Religious faith is woven into the fabric of traditional society, in which individuals have no choice about the roles and rhythms of life. Unravel this fabric, and faith dissolves. That was the position of Europe after the First World War, which undid the great dynasties of Europe and poisoned the ancient loyalties of family, tribe, church, and nation. That is the predicament of the Islamic world today. The philosophers, who had been God's apologists, became God's persecutors. Immanuel Kant demonstrated that God's existence could not be proven, and a century later Friedrich Nietzsche insisted that God was dead. In 1914, Europe believed not in God but in nation and Kultur. By 1918, these gods were toppled, and Europe began to worship the false gods of historical materialism and national socialism. Kant had already destroyed the philosophical proofs of God's existence in 1781, prompting Heinrich Heine's quip that Robespierre merely decapitated a king, whereas a German professor sent the Almighty to the scaffold. Biologists reduced to myth the Biblical story of creation. The Higher Criticism asserted multiple authorship of the Hebrew scriptures. Modern philosophy and science presented themselves as a rational alternative to the sham of religion. Except for the backward or the recalcitrant, traditional faith became impossible.

Along with the great Protestant theologian Karl Barth, Rosenzweig opened a path for a modern faith, a faith strengthened by skepticism as if by inoculation. He turned the tables on the philosophers, the undertakers of faith, arguing that philosophy itself was the sham, the equivalent of a small child stuffing his fingers in his ears and shouting "I can't hear you!" to ward off the terror of death. It was not science that threatened the faith of the West, Rosenzweig explained, but rather a competing idolatry: the resurgent "inner pagan" inside every Christian. Christians are torn between their belief in the kingdom of heaven and their belief in their own blood. It is the Jew, he argued, who converts the inner pagan inside the Christian, because the existence of the Jewish people itself stands surety for God's promise to Christians as well.

Only a "community of blood" (*Blutsgemeinschaft*) provides man with the assurance of immortality, Rosenzweig argued. God's covenant with the physical descendants of Abraham provides such surety to the Jews, and precisely for this reason the Jews provide Christians with proof of God's promise of a New Covenant. By virtue of Christ's blood, Christians become the next best thing to a community of blood, an *ekklesia*, those who are called out from among the nations and, through immersion in water, undergo a new birth to become descendants of Abraham in the spirit. Christianity embraced the Gentiles newly conscious of their own mortality, of the inevitable end of their bloodline. As he wrote in *The Star*:

> Just as every individual must reckon with his eventual death, the peoples of the world foresee their eventual extinction, be it however distant in time. Indeed, the love of the peoples for their own nationhood is sweet and pregnant with the presentiment of death. Love is only surpassing sweet when it is directed towards a mortal object, and the secret of this ultimate sweetness only is defined by the bitterness of death. Thus the peoples of the world foresee a time when their land with its rivers and mountains still lies under heaven as it does today but other people dwell there; when their language is entombed in books, and their laws and customs have lost their living power.

But the contending claims of pagan blood remain in perpetual conflict with the promise of the spirit, and Christianity never entirely suppresses the inner pagan inside each believer. Christianity cannot exist except in symbiosis with Judaism, averred Rosenzweig, to which one might add that Europe's determination to destroy its Jews was an act not just of genocide but of suicide. European Christianity did not survive the regression back to the bloodline of the nations during the middle of the past century. Only in a new nation conceived in the spirit—that is, in ideas, and free of the taint of pagan birth—could Christianity truly flourish, and although Rosenzweig never wrote about America, I believe this assertion is consistent with his views. To see how different faiths—different modes of living—address the fear of death, not only individual but also national, creates a unique vantage point from which to understand how profoundly Christianity, Judaism, and Islam differ from one another.

"Learn Greek, dear reader, and throw my translation into the fire!" wrote the first German translator of Homer's *Iliad*, Count von Stolberg, words that Franz Rosenzweig placed as an epigraph to the preface to his own translation of the medieval Hebrew poet Judah Halevi. Read Franz Rosenzweig, I should like to say, and recycle this book, for the following chapters are but an attempt to put fragments of his thinking before the English-speaking public. Since faith is what ultimately determines the fate of a people, Rosenzweig is of indispensable value for strategic analysis and global theopolitics today.

CHAPTER 2

Jesus versus Siegfried:
Why Europe Chooses Extinction

Since my first essays on faith and fertility appeared in *Asia Times Online*, demographers have recognized the obvious—people of faith have children, and people without faith tend not to—often with dismay. Eric Kaufmann in his book *Will the Religious Inherit the Earth?* (2010) reviews some of the evidence and warns that the high fertility rates of people of faith will turn the world into a fundamentalist theme park. Dozens of books lament the disappearance of Europe. At present birth rates, the number of Germans in the world will fall by 98 percent in two hundred years, which is to say that the German language (and Italian, Polish, and numerous others) will be spoken exclusively in hell. What has brought about this collective suicide, which mocks all we thought we knew about the instinct for self-preservation? The chattering classes have nothing to say about the most unique and significant change in our times. Yet the great political and economic shifts of modern times are demographic in origin. Three examples suffice:

- The great transatlantic rift. Europeans are pacifists, not merely in the Persian Gulf but on their own Balkan doorstep. If they cannot be bothered to reproduce, why should any European soldier sacrifice himself for future generations that never will be born?
- The shift in global capital flows to the United States: Old people lend money to young people. The aging populations of Europe and Japan lend money to younger people in the United States.
- The financial crisis of 2008–2010, as I'll explain in Part 5.

Little enough has been said about the "how" but almost nothing about the "why" of Europe's demographic suicide. Suicidal behavior is common among (for example) Stone Age tribes who have encountered the modern world. One can extend this example to Tamil or Arab suicide bombers. But the Europeans are the modern world. Have the Europeans taken to heart existentialism's complaint that man is alone in a chaotic universe in which life has no ultimate meaning, and that man responds to the anxiety about death by embracing death?

The last five years have brought forth an extensive literature, including several groundbreaking studies from the Max Planck Demographics Institute, showing the close link between faith and fertility. America is the last Christian nation, while Europe is post-Christian. Fifty-nine percent of Americans say that religion is very important in their lives, compared with 11, 21, and 27 percent respectively of the French, Germans, and Italians, according to a report from the Pew Center in 2002. America's fertility rate remains slightly above replacement, at around 2.1 children per female, while Europe will suffer slow extinction at its present fertility of 1.5. The studies show that the fertility of people of faith in Europe and the United States is quite similar; the difference is that there are more people of faith in America.

Here I draw on Rosenzweig. Few Asians (including Jews) can make sense of Christianity's core doctrine—namely, original sin—handed down to all humans from Adam and Eve. Original sin motivates God's self-sacrifice on the cross to remove this stain from mankind; without it, Jesus was just an itinerant preacher with a knack for anecdotes. But what is "original sin," and why (as the medieval rabbis reproached the Christians) should Adam's sin afflict all his descendants, such that nothing less than God's self-sacrifice could atone for it? If we equate sin with death, a deep truth is made visible. All religion, Rosenzweig argued, responds to man's anxiety in the face of death. The pagans of old faced death with the confidence that their race would continue. But tribes and nations anticipate their own extinction just as individuals anticipate their own death. The early Christian Church encountered a great extinction of peoples and their cultures through the rise and fall of the Alexandrian and Roman empires. Who now remembers the Lusitani, the Illyrians, the Sicani, the Quadians, Sarmatians, Alans, Gepidians, Herulians, Pannonians, and a thousand other tribes of Roman times? As nations faced extinction, individuals within these nations came face to face with their own mortality. Christianity offered an answer: The Church called individuals out of the nations and offered them salvation in the form of a life beyond the grave. The Gentiles (as the Church called them) trembled in the presence of original sin, which to them simply meant the sin of having been born Gentile—that is, born to a nation doomed to eventual extinction. The sting of sin is death, said St. Paul, and one might add that the sinfulness of the flesh is cognizance of its mortality. (That is why original sin is self-evident to Christians and incomprehensible to Jews, who think of themselves as an eternal people in the flesh.)

In one respect, Christianity was an enormous success. Its original heartland in the Near East, Asia Minor, and Greece, fell to Islam, but, even while Arabs rode victorious over St. Paul's missionary trail, the Church converted the barbarians of Europe. Christianity made possible the assimilation of thousands of doomed tribes into what became European nations. Something similar is at work in Africa, where Christianity enjoys rapid growth. Yet Christianity's weakness, Rosenzweig added, lay in the devil's bargain it made with the old paganism. Christianity's salvation lay beyond the grave, in the wispy ether of heavenly reward. Humans require something to hang on to this side of the grave. By providing the pagans with a humanized God (and a humanized mother of God and a host of saints), Christianity allowed the pagans to continue to worship their own image. Germans worship a blond Jesus, Spaniards worship a dark-haired Jesus, Mexicans worship the dark Virgin of Guadalupe, and so forth. The result, wrote Rosenzweig, is that Christians "are forever torn between Jesus and Siegfried."

At the political level, Christianity sought to suppress Siegfried in favor of Christ through the device of the universal empire, the suppression of nationality by the aristocracy and Church. The lid kept blowing off the pot. Just when the Habsburgs brought the universal empire to its peak of power in 1519 under Charles V, controlling Austria, Spain, and the Netherlands, Germany revolted under the banner of Reformation. There followed a century and a half of religious wars, culminating in the Thirty Years' War (1618–1648), which wiped out a third of the population of central Europe.

Idolatry in the form of ethnic self-adoration never waned among the European peoples, despite their centuries of Christian tutelage. Was it coincidence that the political backing for Luther's schism came from Saxony, seven centuries after Charlemagne killed the Saxons or converted them at swordpoint? France under Cardinal Richelieu gave a fatal twist to the Christian idea. The French nation would be the standard bearer for, instead of universal empire, Christendom, such that French national interests stood in place of divine providence. All Europe caught the French disease, substituting the warrior Siegfried for the crucified God. Christianity's inner pagan ran amok. A second Thirty Years' War (1914–1944) gave unlimited vent to Europe's pagan impulses and drowned them in blood. The unfortunate Rosenzweig, who saw the fault lines in Christian civilization so clearly, died hoping that Europe still would embrace its Jewish population as a counterweight against its destructive pagan self. It never occurred to him that Europe would choose destruction and take its Jews with it. Siegfried triumphed over Christ during the First World War. No shred of credibility was left in the Christian idea of souls called out of the nations for salvation beyond the grave. In 1914, Europe's soldiers still fought under the illusion of a God that favored their nation. Germany fought the Second World War under the banner of revived paganism.

For today's Europeans, there is no consolation, neither the old pagan continuity of national culture nor the Christian continuity into the hereafter. The French know that Victor Hugo, Gauloise cigarettes, Chateau Lafite, and Impressionist painters one day will become a matter of antiquarian curiosity. The Germans know that no one but bored schoolboys will read Goethe, like Pindar, two centuries hence. They have no ambition but to die quietly, no concerns except for those amusements that might reduce boredom and anxiety en route to the grave. They have no passions except hatred born of envy. They hate America, a new kind of universality that succeeded where the old Christian empire failed. They hate Israel, which makes the Jewish people appear all the more eternal in stark contrast to Europe's morbid temporality. They will pass out of history unmourned even by themselves.

A striking example was given by the two dozen suicides in 2009 at France Telecom, the dullest place in the habitable world, where people go to do nothing and make a living at it. Twenty-four employees at the French telephone monopoly killed themselves in 18 months, and another thirteen attempted suicide. The France Telecom suicide wave—the subject of endless public controversy in France—is one of the iconic events of 2009, the sociological quirk that sets in relief the mortal flaw in the Western character. The mortal sin that motivated the France Telecom suicides was sloth. Dante Alighieri didn't know the half of it. The wolf that barred his way in the Wood of Error at the outset of his *Divine Comedy* represents Lust, who never satiates her dreadful appetite and is hungrier after feeding than before. To evade this predator, the poet journeys through Hell and Heaven, classifying in high Scholastic style the sins of humankind. But lust is the least of the problems in twenty-first-century Europe. The insatiable predator who feeding makes more ravenous is not sex but sloth. Dante doesn't condemn the slothful to Hell; we find them instead in Purgatory, with eventual hope of entry to Heaven. Among the risk averse Europeans, who favor nanny-state paternalism, the most risk averse choose to work for state monopolies. But the global economic crisis has shaken the foundations of state finances in Europe, and bloated entities such as France Telecom must adjust. A consistent pattern informs the suicide notes of France Telecom workers: The fear of downsizing, demotion, and reassignment is too much for them to bear. The desire for security is an addiction: The more security one obtains, the less secure one feels.

France Telecom management "had argued, quite reasonably, that the company had to move with the times: customer demand for mobile phones rather than fixed lines meant massive restructuring was inevitable," wrote Gill Corkingdale in her Harvard Business

School blog. "The company avoided imposing mass redundancies, but asked staff to retrain for Orange call centers and, in some cases, change locations. Fairly reasonable, you might think. Yet this did not stop one worker from stabbing himself repeatedly in the stomach when he was told he was being transferred to another post in the same town."

Although the company went private long ago, telephone workers are considered government employees. Two-thirds of them have civil-service status and cannot be fired. Nonetheless, the monopoly cut 22,000 jobs between 2006 and 2008 and reassigned many more workers to menial jobs with longer hours. One fifty-one-year-old France Telecom employee left a note complaining that he could not bear his new assignment to a call center and jumped off a highway bridge into rush-hour traffic. A telephone worker in Marseille left a suicide note stating, "Overwork, stress, absence of training, and total disorganization in the company. I'm a wreck, it's better to end it all."

A healthy middle-aged man—he ran in marathons as a hobby—with no money problems could not bear the thought of losing an overpaid sinecure at the phone company. For the fretful French, *The Guardian* newspaper wrote, his "suicide note has become the defining message from the grave." Given Europe's fiscal crisis, which is creeping up from the near-bankrupt countries of the Mediterranean (Portugal, Italy, Greece, Spain, now dubbed the "PIGS" by Wall Street wits), the downsizing of France Telecom will be repeated throughout the risk-averse continent. By 2012, Moody's estimates, France and Germany will spend nearly 10 percent of their gross domestic product on debt service. For that matter, the budgetary collapse of U.S. states and cities imperils the one economic sector to add jobs during the past decade. The U.S. private sector shed jobs during the first decade of the twenty-first century, and the slack was taken up by state and local governments riding the real-estate boom.

Lust, contrary to Dante, is the least of today's problems: If only the late France Telecom manager had devoted himself to concupiscence to take his mind off his problems, he would still be alive today. Even the crassest and cheapest sort of sexual relations require a modicum of human intimacy. The modern world, in fact, has found a cure for lust, the she-wolf that Dante considered impassable. It is the desire for nothing, which, after all, is what suicides desire. A favorite theme of postfeminist authors in the United States is the sexless marriage. Japan, in fact, holds the world championship in this league, with more than a third of Japanese couples reporting no sexual relations at all in the past year, and three-quarters reporting that their frequency of relations is no more than once a month. I do not propose to demean Dante, in many respects the greatest of all European poets, perhaps the greatest poet of all time. But he wrote for a world in which certain things, such as the desire for life, were taken for granted. The sin of suicide draws his passing attention in canto 13 of the Inferno, where he passes through a wood of gnarled and brittle trees encasing the souls of those who took their own lives.

Following Aristotle, who argued that dissipation of one's wealth was a form of suicide, Dante depicts a pair of notorious contemporary spendthrifts who killed themselves. But it is not dissipation of one's substance but rather the desire for security that accounts for the two dozen suicides at the French telephone company. It seems inexplicable that healthy and affluent people would end their lives over the prospect of having to go out and find a new job, unless we consider that there is a bit of death built into the craving for security to begin with. Life is risky, and to withdraw from it is to embrace death. That is why the sort of person who seeks a lifetime sinecure at a state monopoly is more likely to tumble into despair at the first intrusion of uncertainty. In the modern world, we observe that love of life and willingness to assume risk go together with religious faith. By "modern world" I mean those countries in which education and occupation are determined by choice and talent rather than by tradition and compulsion—the industrialized nations, in short.

The United States and Israel produce the most babies and the most entrepreneurs per capita in the industrial world and are also the only two industrial countries in which religious faith still occupies the public square. This is true by construction: Israel and the United States, uniquely in the world, were created by immigrants motivated in large measure by religious faith. Unlike the peoples of Europe, who were assimilated into the Christian religion by political agreement more than by individual conversion, the founders of the United States and Israel selected themselves as citizens of a new country. If we construct a crude "love of life" index by comparing the fertility rate (on the premise that people who love life also love babies) against the suicide rate, Israel is off the charts in the upper-left-hand quadrant; the United States has the second-highest fertility rate and one of the lowest suicide rates. Israel and the United States share another distinction: They are the world's principal venues for entrepreneurship. As Reuven Brenner of McGill University wrote in the February 2009 issue of *First Things*,

> today Israel's venture-capital industry still raises more funds than any other venue except the United States. In 2006 alone, 402 Israeli high-tech companies raised over $1.62 billion [US]—the highest amount in the past five years. That same year, Israel had 80 active venture-capital funds and over $10 billion under man-

agement, invested in over 1,000 Israeli start-ups. By 2007, with 71 companies listed on NASDAQ, Israel had become second only to the United States, having leapfrogged now-third-place Canada.

There is a deep affinity among love of life, risk-friendliness, entrepreneurship, and religious faith. To misquote G. K. Chesterton: If you cease to believe in God, you will believe in anything. In Spengler's corollary to Chesterton's doctrine, if you cease to fear God, you will fear everything. Why should we take risks to begin with? Life is not only risky but, by definition, it is a losing proposition, because it will end in failure (namely, death) despite our best efforts to the contrary. Life, moreover, is uncertain at the best of times. If anything can happen (and it usually does), nemesis may strike at any moment, and everything is a prospective source of terror. The pagan, as Étienne Gilson put it, lived in a god-infested world; modern neopagans live in a world infested by demons. People of faith believe that, although God's purpose is unknowable to human reason, a plan of salvation for mankind somehow underlies the seemingly random procession of triumphs and disasters that constitute life. Life is risky—fleeting, or *hevel*, in the word of Ecclesiastes—and we are better off if we cast our bread upon the waters.

No mainstream current of Christianity or Judaism promises that the prayers of the pious always will be answered. The Book of Job is there to instruct Christian and Jew that God's purposes are so obscure to us as to make pointless the attempt to justify them. But the belief that there exists an ultimate purpose is high motivation to take a chance on the strength of our own efforts. If we do not see God's purpose in our own isolated corner of the battlefield, our children will, or our children's children. Even if death closes out our part in the drama, God will redeem us from death. People of faith tend to have children; those who are persuaded of the randomness of existence tend not to. I cannot prove the validity of the point of view of faith, but it is instructive to consider the alternatives. The most onerous expression of idolatry in the modern era was the communist conceit that the scientific ordering of society can eliminate uncertainty. Scientific socialism was supposed to eliminate economic crisis and war; instead, it brought about 100 million deaths and reduced once-prosperous countries to penury. Seventy years after its founding, the entire value of the industrial plant of the Soviet Union and its satellites was less than its scrap value, when the costs of environmental cleanup were taken into account. The life expectancy of Russian men has fallen to only fifty-five years, and the most frequent cause of death is alcoholism. Russia and its former satellites have such low fertility that their populations will fall by between one-third and one-half by midcentury. Europe's nanny-state version of social democracy is a low-grade version of the same infection.

J. W. Goethe's fictional devil Mephistopheles declaimed a fitting epitaph for communism when he admonished God for giving man "the spark of heaven's light he calls reason," which "he uses only to be beastlier than any beast." Whether Goethe compares to Dante as a poet is beside the point; his masterwork *Faust*, written at the turn of the eighteenth into the nineteenth century, speaks to the central concern of the age of sovereign individual choice. Offered anything he wants, modern man in his freedom will tend to choose—nothing. As God instructs Mephistopheles in the drama's prologue in Heaven, "All too easily, human activity simply goes to sleep / Man first of all will choose unconditional rest." That, God explains, is why he has given man a devil for a companion: to provoke him out of his torpor.

The devil is a nihilist. He is the same devil of the Hebrew Bible who tormented Job, but with this difference: Whereas Satan tortured ancient man by taking away what he required, he tortures modern man by offering him whatever he wants. He offers Faust his choice of pleasures—women, fame, money, and so forth. Faust rejects these; he wants to embrace life in all of its dimensions. At this the devil expresses astonishment: Life, he tells Faust, simply isn't designed for human beings.

> Believe me, who for millennia past
> Has chewed on this hard crust:
> From cradle to the grave
> No man ever has been able to digest this sourdough!
> Believe our kind: this whole
> Was made only for a God!
> He basks in light eternal.
> Us he brought down into darkness,
> While all you get is—day and night.

Faust, of course, vows to fight the devil to the end. All his endeavors fail, but he dies saved, with this motto on his lips: "I am wholly dedicate to this purpose / Which is the final conclusion of wisdom: / Only he deserves freedom as well as life / Who must conquer them every day!"

Not so the little people who inhabit the barrows of the state monopolies. Oswald Spengler, who characterized Western culture as "Faustian," would have been astonished to see today's Europeans nod in assent with Mephistopheles' refutation of life. Dante might have expanded his tour of the Inferno with something like the following (pardon a scenario without terza rima):

The Boiling Pots of the Slothful: Dante and Virgil enter an enormous cavern in Hell containing hundreds of boiling pots of pitch. In each pot are thousands of tortured souls writhing in unspeakable agony. Around each pot are a legion of devils with pitchforks. From time to time, a soul will attempt to crawl out of the pitch, and the nearest devil pokes him back into the pot.

"Who are these souls who suppurate in boiling pitch, O Master?" Dante inquires.

"These are the slothful, who bathed in indolence during their lifetime, and for eternity must bathe in foul and stinging pitch." Dante notices one pot in the corner boiling along by itself, with no devils surrounding it. "Why, O Master," he asks, "is that pitchpot over there unguarded?"

"Oh, that's France Telecom," Virgil replies. "When one of them tries to crawl out, the others pull him back in."

CHAPTER 3

The Sacred Heart of Darkness

In the Black Legend of Whig historiography, no phenomenon in modern history evinced more irrational cruelty than the Spanish Inquisition. The Inquisition was monstrous, to be sure, but it was a response to irrationality as much as the cause of it. Catholic apologists still offer a touching defense of the institution; the Vatican claimed not long ago that the Holy Office burnt at the stake less than 1 percent of the 125,000 accused heretics brought before it. A more realistic number is 10,000, but in any case, in comparison to the many millions killed in the religious wars of the sixteenth and seventeenth centuries, the number is small. Catholic publicists have been campaigning to rescue the Inquisition's good name from the besmirchment of Protestant propaganda. Wrote Thomas F. Madden of St. Louis University in October 2003: "The Spanish people loved their Inquisition. That is why it lasted for so long." Silly as he sounds, Madden has a point. People in general do nasty things not because they are negligent or bloody-minded but rather because they cannot avoid doing them. That is why we call such things tragic. Spain's inquisitors were not the horror-movie sadists of popular myth but sad little functionaries seeking to prevent the sort of religious war that plagued Europe during the sixteenth and seventeenth centuries. Not the boorish Germans but rather the agile Latins first opened the Pandora's Box of religious reform. If we accept that Spain's Inquisition was tragic rather than arbitrary, we must—I believe—also reach the conclusion that Christianity can flourish only on the American model. Neither Catholic empire nor the Protestant nation-state could do anything except destroy itself. But this is to get ahead of the story; we have only just tugged at the loose thread.

Before it burned heretics, the Spanish Inquisition burned books. Only one leaf remains of Bonifacio Ferrer's Spanish translation of the Bible in 1478, for the Inquisition hunted down every copy printed. Bible reading, they knew, led to Protestantism, and Protestantism led to religious war. Then the Inquisition hunted down Jews, for Jews knew Hebrew and might teach it to Protestants, who then might translate the Bible (which happened in Luther's Germany). As *The Catholic Encyclopedia* of 1911 puts it, the Inquisition sought to prevent the "Judaizing of all of Spain"—that is, the spread of Protestantism—and so persuaded the Catholic monarchs to expel the Jews in 1492.

Was the Spanish Inquisition wrong? On the contrary. Religious war devastated France during the sixteenth century, and during the seventeenth century it reduced the population of Germany by more than half. England's Civil War shed less blood but left its business unfinished. Cavalier and Roundhead diehards emigrated respectively to Virginia and Massachusetts, sowing the seeds of America's devastating Civil War two hundred years later. (See chapter 14; also

David Hackett Fischer, *Albion's Seed* [1989].) Not until 1936 did the lid blow off, and Spain fought a long-delayed religious war between Catholicism and atheism, in which the firing squad claimed more than a fifth of the estimated half-million violent deaths. The Spanish Civil War reduced a formerly martial nation to the feckless, infertile hedonists of today whose only claim to fame is Western Europe's lowest birthrate. It was not always so. Thanks to the Inquisition, the likes of Luther and Calvin got all the credit for the Reformation, but there is reason to believe that, given a chance, the Spanish variant would have been far more intrepid. After the American Revolution, Massachusetts Puritans became overt Unitarians. Like George Washington, John Adams, Thomas Jefferson, and Benjamin Franklin, they believed in a Creator but not in the divinity of Jesus. As such they traced their spiritual ancestry to the Spaniard Michael Servetus, whom John Calvin burned slowly at the stake at Geneva in 1553. Calvin deserves censure for the killing of Servetus no more than does the Inquisition for burning its own heretics. Necessity, not bigotry, made Calvin kill Servetus. More radical still was Fernando de Rojas, whose tragicomedy *La Celestina* of 1499 became, at least proportionally, the biggest fiction bestseller of all time, with multiple editions in all the European languages. The tiresome race of cultural historians likes to think of an orderly evolution of literary styles. On the contrary, with de Rojas modernism sprang fully grown from the Spanish crisis of 1492, like Athena from the head of Zeus. De Rojas, a barrister, defended an uncle accused by the Inquisition of covertly practicing Judaism, suggesting that his family was among the Jews who chose conversion rather than exile in 1492.

De Rojas's protagonist is a perverse old procuress next to whom Shakespeare's Iago or Marlowe's Barnabas seem like mischievous children; only Goethe's Mephistopheles can be termed a worthy successor. Engaged by a social-climbing nobleman to obtain access to the daughter of a high and ancient family, Celestina evinces tactical genius and steely nerve. Many passages are funny and frightening at the same time, a true mixture of genres Shakespeare never attempted. Celestina sets in motion a series of events that kills the lovers as well as most of the remaining characters. De Rojas portrays a world of greed, lust, self-delusion, and hypocrisy that deserves its own doom. From Spain at the turn of the sixteenth century, that is, we already obtain the theology of the Enlightenment from Servetus as well as a mixed-genre satire not reencountered until Goethe's *Faust* or Mozart's *Don Juan*. Despite the best efforts of the prudent inquisitors of the Spanish Church, Spain still managed to produce the greatest satire of all at the turn of the seventeenth century, Cervantes's *Don Quixote*. A remnant of de Rojas's savage sense of humor stayed alive in Spanish literature. The auteur Luis Buñuel was his last spiritual descendant. The price of religious peace, in short, was to turn Spain from a nation of spiritual conquistadors into Europe's laughingstock. When Pierre Caron de Beaumarchais put on stage his lampoons of the French monarchy, the censors gave him leave because he set the plot in Spain. Even the doomed aristocrats of France had no objection to portraying the Spanish nobility as buffoons.

Nonetheless, Spain's inquisitors were right to fear what Protestantism might bring. Sir Thomas More, portrayed for posterity as a martyr to freedom of conscience, had the great English Bible translator William Tyndale burned at the stake for the same reason. Protestantism presented a double danger. By its nature it spoke to the conscience of the individual seeking grace in the word of God. A Protestant state religion is a contradiction in terms, yet no one (except the unfortunate Servetus) then envisioned a separation of church and state. When Luther allied with the German princes against pope and empire, he opened a path for a nationalist Christianity whose deplorable consequences plagued Europe into its decline. By replacing the magisterium of the Church with the Bible-reading of the individual, Protestantism puts at risk the slender flame of faith. Influenced by the Jewish critique of original sin, Luther well knew that it could not be reconciled with free will. Christianity cannot do without original sin, which motivates Christ's sacrifice to begin with. Luther instead excised free will in favor of the unsatisfactory doctrine of predestination. Otherwise Protestantism must take the path indicated by Servetus, which ultimately must lead to loss of faith. Doctrinal questions of this sort arise when under a state religion; in this case heresy implies disloyalty to the state. The fundamental responses of Christianity and Judaism are not logical but rather existential. Nothing could be further from logic than the doctrine of election—the notion that God specifically chose the Jews as His People. Yet the Jews have persisted through millennia in the faith that Abraham's seed would not fail once God established His covenant with their forefather.

Neither Christian nor Jew cares much about the logic of salvation. The soul stands in fear and trembling, sick unto death—which is the same as sin—and reaches out for grace. The Jews do this as a kinship community—*Blutsgemeinschaft*, in Franz Rosenzweig's word. Christians must do so as individuals, because as Christians they abandon the doomed ties of Gentile kinship and instead join the assembly (*ekklesia*) that calls them out from among the nations. The remnants of Christian state religion rot and stink on the dying continent of Europe. Christianity cannot persist except as a continuing revival, a recurring conversion—as a sequence of singular events rather than as an orderly process. Awaiting execution in Hitler's prisons, the German theologian Dietrich Bonhoeffer wrote that, in a world come of age, the Christian religion no longer could exist as organized practice but only as an expression of individual conscience. America was created for precisely this purpose, to replace state religion on the European model with a religion of individual conscience. Such a religion must be schismatic, multisectarian, short on doctrine but long on inspiration. America's kaleidoscope of Protestant denominations, so bewildering to Europeans, constitutes the only type of milieu in which Christianity has flourished during the past generation. Although Christian communities are burgeoning throughout the world, they seem to succeed best in emulation of the American version. With right the Vatican may defend the record of the Spanish Inquisition, but it alters not a jot or tittle of the awful sentence—oblivion—that history has passed on European Christianity.

Friedrich Schiller (1759–1805) wrote tragedies about Europe's wars of religion that serve as Europe's epitaph. English speakers know Schiller mainly through bad translations of the first stanzas of one of his poorer poems, the "Ode to Joy," stanzas that Ludwig van Beethoven set in the Ninth Symphony. It was not always so. The English Romantic poets drank Schiller with their mother's milk. Schiller created a new kind of tragedy, in which the flaw applies to the people as much as to the protagonists. The hand of destiny is revealed as the tramp of boots on the ground worn by human beings with real needs and passions. The chorus itself becomes a tragic actor.

There are few moments in theater more chilling than the concluding chorus sung in *Wallenstein's Camp*, the first of Schiller's Wallenstein trilogy, by the Soldateska, the "new people" whom the imperial field marshal of the Thirty Years' War has summoned together from every corner of Europe. A minor Bohemian noble,

Wallenstein crushed the Protestant revolt against the Austrian empire by raising a mercenary army that was large enough to live off the land. But his success ruined civil society and turned the Thirty Years' War into a horror that killed more than a third of the population of central Europe.

As the play opens in 1634, the Austrian court has decided to excise the Protestant cancer, Wallenstein meanwhile is negotiating secretly to betray the imperial army to the Protestant Swedes, and imperial agents in his own camp are preparing his ruin. His soldier folk, a diabolical caricature of the "new people" of Christendom, prepare to assert themselves against civil society and imperial authority. *Die Freiheit ist bei der Macht allein*—"You get freedom only with power," declares a cuirassier. "I'll live and die with Wallenstein!" The empire pawned its moral authority by calling Wallenstein and his monstrous army to its service, bringing more misery to its own people than ever did the invading Protestants. Schiller has the soldiers sing:

Aus der Welt die Freiheit verschwunden ist,
Man sieht nur die Herren und Knechte;
Die Falschheit herrscht, die Hinterlist
Bei dem feigen Menschengeschlechte.
Der dem Tod ins Angesicht schauen kann,
Der Soldat allein ist der freie Mann!

(Freedom has disappeared from the world,
And you see only masters and slaves;
And perfidy reigns, and deceitfulness,
Among the cowardly human race
He who can look death in the face,
The soldier alone, is a free man!)

Wallenstein's army stands opposed to civil society—indeed, it is consuming civil society—but its soldier citizens will risk their lives to perpetuate it.

These are the outcasts of Europe to whom Wallenstein has given hope and purpose, and we are drawn into their enthusiasm even when we know that their hope is perverse and their purpose is malignant.

The superstitious Wallenstein imagines that he is the captive of his stars; in fact, his destiny is the terrible army he has brought into being and whose ambitions he must fulfill or he will perish. There is no tragedy in literature quite like that of Wallenstein, the greatest man of seventeenth-century Germany but also the most destructive. The drama has some dreadful weaknesses, including a cloying romantic subplot, but it illuminates European history like few other works of literature. Schiller wrote the trilogy in 1799, and his audience knew that the protagonist was not so much Wallenstein as Napoleon Bonaparte, who again would summon the freebooters and malcontents of Europe into a multinational army that threatened to eradicate civil society. Both were tragic figures. Europe had the capacity to bring forth a new people, and instead it gave rise to a murderous horde. Europe strains for universality, and, in the absence of universal Christian empire, a different and dire species of universality would arise. Wallenstein, Napoleon, Joseph Stalin, and Adolf Hitler would send the rough hordes raging across Europe again and again until only a moral ruin remained of Christendom.

Schiller, to be sure, hoped against hope that Napoleon would somehow escape Wallenstein's tragedy. But the great tragedian nonetheless missed the most important dimension of the case. The lacunae in Schiller's account are filled by Aldous Huxley's biography (1942) of the seventeenth-century French diplomat and spymaster Père Joseph. Huxley, who in his celebrated dystopia *Brave*

New World foresaw a hideous fate for civilization, struggled with the origins of the terrible world war then consuming Europe. The red thread of his research took him back to Father Joseph du Tremblay, the original "Grey Eminence." Father Joseph's skullduggery on behalf of Louis XIII and Cardinal Richelieu became the stuff of legend, thanks in part to Alexander Dumas' historical fiction. Huxley was half-mad with mysticism by the time he fixed his gaze on Father Joseph, but sometimes it takes one to know one. Richelieu's diplomat and spymaster trained in a school of mystical "self-annihilation" that substituted the interests of France for the plans of divine providence. France herself was God's instrument for the salvation of humanity, Father Joseph believed, such that her interests justified any means, no matter how horrible.

Not merely the temporal interests of the French state, but a self-deifying delusion prompted these French clerics to prolong the religious wars of the 1620s into the terrible Thirty Years' War, killing most of the population of central Europe. Richelieu and Père Joseph bribed and manipulated Protestant and Catholic alike to extend the conflict. Wallenstein's *levee en masse* crushed the Protestants after ten years of war, so Richelieu subsidized the Swedish intervention on the Protestant side. Notoriously, Father Joseph duped the Austrian emperor into dismissing his best general, Albrecht Wenzel Eusebius von Wallenstein, in order to give Sweden a freer hand. Father Joseph and his spies probably had a hand in the Austrian decision to assassinate Wallenstein after he tried to make a separate peace with the Swedes. In the greater interest of France, this Catholic fanatic paid Protestant and Turk to harass the Habsburgs.

Huxley, searching for the causes of the terrible world wars of the twentieth century, concluded that their source was to be found in this horrifying period. French clerical mysticism was the sacred heart of darkness. In fairness to the French, the Spanish had much the same idea. All nationalism worships God in the carnival mirror of its own reflection. The exception is the Jewish nation, which understands itself to exist because God called it to his service. As Franz Rosenzweig observed, once the Gentile nations embraced Christianity, they abandoned their ancient fatalism regarding the inevitable extinction of their tribe. It is the God of Israel who first offers eternal life to humankind, and Christianity extended Israel's promise to all. But the nations that adhered to Christendom as tribes rather than as individuals never forswore their love for their own ethnicity. On the contrary, they longed for eternal life in their own Gentile skin rather than in the Kingdom of God promised by Jesus Christ. After Christianity taught them the election of Israel, the Gentiles coveted election for themselves and desired that their own people be the chosen people. That set ethnocentric nationalism in conflict both with the Jews—the descendants of Abraham in the flesh—and with the Church, which holds itself to be the new People of God.

Christian universal empire, from Charlemagne in AD 800 to the Habsburgs in 1914, was by definition multinational, if not antinational. The Christians were the *ekklesia*, those called out of the nations, and only a truly universal elite could rule them.

As Rosenzweig put it:

Precisely through Christianity the idea of Election has gone out amongst the individual nations, and along with it a concomitant claim upon eternity. It is not the case that such a claim upon eternity conditioned the entire life of these peoples; one hardly can speak of this. The idea of Election, upon which such a claim [on eternity] uniquely can be based, becomes conscious for the peoples only in certain exalted moments, and in any case is more of a festive costume than their workaday dress.... Still, there sleeps upon the foundation of one's love for one's own people the presentiment that someday in the distant future it no longer will be, and this gives this love a sweetly painful gravity.

Nationalism was to be suppressed. That is why the sixteenth-century Church did not tolerate translation of the scriptures into the vernacular. Charles V himself, the most powerful man in the world, had to ask the Inquisition's permission to keep a French translation of the Bible. Richelieu and Father Joseph overthrew this. They proposed, in place of universal empire, a Christian empire led by a particular nation divinely appointed for world mastery—namely, France. Between the Sun King Louis XIV and Napoleon Bonaparte, it became a going proposition for the better part of two centuries.

France, to be sure, was not the only nation that mistook itself for God. Adolf Hitler turned the idea into something unspeakably worse than the French ever could have imagined. The Greek-speaking remnant of the Roman Empire in Constantinople, the "Second Rome," saw itself as the legitimate savior of the world. As Huxley observes, Father Joseph's vision of France as the instrument of providence was of one piece with his vision of a French-led crusade to liberate Constantinople from the Turks. Nineteenth-century Russia suffered from the same delusion of a liberated Constantinople. By some perverse twist of fate, the French ambassador to the court of the czar in 1914, Michael Paleologue, descended from the last ruling family of Constantinople. He spurred Russia toward a war that, he hoped, would wipe out the hated Habsburg monarchy of Austria forever.

Habsburg Austria, the embodiment of the medieval Catholic empire, became the target of the French messianists, because it was precisely this model that the French desired to supplant. Catholic universal empire, the "prison of the nations" in its nineteenth-century Habsburg expression, ultimately was a failure. By contrast, the United States, a melting-pot nation of immigrants, achieved a transcendent kind of universality and thereby became the world's dominant power. It is this that France cannot abide in its sacred heart of darkness. Habsburg Austria was a competitor, but America is an obsession. That America twice saved France during the twentieth century merely reinforces the French sentiment of ultimate irrelevance. Centuries of accumulated bile ooze and gurgle in mortification. None of it matters. France has no military power and a sclerotic economy. Along with the rest of Europe, its population is aging and soon will decline. Its protest against American hegemony is the last echo of an evil age in Europe whose passing will go unmourned. The tragedy in the wars of religion was the death of Catholic universalism, and the tragedy of a mediocre people that could find nothing to replace it with—until the American Revolution.

CHAPTER 4

National Extinction and Natural Law

When nations go willingly into that dark night, what should we conclude about human nature?

In the ancient world of perpetual war, nations perished by violence, and it was assumed that they would have preferred to survive. The modern world, with few exceptions, removes the violent threat to the national existence of small peoples, yet the rate of their extinction by strictly voluntary means is faster than ever before in history. We find it hard to come to terms with the suicide of an acquaintance; how do we come to terms with the suicide of a nation? In the aftermath of the First World War, Sigmund Freud claimed that human beings possessed a death drive as much as an instinct for self-preservation. If we judged by the numbers alone, we would have to agree with Freud, given that most of the world's cultures, advanced as well as aboriginal, seem likely to annihilate themselves. Freud offered in effect a Satanic parody of the old-fashioned Catholic view of "natural law" (today's Catholic view is more nuanced).

The Catholic Encyclopedia of 1911 defined it as "those instincts and emotions common to man and the lower animals, such as the instinct of self-preservation and love of offspring. In its strictly ethical application—the sense in which this article treats it—the natural law is the rule of conduct which is prescribed to us by the Creator in the constitution of the nature with which He has endowed us." Sadly, most human societies evince no instinct for self-preservation, and certainly no love of offspring, for they do not bother to have sufficient offspring to survive.

No matter what assumption we make about God and human nature, we land in logical trouble. If our nature inclines us toward the moral law without the help of revelation, it is not clear why God is strictly necessary. That was the position of the Catholic Church as of the First Vatican Council (1870), which proceeded from the view of St. Thomas Aquinas. Again, *The Catholic Encyclopedia*:

> Theoretically speaking, man is capable of acquiring a full knowledge of the moral law, which is . . . nothing but the dictates of reason properly exercised. Actually, taking into consideration the power of passion, prejudice, and other influences which cloud the understanding or pervert the will, one can safely say that man, unaided by supernatural revelation, would not acquire a full and correct knowledge of the contents of the natural law (cf. Vatican Council, Sess. III, cap. ii).

In this system, God isn't strictly necessary, merely convenient, because humankind is "capable of acquiring a full knowledge of the moral law," although we are prone to mistakes without the aid of supernatural revelation. That helps explain why a certain kind of Marxist philosopher always has found it easy to become a certain kind of Thomist; in both cases, nature is in the driver's seat. Either human reason can work out everything out on its own, or it can't. Natural theology leaves humankind half-pregnant with reason. It does not help much to reject natural theology and argue instead for "divine-command ethics"—in other words, to assert that what is good is simply what the Bible (or some other preferred scripture) tells one to do. That, the divine-command view, was articulated by Karl Barth, the great Reformed theologian of the twentieth century.

Whatever the Bible might require, humankind still is God's creation, and, if God intended us to hearken to his revelation, he must have made us capable of responding to it in some fashion. There must be some correspondence, in other words, between the nature of human beings and any divine revelation that makes it possible for humans to accept grace. We know that there is a correspondence between nature and the human imagination, or we would not have discovered planetary orbits or split the atom; why should there not be a correspondence between nature—that is, Creation—and the imagination of our hearts? If it is divine love that elicits from us a response to grace, how can we separate our nature from our capacity to respond to love?

Part of the answer to this question, I believe, lies in our understanding of nature itself. The pagan sees nature as given and worships it; the ancient Hebrews saw nature as created and contingent, as in the 102nd Psalm:

> In the beginning you laid the foundations of the earth,
>> and the heavens are the work of your hands.
> They will perish, but you remain;
>> they will all wear out like a garment.

Like clothing you will change them
    and they will be discarded.
But you remain the same,
    and your years will never end.
The children of your servants will live in your presence;
    their descendants will be established before you.

The idea that the universe was finite in time and entropic—that it would wear out like a suit of clothes—was an ancient theological precept before it was a discovery of twentieth-century science. In Jewish thinking, nature itself is flawed, and Jewish prayers envision a repair of the flaws in the cosmos itself at the coming of the Messiah, as Rabbi Joseph Dov Soloveitchik observes regarding the prayers for the new month in his book *Halakhic Man*.

The trouble with asserting a "natural law" lies in our relationship to nature itself. Since Athens in the fifth century BC, philosophers have debated whether ideas in our mind have a "real" existence simply because we can define them mentally. Or must we first instantiate such ideas in order to establish their reality? Through St. Thomas Aquinas, Aristotle's vision of nature as a complete and coherent entity, and of our perception of nature as impressions on a *tabula rasa*, forms the basis for natural law: We observe what is in nature and order our actions in correspondence with nature. That is a compelling and persuasive idea, which suffers from two main deficiencies. One is that there is very good reason to believe that there are "true" ideas that exist in our minds but do not derive from the senses and cannot be instantiated through empirical observation. The second is that, at the deepest level of ontology, nature itself remains ineffable and beyond the grasp of human sense perception. If we cannot quite understand nature, how can we base judgment on "natural law"? And if our ability to perceive and understand nature is flawed—if we encounter an insuperable epistemological barrier—how can we exclude the possibility that nature itself is flawed?

The ancient Greeks were painfully aware of these problems. Of all the ideas that exist in our mind but cannot be instantiated empirically, the Infinite is the oldest and least tractable. What Aristotle called an "actual infinity" may be imagined but cannot be comprehended empirically, for we never can finish counting it. Physical reality thrust the problem of the infinite on the mathematicians. Aquinas dismissed Plato with the quip that knowing the essence of the mythical Phoenix does not mean that such a bird actually exists. Mathematics, though, presents problems of a different kind: objects that exist in the mind but cannot possibly derive from the senses and yet have a manifest relationship to the real world. That is why we distinguish "strong Platonism" (the claim that essence implies existence) from "weak Platonism"—from, that is, the far more restricted claim that certain kinds of ideas (notably, well-ordered mathematical concepts) are real. The ancients and the Scholastics fought about abstractions. After the fifteenth century, though, metaphysics was compelled to respond to physics. The "actual infinite" that Aristotle eschewed forced itself on the philosophers.

Curiously, the first intimation of the actual infinite appeared in music. During the 1430s, musicians began tempering musical intervals, using string lengths that corresponded to irrational numbers. Because the results were audibly harmonious, Nicholas of Cusa asserted that irrational numbers therefore must be real, after the fashion of Augustine's "numbers in the mind of God" that were "too simple" for us to grasp directly. This provoked a crisis in mathematics as well as metaphysics. Aristotle knew that an irrational number could be represented as an infinite series of rational numbers and that the irrationals therefore implied the existence of an actual infinite, which of course could not be grasped by the senses. He rejected the concept, and, under his influence, fifteenth- and sixteenth-century mathematicians and music theorists agonized over whether to admit the irrationals into musical tuning. The discovery of the calculus in the second half of the seventeenth century, though, introduced a new kind of "real" object that was in the mind and not derived from the senses. The calculus gives us the exact sum of an infinite number of infinitesimal quantities, which by definition are imperceptible. We cannot perceive vanishingly small quantities, yet in the calculus their sum is a definite number. The physics that issued from the work of Newton and Leibniz transformed the world. That made it more difficult (if not quite impossible) to dismiss infinitesimals as the mere imaginings of mathematicians. At issue was not a mythical bird but rather the precise calculation of ballistic trajectories and planetary orbits. Leibniz embraced the "actual infinite" that Aristotle abhorred.

Leibniz did not "prove" the existence of an actual infinite in the form of infinitesimals, for there is no proof that mathematical objects "exist" in the same way that thistles and marmalade exist. There still are dissenters among mathematicians—namely, the Constructivist school—who cleave to Aristotelian "realism." But the revolution in mathematics and physics made for a different sort of debate from what had occurred among the ancients or the Schoolmen. Plato's theory of species, with its borrowings (for example, in the *Timaeus*) from Pythagorean mysticism, was speculation, not physics. The infinitesimals, by contrast, were not simply a new sort of Platonic number mysticism but rather a working principle that transformed the world.

As noted, natural-law theory—the contention that natural reason allows humankind to discover the laws of ethics without the aid of revelation—hearkens back to St. Thomas Aquinas and indirectly to Aristotle. An alternative approach is found in Augustine, who argued that concepts in the mind that cannot be derived from the senses are given to us through Divine Illumination. This became a practical rather than a Scholastic issue in consequence of the new mathematics and physics of the sixteenth century, which roused the philosophers to explain the existence of objects in the mind that were not in the senses. Descartes's "innate ideas" looked back to Augustine's theory of Divine Illumination. Immanuel Kant, by contrast, proposed an inborn ("a priori") capacity for transcendental reason—reason that transcends sense perception—in order to do, without the inconvenient presence of God, what Augustine had proposed.

That is why Kant triumphed over the Scholastics, the ancients, and the empiricists: His followers quickly learned how to use his theory to explain Newtonian natural science. The neo-Kantian school that dominated Continental academic philosophy from the last quarter of the nineteenth century through the first quarter of the twentieth hung its hat on the problem of infinitesimals. "The infinitesimal magnitude, thought of as reality, becomes the idealistic lever of all knowledge of nature," wrote Hermann Cohen, founder of the neo-Kantian school, in 1883.

And it got stranger still. Leibniz's troublesome infinitesimals turned out to be only one among an infinity of "actual infinities." The theory of infinite sets proposed by the great nineteenth-century mathematician Georg Cantor was a response to anomalies in the calculus. By the early nineteenth century, mathematicians had learned that "spiky" functions—for example, functions that shift sign at arbitrarily small intervals—cannot be analyzed with Leibniz's infinitesimals. Somehow the infinitely small intervals that the calculus integrates into a finite sum were not quite "small" enough to capture such functions. There was the infinitely small and the infinitely smaller still—and that is what Cantor proved: Different orders, or densities, of infinity do in fact exist. That is why infinite sets became so important—not because mathematicians sat around staring at the ceiling and thinking of the infinite. Cantor named the different infinities "transfinite numbers." Kurt Gödel—a deeply religious man—set out to demonstrate, in turn, that we cannot prove with formal logic everything that we know to be true in mathematics. The nub of his Incompleteness Theorems is that there are things that we can define to be true in a mathematical system but that we cannot capture in a formal proof. If we concede that mathematical objects are in some way real, Gödel requires us to concede as well the existence of some higher source for the intuition that sees a mathematical truth that transcends formal logic.

Since then mathematicians have proved that there exists an infinite number of transfinite numbers. Thanks to the work of Gödel and Paul Cohen on the independence of the Continuum Hypothesis, we know that we cannot know how dense they are or in what order they should be arranged—not, at least, within any existing framework of mathematical logic. Whereas Aquinas had argued that there are things we can imagine but that do not exist, Gödel proved that there are things that exist that we cannot imagine. The latter seems rather more pertinent. The Thomists, to be sure, can argue their way out of this corner, but the strain shows.

Natural-law theory thus has two Achilles' heels. The first, as Descartes, Leibniz, and Kant demonstrated, is that we cannot attribute to "unaided reason" the sort of conclusions that Aquinas wished to draw—not about the most fundamental questions of how we perceive reality. The second is the breakdown of the deterministic model of the universe itself. The new German science of the 1920s made a shambles of Cohen's neo-Kantian world. In his book *Halakhic Man*, Soloveitchik saw an historic opportunity in the collapse of scientific determinism and Kantian objectivity. The end of the Newtonian determinism "has helped deliver the philosopher from his bondage to the mathematical sciences." He praised the Danish physicist Niels Bohr for "exploiting Heisenberg's Indeterminacy Principle to [undertake] the refutation of the time-hallowed myth of the insularity of the physical world."

Heisenberg's famous "observer effect" proved that we cannot "look" at the subatomic world without altering it, for "looking" meant sending a photon of light to collide with the particles we wished to observe, and the collision would alter the position of the observed particle. Ultimate reality, moreover, could no longer be described deterministically in the quantum universe but only according to probabilities. Strange as the quantum world appears, the theory has proven itself through innumerable new technologies, notably solid-state electronics. Nature, as Soloveitchik observed, is no longer a remote object of contemplation. If the natural order were perfect and self-contained, we could not distinguish between nature and God—which is the whole thrust of Enlightenment philosophy. Nature that is not quite perfect and not perfectly comprehensible, by contrast, is only the perishable garment of its creator. And our most important thoughts about nature cannot derive from unaided reason, at least not reason defined by formal logic, for, as Gödel demonstrated, there are propositions that we know with certainty to be true in mathematical systems but that we cannot formally prove.

Nonetheless, the debate between "natural theology" and "command ethics" continues around the circle, and I see no end to it.

Of course, we can argue that some people are preprogrammed to receive grace and others are preprogrammed to reject it, but that is no more satisfying than Freud's contention that some people follow Eros while others follow a death drive. We are left watching a majority of the world's cultures simply will themselves out of existence, largely through the individual decision of their members not to rear offspring, and wondering why this should be the case.

What is it that makes human beings different from animals?

Unlike humans, healthy animals universally show an instinct for self-preservation and the propagation of their species. We do not observe un-neutered cats deciding not to have kittens the better to pursue their careers as mousers, nor do they abandon their kittens at the church door. Nor is it quite true that humans are the only species that is sentient of death. Elephants evidently grieve for their dead, and domestic animals grieve for dead human companions. Humans may not be the only animals who are sentient of death, but they are the only animals whose continuity depends on culture as much as it does on genes. I do not mean to suggest that humans of different cultures belong to different species—on the contrary, the child of a Kalahari Bushman will thrive if raised in the family of a Glaswegian ship's engineer. I consider secondary, if not trivial, the genetic differences among the races of *Homo sapiens sapiens*. But culture performs a role among humans similar to the role species does among animals. An adult Bushman never would make sense of industrial society, any more than a Glaswegian ship's engineer would last a fortnight in the Kalahari. Individual human existence has no meaning outside the culture that nurtures, sustains, and transmits our contribution to future generations. Culture is the stuff out of which we weave the hope of immortality, not merely through genetic transmission but through intergenerational communication. That communication, I hardly need add, ends with the extinction of language. That is why I keep returning to Rosenzweig's remarkable insight that humans are sentient of the death of their cultures as much as they are of their own physical death.

A sick cat or dog will crawl into a hole to die. The members of sick cultures do not do anything quite so dramatic, but they cease to have children, dull their senses with alcohol and drugs, become despondent, and too frequently do away with themselves. This is not due to an inborn death drive, contrary to the odious Freud, but rather is a symptom of a culture's mortal illness.

That is also why pagans become Christians. That is, individuals embrace Christianity when their pre-Christian culture no longer can transmit their memory as well as their genes can to future generations. Christianity, in that sense, succeeds precisely where "natural law" fails. Self-confident and secure pagans do not seek life eternal through belief in Jesus Christ, for they are quite happy to believe in themselves. It is when they have reason to cease to believe in themselves, when the depredations of the empires, or the great tide of globalization, overrun their defenses and expose their mortal fragility. We observe two great and related phenomena in the Global South: the fastest rate of cultural extinction in history as well as the fastest rate of Christian evangelization in history. I do not mean to minimize the tragedy of declining cultures, but it is only because of the terrible depth of that tragedy that hundreds of millions of souls turn in fear and trembling to a religion that represents itself as standing above all human cultures: the *ekklesia* of individuals called out from among the nations to the Kingdom of God. Whence come the fear and trembling? Christians are the adoptive children of the Jewish patriarch Abraham. In an important sense, the new

Christians of the Global South relive the life of Abraham, who, at divine command, left behind clan and kindred in the world of four thousand years ago, when clan and kindred were everything. Given a son in old age, Abraham was told to sacrifice that son, thereby destroying his links to the future.

Among peoples facing both the erasure of their links to the past and uncertainty about their future, Abraham's frame of mind on Mount Moriah must seem much less remote than it does to the comfortable Christians of the North. The Hebrew Bible has a personal meaning for the new Christians of the South because in a sense they relive the experience of the patriarch. Like the myriad tribes of the Roman Empire and the invading barbarians of the Middle Ages, hundreds of peoples will give up their tribal identity and in compensation receive Christianity. Opinions will remain divided as to whether this is a good thing or a bad thing, but it very well may be the main thing occurring in our present century.

This phenomenon completely overthrows the trifling calculus of political science. Theology was dethroned as queen of the sciences two centuries ago, but there is a strong case for its restoration. The world has buried Karl Marx's economic man and Sigmund Freud's libidinous man, and the shovel is ready for Martin Heidegger's "authentic" man. To make sense of what's happening in the world, we need to look instead toward biblical man.

The splendid book *Resurrection: The Power of God for Christians and Jews* by Kevin J. Madigan and Jon D. Levenson shows us biblical man in his confrontation with death and, in so doing, holds up a mirror to us. Life and death to the ancient Hebrews were moral conditions more than medical, as the authors explain. Enslavement and looming cultural extinction were felt as the grave, as was childlessness. National redemption and the covenantal promise of the continuity of Abraham's line were a restoration of life, a resurrection in the earliest stirring of Hebrew religious sensibility. The modern materialist view of life and death, the authors remind us, has little in common with the way in which ancient readers of the Bible understood existence. One might go further and assert that the biblical understanding of life and death still prevails today among most of the world's six billion souls. The materialism of modern political science sadly misjudges the demands of the human heart. Nations are willing to fight to the death because their national life already has become a living death, in just the way the Bible saw it. In their hearts they already have gone down to Sheol, and the world holds no greater terror for them than what they live each day.

Resurrection draws a red line from the earliest response to death in the Hebrew Bible to the promise of resurrection in the flesh in the Book of Daniel in the second century BC and in Christian doctrine. Madigan and Levenson show how basic to Jewish and Christian belief is the promise that a loving God will redeem his faithful from death, in the full unity of body and soul. This is the promise of redemption that has sustained Jews and Christians through the centuries and given them a perception that their life in this world participates in eternal life. And so they are alive even in death.

But what of those who feel abandoned to death? By the same token, they are dead even in life.

Here is the authors' portrait of the biblical view:

> The sources in the Hebrew Bible have a broader definition of death and of life than we do. That is why they can see exile, for example, as death, and repatriation as life, in a sense that seems contrived (to put it negatively) or artful (to put it positively) to us, but probably did not so seem to the original authors and au-

diences. In part, this is because *the ancient Israelites, altogether lacking the materialist habit of thought so powerful in modernity, did not conceive of life and death as purely and exclusively biological phenomena. These things were, rather, social in character and could not, therefore, be disengaged from the historical fate of the people of whom they were predicated.* (Emphasis added)

Levenson and Madigan add:

To be alive inevitably entailed more than merely existing in a certain physical state. It also entailed having one's being within a flourishing and continuing kin group that dwelt in a productive and secure association with its land. Conversely, to be widowed, bereaved of children, or in exile was necessarily to experience death.

Ancient Israel felt Egyptian slavery as a living death, and redemption as a resurrection from this death. That is what the author of 1 Samuel meant by these words: "The Lord deals death and gives life / Casts down into Sheol and raises up" (1 Sam 2:6). When Ezekiel in the sixth century BC saw a vision of a valley of dry bones brought back to life, he did think in terms of the resurrection in the flesh of each individual, as prophesied by the prophet Daniel three centuries later. The authors explain:

What does not die is the people Israel, because God has, despite their grievous failings, honored his unbreakable pledge to their ancestors. Israelite people die, like anyone else; the people Israel survives and revives because of God's promise, despite the most lethal defeats.

Because existence was not individual but social in ancient Israel, national restoration and individual resurrection occur as the same thought in Second Isaiah when the return of Israel to Zion is prophesied:

> He will destroy death forever.
> My Lord GOD will wipe the tears away
> From all faces
> And will put an end to the reproach of His people
> Over all the earth—
> For it is the LORD who has spoken.
>   —Isaiah 25:8

The leap from Ezekiel and Second Isaiah to the Book of Daniel, which offers the hope of resurrection in the flesh to all of the righteous, is far narrower than standard scholarship has claimed, in the authors' view.

Why Christianity and Judaism stood their ground on the issue of resurrection in the flesh against internal and external skeptics requires a second thought. Neither religion, observe the authors, can claim a "radical uniqueness" with respect to the other. The priestly elite of Second Temple Judaism, the Sadducees, denied resurrection, as did the Gnostics against whom the Church fathers fought so bitterly during the first three centuries of Christian life. "In rabbinic theology God was not thought to have fulfilled his promises until the whole person returned, body included ... the person is not 'the ghost in the machine' (that is, the body) but rather a unity of body and soul."

For Christians the bodily resurrection of Jesus Christ is the revelation on which the faith is founded. Resurrection in Christian doctrine is the reward of the individuals who leave their Gentile nations to take part in the new people of God and become part of Christ's resurrection. Christian identity is just as social as Jewish identity, for Christians believe they are saved through adoption into a new people. Madigan and Levenson show that the sacrament of baptism for early Christians was inextricably tied to rebirth and resurrection. Thus Christians rescued themselves from the maelstrom of death that took hold of the late Roman Empire.

It is a conceit of modern materialism that identity no longer is social but rather individual; we choose our pleasures, and, if the mood strikes us, shop for a religion the way we might choose a neighborhood. We fancy ourselves rational beings. If we are not quite beyond good and evil, for law and custom still discourage rapine and murder, we certainly are beyond sin and redemption, which we have replaced with stress and therapy. Modern materialism has weaned the industrial world off spiritual food, like the thrifty farmer who trained his donkey to eat less by reducing its rations each day. "Just when I thought I had him trained to live on nothing," the farmer complained, "the donkey had to die!" Like the donkey, the modern world has died after its spiritual rations were cut to nothing. We refuse to acknowledge that our deepest needs are no different from those of biblical man. We fail to nourish them and we die.

What Benedict XVI calls the anti-culture of death will reduce most of the industrial world to a geriatric ward by the latter half of this century and, not long thereafter, to ruins to be picked over by immigrants. We experience death in life, but our intellect and our technology enable us to deny the prospect of death. Not so the peoples who, blinking, emerge into the modern world from the wreckage of traditional society. Globalization spells the end of traditional society, and no amount of sentimentality will save it. In many ways the traditional peoples are much closer to the social view of iden-tity expressed in the Bible than are we. They experience death as a palpable and everpresent horror. Among contemporary poets, none portrays this horror more vividly than the Syrian Arab poet who calls himself Adonis.

In one interview, he described the three hundred million Arabs as already an extinct people: "We have become extinct.... We have the masses of people, but a people becomes extinct when it no lon-ger has a creative capacity, and the capacity to change its world.... The great Sumerians became extinct, the great Greeks became ex-tinct, and the Pharaohs became extinct."

Adonis is the greatest poet in the Arab language, the only Arab writer on the short list for a Nobel Prize, and his song is of living death. Outbursts like the following are characteristic of his poems:

Each day is a child
who dies behind a wall
turning its face to the wall's corners. When I saw death on a road
I saw my face in his. My thoughts resembled locomotives
straining out of fog
and into fog.

Strangled mute
with syllables
voiceless,
with no language
but the moaning of the earth,
my song discovers death
in the sick joy
of everything that is

for anyone who listens.
Refusal is my melody.
Words are my life
and life is my disease.

Modern Westerners endure a living death no less terrifying than the awful images of Adonis. Perhaps that is what makes vampires and zombies perennially popular in Western entertainment. The presentiment of death lurks in Western consciousness and leers out through the television screen. Westerners avert their eyes from the horror that prevails in the traditional world, flipping channels from massacres in Darfur or bombings in Iraq to the "Attack of the Teen Vampire Zombies." Only on occasion—for example, September 11, 2001—does the horror crawl out of the screen and impose itself on Western consciousness. What passes for political science takes as a point of departure Immanuel Kant's claim that he could devise a constitution for a race of devils, "if only they be rational." Persuading the peoples of the Global South to accept modern materialism has proven to be a failure. If only the donkey hadn't died after learning to eat nothing, complain the farmers who populate the political science faculties of the West. Modern political science has encountered the raw hopes and fears of biblical man and shied away in consternation. The hope of traditional society for life on this earth—for men cannot tolerate life on this earth without the promise of eternal life—is precisely the same as it was in late antiquity. Four hundred million Christian converts in Africa and perhaps a hundred million in China are evidence enough that much of the world will abandon broken traditions and embrace the promise of life. Man is still biblical man, and the Bible yet again may prove a guidebook to life as it did two millennia ago.

Theology should reclaim its throne as queen of the sciences because it is our guide to the issues that will decide the life and death of nations.

CHAPTER 5

Rings of Power
and the
Remnants of the West

It may seem a stretch to found an analysis of present-day politics on Franz Rosenzweig's sociology of religion. In fact, we can derive the crucial idea—the extinction of the nation and its effect on the individual member of the nation—from one of the most popular books of the twentieth century, the book that, in fact, Amazon.com readers in 1999 voted their favorite of the twentieth century: J. R. R. Tolkien's *The Lord of the Rings.*

Alone among twentieth-century novelists, Tolkien concerned himself with the mortality not of individuals but of peoples.

The young soldier-scholar of the First World War viewed the uncertain fate of European nations through the mirror of the Dark Ages, when the life of small peoples hung by a thread. In the midst of today's Great Extinction of cultures, and at the onset of civilizational war, Tolkien creates an uncanny resonance among today's readers. With *The Lord of the Rings* he wrote not a fantasy but rather a roman á clef. Additionally, his epic serves as an "anti-*Ring*" to repair the damage that Wagner had inflicted on Western culture.

No serious critic will give Tolkien a place in the literary canon, because his characters generally are stick figures speaking in stilted declamation. But that is beside the point. He has little time to waste on the petty concerns of the sort of character that populates modern fiction. His concern is the doom of peoples, or, to coin a phrase, the decline of the West. Despite his huge readership, Tolkien during his lifetime never published *The Silmarillion*, the tragedy of immortals that underlies *The Lord of the Rings*. Instead he hit on the genial device of leading the reader to the elements of his story through the eyes of the Little People who are entangled in it. It is as if Shakespeare had published something like Tom Stoppard's *Rosenkrantz and Guildenstern Are Dead* rather than *Hamlet*.

Tolkien took by the horns the great ideological beast of his time. After the Great War, the newly hatched existentialist philosophers were shocked to discover that human beings fear for their mortality. In fact, it is quite a commonplace thing to die for one's country, provided that one believes that one's country still will be there. The pull of cultural identity is so strong that men will fling themselves into the jaws of death if they believe such actions will preserve their culture. But what if culture itself—the individual's connection to past as well as future—is in danger? Now, that is really being alone in the universe. Death to preserve one's people is quite a tolerable proposition. The prospective death of the entire people along with its culture is what creates a particularly nasty type of existential angst, the sort that produces a Hitler or an Osama bin Laden.

Small peoples of the Dark Ages, such as Beowulf's Geats, had to think about such things, because extinction was the normal outcome. The old woman's lament at Beowulf's funeral pyre, for example, foresees the destruction of his Geats after the death of its hero and protector. As it turned out, Tolkien's early medieval sources (he had translated *Beowulf*) mirrored the existentially challenged world after the Great War, precisely because the subject of national extinction had forced its way back to the surface. The theme of national extinction permeates the entire work. "It is not your own shire," the High-Elf Gildor reproaches Frodo at the outset of his journey in the forests of the shire. "Others dwelt here before hobbits were; and others will dwell here again when hobbits are no more." A people vanishes from the earth when its language no longer is spoken. Tolkien did not simply invent languages but recreated the linguistic maelstrom of the early Middle Ages, when the high speech of great civilizations faded from memory while the dialects of small peoples dissolved into larger language groups. Tolkien's great philological skills created a unique means of portraying the temporality of the nations.

Tolkien invented a deathless and noble race as a foil to human mortality. His Elves suffer from satiety with immortal life. They no longer reproduce. We meet no Elf younger than a millennium. Tolkien's Fair Folk, endowed with marvelous powers of mind and body, possessors of a radiant high culture, merely mark the time before they must leave Middle-Earth. More than anything else, *The Lord of the Rings* is the tragedy of the Elves and the story of their renunciation.

Minas Tirith, for that matter, houses only half the population it could comfortably hold, as its ancient race of men fails to bring children into the world. Gondor's military weakness stems from its declining population; the army Aragorn leads to the Black Gate in the last battle numbers fewer than the vanguard of the army of Gondor in its prime. Mordor encroaches because Gondor cannot man its borders.

In Tolkien's Anglo-Saxon sources, the extinction of the nation lurks behind every setback. From the vantage point of the trenches of the Great War, though, this echo of the Dark Ages took on a new and terrible meaning.

Here is a summary of the mythic tragedy behind *The Lord of the Rings*: Immortality was not enough for Tolkien's "Light-Elves" (*Licht-Alben*, precisely what Wagner calls his gods). Possessive love for their own works led them to tragic errors, first among which is Feanor's ill-advised quest for his stolen jewels, the Silmarils. That motivates the Elves' exile in Middle-Earth. Later, the Elvish Smiths of Middle-Earth accept the assistance of the evil Sauron in forging the Three Elven Rings of air, fire, and water. In some way or other, the vague association with Sauron contaminates the Three Rings such that, when Sauron's One Ring is destroyed, the power of the Three Rings must fade as well. That means the end of the magical wood of Lothlorien, which Galadriel has preserved in a sort of perpetual spring, and the demise of Rivendell, which Elrond maintains as the last bastion of lore and art. Presumably Gandalf, who bears the ring of fire, will lose some of his power as well. Sauron furthermore corrupted the Numenoreans, a noble race of Men, by convincing them they could wrest immortality from the Valar (the gods) by invading their Blessed Realm, Valinor.

The Nine Rings granted to mortal Men produce a vampirelike caricature of immortality, as the bearers fade into wraiths. The One Ring bestows a perverse sort of immortality on its owner, whose body ceases to age while his soul decays, like Dorian Gray and his portrait. It is a warped version of the Elves' immortality within the mortal world of Middle-Earth. Once touched, it cannot easily be relinquished; Isildur, heir of the Numenorean "faithful," cannot bear to destroy it. The Hobbits' great virtue is the inner strength to part with the Ring. But all of the three Hobbits who have borne it, Bilbo, Frodo, and Samwise, ultimately must abandon Middle-Earth. Immortality, once tasted, poisons the joy of Middle-Earth even for Hobbits. Galadriel redeems herself by renouncing her works, although in consequence she and her people must leave the mortal realm, that is, Middle-Earth. She refuses the offer of the One Ring ("I will diminish, and remain Galadriel"). The "faithful" survivors of the ruin of Numenor, of whom Aragorn is the heir, accept mortality and therefore are redeemed.

It is tricky, of course, to draw analogies between the pride and folly of Feanor or the Numenorians in Tolkien's fantasy and the pride and folly of the European nations in the First World War. But it was a commonplace observation after 1918 that the great European tragedy began with a misguided attempt to cheat mortality through the assertion of national supremacy. One cannot make sense of Hitler's rise to power without observing that many Germans believed with all their heart that the existence of the *Volk* was in jeopardy. Martin Heidegger gave (and never retracted) his wholehearted support to Hitler, believing that immersion in the *Volk* was a legitimate answer to the existential crisis.

Immortality was not enough for the Europeans. That is, Christianity at the altar, and universal Christian empire in politics, offered the Europeans a form of immortality beyond the existence of the nation. Europe fell from grace when its great constituent nations decided that this sort of immortality was not enough for them and that they should instead fight for temporal dominance on the earth. Exhausted from their wars, the peoples of Europe sank into a torpor that is destroying them slowly but with terrible certainty.

Tolkien was the most Christian of twentieth-century writers, not because he produced Christian allegory and apologetics like his friend C. S. Lewis but because he uniquely portrayed the tragic nature of what Christianity replaced. Tolkien's popular *Ring* trilogy sought to undermine and supplant Richard Wagner's operatic *Ring* cycle, which had offered so much inspiration for Nazism.

Tolkien well may have written his epic as an "anti-*Ring*" to repair the damage that Wagner had inflicted upon Western culture. Consciously or not, the Oxford philologist who invented Hobbits has ruined Wagner for the popular audience. It recalls the terrible moment in Thomas Mann's great novel *Doktor Faustus* when the composer Adrian Leverkuhn, finishing his Faust cantata in the throes of syphilitic dementia, announces, "I want to take it back!" His amanuensis asks, "What do you want to take back?" "Beethoven's Ninth Symphony!" cries Leverkuhn. Leverkuhn (on the strength of a bargain with the devil) has written a work whose objective is to ruin the ability of musical audiences to hear Beethoven. Tolkien has taken back Wagner's *Ring*.

It is hard for us today to imagine what a cult raised itself around Wagner after the premiere of his *Ring* cycle in 1876. Compared to it, the combined fervor for Elvis, the Beatles, Madonna, and Michael Jackson seems like a band concert in the park. Perfectly sensible people attended a Wagner opera and declared that their lives had changed. Bavaria's eccentric King Ludwig II fell in love with the composer and built him the Bayreuth Festival, to which the elite of Europe repaired in homage. It was something like the mood that swept the youth of the West in the late 1960s but on an order of magnitude more powerful.

In 1848, Wagner was a disgruntled emulator of French grand opera who stockpiled hand grenades for revolutionaries, a fugitive from justice after that year's uprising. A quarter-century later he stood at the pinnacle of European culture. What precisely did he do? Wagner announced the death of the old order of aristocracy and Church, of order and rules. Not only was the old order dying, but also it deserved to die, the victim of its inherent flaws. As the old order died, a New Man would replace the servile creatures of the old laws, and a New Art would become the New Man's religion. The New Man would be fearless, sensual, and unconstrained, and could make the world according to his will. Wagner's dictum that the sources of Western civilization had failed was not only entirely correct but also numbingly obvious to anyone who had lived through the upheavals of 1848. But how should one respond to this? Wagner had a seductive answer: Become your own god! Using elements of old Norse sagas and medieval epic, he cobbled together a new myth. The Norse god Wotan personifies the old order: He rules by the laws engraved on his spear, by which he himself is bound. To build his fortress Valhalla, he requires the labor of the giants, and to pay the giants he steals the treasure of the Nibelung dwarf Alberich. Alberich won the treasure with a magic ring he fashioned from the stolen gold of the Rhine River. Wotan covets this ring, which gives its bearer world mastery, but is compelled to give it to the giants.

Wagner's audience had no trouble recognizing in Wotan and the other immortal gods the ancient aristocracy of Empire and Church, who made a fatal compromise with capital (the Ring of world domination) and thus sealed their own doom. Siegfried (Wotan's grandson) takes the Ring back from the giant Fafner and then shatters the god's spear and wins as his bride Brunnhilde the immortal Valkyrie. Through the rest of a silly plot full of love potions and magic disguises, Siegfried is betrayed and stabbed in the back. Brunnhilde immolates herself on Siegfried's funeral pyre, and the flames burn down Valhalla as well, gods and all. A New World Order emerges on the basis of heroic will. It is not hard to see how appetizing this stew was for Hitler.

Tolkien himself despised Wagner (whom he knew thoroughly)

and rejected comparisons between his *Rings* and Wagner's cycle. ("Both rings are round" is the extent of his published comment.) But the parallels between the two works are so extensive as to raise the question as to Tolkien's intent. The Ring of Power itself is Wagner's invention (probably derived from Friedrich de la Motte Fouque, a German Romantic). Also to be found in both works are an immortal woman who renounces immortality for the love of a human, a

Wagner versus Tolkien

Der Ring des Nibulungen	The Lord of the Rings
Alberich forges a Ring of Power	Sauron forges a Ring of Power
Wotan needs the giants to build Valhalla	The Elves need Sauron to forge their Rings of Power
The Ring gives the bearer world domination	The Ring gives the bearer world domination
Wotan uses the Ring to pay the giants	Sauron betrays the Elves
The Ring is cursed and betrays its bearer	The Ring is evil and betrays its bearer
Fafner kills brother Fasolt to get the Ring	Smeagol kills friend Deagol for the Ring
Fafner hides in a cave for centuries	Smeagol-Gollum hides in a cave for centuries
Siegfried inherits the shards of his father's sword	Aragorn inherits the shards his father's sword
Brunnhilde gives up immortality for Siegfried	Arwen gives up immortality for Aragorn
Wotan plays "riddles" for the life of Mime	Gollum plays "riddles" for the life of Bilbo
A dragon guards the Nibelungs' hoard	A dragon guards the dwarves' hoard
The gods renounce the world and await the end	The Elves renounce the world and prepare to depart
The Ring is returned to its origin, the River Rhine	The Ring is returned to its origin, Mount Doom
Hagen falls into the river	Gollum falls into the volcano
The immortals burn in Valhalla	The immortals leave Middle-Earth
A new era emerges in the world	A new era emerges in the world
Men are left to their own devices	Men are left to their own devices

broken sword reforged, a life-and-death game of riddles, and other elements that one doesn't encounter every day.

For those who don't know the details of the Tolkien *Ring*—well, you will before long, because it is a story that everyone will learn. The details are far less important than the common starting point: the crisis of the immortals. Wagner's immortal gods must fall as a result of the corrupt bargain they have made with the giants who built Valhalla. Tolkien's immortal Elves must leave Middle-Earth because of the fatal assistance they took from Sauron. What Tolkien has in mind is nothing more than the familiar observation that the high culture of the West arose and fell with the aristocracy, which had the time and inclination to cultivate it. With the high culture came the abuse of power associated with the aristocracy; when this disappears, the great beauties of Western civilization and much of its best thought disappear with it.

Tolkien enthusiasts emphasize his differences with Wagner, as if to ward off the disparagement that *The Lord of the Rings* is a derivative work. As Bradley Birzer, David Harvey, and other commentators observe, Tolkien detested Wagner's neopaganism. He was a devout Roman Catholic, and explicitly philo-Semitic where Wagner was anti-Semitic. But this defense of Tolkien obscures a great accomplishment. He did not emulate Wagner's *Ring*, but he recast the materials into an entirely new form. "Recast" is an appropriate expression. A memorable scene in Wagner shows Siegfried filing the shards of his father's sword into dust and casting a new sword out of the filings. That, more or less, is what Tolkien accomplished with the elements of Wagner's story. Wagner will still haunt the stages of opera houses, but audiences will see him through Tolkien's eyes.

Tolkien is a writer of greater theological depth than his Oxford colleague C. S. Lewis, in my judgment. Lewis is a felicitous writer and a diligent apologist, but mere allegory along the lines of the Narnia series can do no more than restate Christian doctrine; it cannot really expand our experience of it. Tolkien takes us to the dark frontier of a world that is not yet Christian, and therefore is tragic, but has the capacity to become Christian. It is the world of the Dark Ages, in which barbarians first encounter the light. It is not fantasy but rather a distillation of the spiritual history of the West. Whereas C. S. Lewis tries to make us comfortable in what we already believe, by dressing up the story as a children's masquerade, Tolkien makes us profoundly uncomfortable. Our people, our culture, our language, our toehold on this shifting and uncertain earth are no more secure than those of a thousand extinct tribes of the Dark Ages, and a greater hope than that of the work of our hands and the hone of our swords must avail us.

It is useful to contrast Tolkien's purpose to that of T. S. Eliot, too often held up as the exemplary Christian poet of the twentieth century. Eliot sifted through the detritus of the pagan past in the cellars of Christianity. As he wrote in his notes to "The Waste Land" (1922): "To another work of anthropology I am indebted in general, one which has influenced our generation profoundly; I mean *The Golden Bough*" of James Frazer. Frazer attempts to show that all Christian imagery and ritual derive from pagan myth—for example, the commonplace idea of a sacrificed god. His conclusions have been rejected by later scholars, but the relevant point regarding Eliot is that he embraced the pagan antecedents of Christianity as he thought they were (even though they turned out to be something other than what he thought).

Tolkien knew far more about the pagan past than Eliot did; as the great philologist of his time, he produced the first readable translation of *Beowulf* as well as seminal editions of the most important

Anglo-Saxon classics. He loved the material more than any man living, but, unlike the dilettantish Eliot, the authority Tolkien sacrificed his love for the Anglo-Saxon sources and chose to transform the modern memory of it by creating a variant of it more congenial to Christianity.

Part Two

Symptoms and Distractions

CHAPTER 6

Green Presentiments

The imminent death of one's culture is often too awful to contemplate, so the dread is evaded, medicated, or deflected. This observation explains a wide range of cultural phenomena and even whole political movements.

In this light, I have come to the conclusion that the Climate Change camp is a loony cult. The scientific controversy is beyond me, but at a hundred paces I can recognize the fixed stare, the strained voice-throb, and the rigid jaw of a madman. The Greens hector us about the impending end of the world. I put it to them: Perhaps it is not the end of the world but just the end of you.

In various places, 2010 had some of the coldest winter days on record. Then, 2010 had some of the hottest summer days on record, with Russia battling heat-induced wildfires. Londoners frolicked on the frozen Thames in the days of Samuel Pepys. A few hundred years earlier, in the early Middle Ages, wine grapes were grown in southern Scotland. We could line up hundreds of such factoids.

However, analysis of global weather patterns is a subtle issue about which reasonable men might in good faith reach different conclusions. Clearly, then, the evangelical zealotry that motivates the global-warmers (Al Gore, the book-cooking scientists of East Anglia, the Nobel Prize Committee) has a source other than the facts.

For the same reason that men cannot live without the hope of immortality, they cannot bear their gray, miserable lives without some sense of exaltation—religion, art, music, poetry, sex, drugs, violence, whatever. With the decline of Christianity and its bodyguard—the high culture of the West—sex, drugs, and (simulated) violence predominate. These devices eventually leave the user all the more anxious.

But not only anxiety plagues them. By living on the underside of popular culture, the young people of the West make themselves feel worthless and insignificant. In the animated film *Antz* (1998), an ant (with Woody Allen's voice) complains to an ant psychiatrist, "I feel so insignificant," to which the psychiatrist replies, "That's a breakthrough. You are insignificant." To be truly convinced of your insignificance, however, is an unbearable, if not suicidal, thought. The human mind resists its own destruction by wishing away its sense of insignificance. One such device is paranoia, which attributes significance to insignificant objects and events; we imagine that the fellow at the next table is a secret-police agent. It is more comforting to believe that occult forces are persecuting us than that no one cares about us. In the United States, many blacks believe that evil white doctors invented AIDS to wipe out the black population. Adolf Hitler believed that syphilis was a Jewish plot to poison Aryan blood. Egyptian high-school textbooks teach that American pilots and spy technology secretly won the 1967 war for Israel, and so forth.

Today's educated Westerners do not normally believe in such

bizarre ideas, but they are susceptible to subtler forms of the same malady. After rejecting revealed religion, modern people seek a sense of exultation in nature. The sense of the transcendent they derive from contemplating nature is of existential importance. *It is not that I will pass from the earth without leaving so much as a grease spot to mark my stay*, thinks the Green. *It is the earth herself who is in danger. The German forest is dying! The rainforests will vanish! The whales will become extinct! The ice caps are melting!* The Green projects his own presentiment of death onto the natural world. Fear for the irreversible destruction of the natural world—trees, whales, polar ice caps, Siberian tigers, pandas—substitutes for the death anxiety of the individual. Post-Christian Westerners confound their own sense of mortality with the vulnerability of the natural world. Sadly, it is not the end of the world. It is just the end of you.

In the extreme case, the Green becomes the enemy of industrial civilization in general and comes to regard modern humans as a cancer of the biosphere. Of course I do not oppose sensible measures to protect rainforests, preserve habitat for the spotted owl (which an acquaintance has assured me tastes just like chicken), prevent overfishing, and so forth, but I am weary of the fanaticism that distinguishes the conservationist from the environmental fanatic who has turned against civilization. It should come as no surprise that, broadly speaking, Americans have shown less concern over apocalyptic climate-change scenarios than have Europeans. Unlike the Europeans, most Americans cling to the old Judeo-Christian religion and have other means to address the matter of mortality. For them, the sun and moon are merely lamps and watches in the display cases of the creator's shop window. What is transcendent is not nature but a creator who is not himself part of nature.

This mechanism of substituting mortal anxiety also serves to explain the brisk sales of books such as Jared Diamond's *Collapse: How Societies Choose to Fail or Succeed*. Why people read a certain book often contains more information than the book itself. Diamond picks out of the rubbish bin of history a few cases of nugatory interest in which environmental disaster overwhelmed a society otherwise desirous of continued existence. Diamond avers that the problem was in breeding too fast and cutting down too many trees. The silly Vikings of Greenland refused to eat fish, disdained the hunting techniques of the Inuit, and consumed too much wood and topsoil. As a result their colony collapsed during the fifteenth century and they all died. One feels sorry for the Greenlanders, though not for their cousins on the Scandinavian mainland, who just then stood at the cusp of their European power.

Something similar happened to the Easter Islanders, who chopped down all their palm trees, and to the Mayans of Central America, who burned their forests to build temples. Apparently, this should serve as a warning to the inveterate consumerists of the United States, who presumably also face extinction should they fail to erect legal barriers to suburban sprawl. Ideological reflex is too mild a word for this sort of thinking; perhaps the term *cramp* would do better. Given that America returns land to the wilderness each year, the danger to American survival from deforestation must be on par with the risks of being hit by a large asteroid. The fact that a geography professor's book on the peculiar circumstances that killed obscure populations turned into a best seller does illustrate, however, that the topic of mass extinction commands the attention of the reading public—although the reading public wants to look for the causes of mass extinction in all but the most obvious place, which is the mirror. Diamond's books appeal to an educated, secular readership—that is, precisely the sort of people who have one child or none at all. If you have fewer than two children, and most of the people you know have fewer than two children, Holmesian deductive powers are not required to foresee your eventual demise.

In fact, the main reason societies fail is that they choose not to live. Small cultures die out for any number of reasons. They are conquered, or ravaged by plague, or run out of whatever it is that they hunt and gather. Large and successful cultures, though, can only destroy themselves. That is a horrifying thought to absorb, and the average reader would much rather delve into the details of obscure ecosystems of the past than reflect on why half of Eastern Europe will die out by midcentury. To "die out" is a euphemism; suicide is closer to the truth. Suicide is a rare occurrence at the individual level but a typical one at the level of nations. We know little of small peoples who died out in antiquity or even the Middle Ages, but the case histories that have come down to us are compelling, precisely because they include the most successful civilizations of the West, namely classical Greece, Rome, and Byzantium. As Robert Marcellus wrote in the *Human Life Review*:

The Greek geographer and historian Strabo (63 BCE–21 CE) described Greece as "a land entirely deserted; the depopulation begun since long continues. Roman soldiers camp in abandoned houses; Athens is populated by statues." Plutarch observed that "one would no longer find in Greece 3,000 hoplites [infantrymen]." The historian Polybius (204–122 BCE) wrote: "One remarks nowadays all over Greece such a diminution in natality and in general manner such a depopulation that the towns are deserted and the fields lie fallow. Although this country has not been ravaged by wars or epidemics, the cause of the harm is evident: by avarice or cowardice the people, if they marry, will not bring up the children they ought to have. At most they bring up one or two. It is in this way that the scourge before it is noticed is rapidly developed. The remedy is in ourselves; we have but to change our morals."

Sparta, the model of slave-based military oligarchy, had five thousand land-owning families at the time of the Peloponnesian War but only seven hundred by the third century AD, after Epiminondas broke the Spartan hold over its helot population. Rome's population fell to perhaps 100,000 during the seventh century, from one million in the second century. Between AD 150 and 450, the population of Rome's Western empire fell by about four-fifths. Constantinople held between 600,000 and one million during the twelfth century, yet it had fallen to only 100,000 when the Turks took it. There is endless debate about such data. Roman population data are somewhat conjectural, and Strabo's estimates have been disputed by some scholars. Explanations have been forwarded that range from the collapse of the slave-based agricultural system to mass infanticide and venereal disease. Nonetheless, it seems clear that the Romans did not so much conquer Greece as occupy its shell, that the Germanic tribes did not so much conquer Rome as move into what remained of it, and that the Arabs did not so much conquer the Byzantine hinterland as migrate into it. In one form or another the antecedents of Western civilization died of existential causes rather than external or environmental ones.

Perhaps the will to live among seventeenth-century Easter Islanders burned brightly as they chopped down their last palm tree. It is hard for us to fathom, for we have very little in common with the Easter Islanders. But we have a great deal in common with the residents of the classical Greek polis and with the Romans as well as their Byzantine offshoot.

CHAPTER 7

The Fraud of Primitive Authenticity

Closely associated with the nature worship of modern Westerners is the cult of primitive authenticity. Regarding its own history as one of oppression, the West has looked toward the primitive man as an exemplar of purity and nobility and has done so at least since Rousseau gave us his version of the noble savage. Perhaps we should take a closer look. Two billion war deaths would have occurred in the twentieth century if modern societies suffered the same casualty rate as did primitive peoples, according to the anthropologist Lawrence H. Keeley. He has calculated that two-thirds of primitives were at war continuously, typically losing half of a percent of their population to war each year. This and other noteworthy prehistoric factoids can be found in Nicholas Wade's *Before the Dawn*, a survey of genetic, linguistic, and archeological research on early man. Primitive peoples, it appears, were nasty, brutish, and short, not at all the cuddly children of nature depicted by popular culture and postcolonial academic grievance studies.

The ubiquity of war may also explain the proliferation of languages in the world. Linguists believe, for credible reasons too complex to review here, that present-day languages descend from a small number of early prototypes and splintered into many thousands of variants. Wade points out that:

> "this variability is extremely puzzling, given that a universal, unchanging language would seem to be the most useful form of communication. That language has evolved to be parochial, not universal, is surely no accident. Security would have been far more important to early human societies than ease of communication with outsiders. Given the incessant warfare between early human groups, a highly variable language would have served to exclude outsiders and to identify strangers the moment they opened their mouths."

The ostensible culprit in the extermination of the noble primitive peoples who survived up to the modern age is Christianity, whose missionaries (now a term of disparagement) attempted to spread civilization around the globe. Yet even in Christianity's darkest hours, when the Third Reich reduced the pope to a prisoner in the Vatican and the European peoples turned the full terror of Western technology on one another, the Nazis managed to kill a small fraction of the proportion that routinely and normally fell in primitive warfare.

American Indians, Eskimos, and New Guinea Highlanders as well as African tribes slaughtered one another with skill and vigor. Their acumen was such that they frequently won their first encounters with modern armed forces. "Even in the harshest possible environments [such as northwestern Alaska] where it was struggle enough just to keep alive, primitive societies still pursued the more overriding goal of killing one another," Wade notes. A quarter of the language groups in New Guinea, home to 1,200 of the world's six thousand languages, were exterminated by warfare during every preceding century, according to one estimate Wade cites. In primitive warfare, "casualty rates were enormous, not the least because they did not take prisoners. That policy was compatible with their usual strategic goal: to exterminate the opponent's society. Captured warriors were killed on the spot, except in the case of the Iroquois, who took captives home to torture them before death, and certain tribes in Colombia, who liked to fatten prisoners before eating them."

However badly civilized peoples may have behaved, the hundred million or so killed by communism and the fifty million or so killed by National Socialism seem modest compared with the couple billion or so who would have died if the casualty rates of primitive peoples had applied to the West. In spite of this, Hollywood grinds out stories of wise and worthy American Indians, African tribesmen, Brazilian rainforest people, and Australian Aborigines, and, most recently, the primitive aliens of *Avatar*, not because Hollywood studio executives hired the wrong sort of anthropologist but because the public pays for them. A slightly more middlebrow public gets the same message from books, such as Jared Diamond's *Guns, Germs, and Steel*, which attributes civilization to mere geographical happenstance, turning a mendacious apology for the failure of primitive society into a bestseller. Research reported by Wade refutes Diamond on a dozen counts, but his book never will reach the vast audience that takes comfort in Diamond's pulp science. The same public whose middlebrow contingent reads Jared Diamond also pays for screenings of *Avatar* and buys *Dances with Wolves* at the Wal-Mart checkout for $5.99. Which raises the question: Why, in the face of overwhelming evidence to the contrary, does popular culture portray primitives as peace-loving folk living in harmony with nature, as opposed to the rapacious and brutal civilizations they were—and, in some places, still are? Why is it that the modern public revels in a demonstrably false portrait of primitive life?

The overwhelming consensus in popular culture holds that primitive peoples enjoy a quality—call it authenticity—that moderns lack and that, by rolling in their muck, some of this authenticity will stick to us. Colonial guilt at the extermination of tribal societies does not go very far as an explanation. The Westerners who were close enough to primitives to exterminate them rarely regretted having done so. Modern Westerners have grown up on *The Lion King* and the ruggedly virtuous Ewoks from *Star Wars*; the missionaries, colonizers, and fortune seekers met the real thing and had few qualms about ridding the world of their diverse traditions. The modern hunger for authenticity has another source then mere colonial guilt.

What brought about civilization—that is, large-scale communication and political organization? Conquest is too simple an explanation. We have from Latin five national languages and dozens of dialects but no comparable development out of the Greek of the earlier Alexandrian empire. Latin and its offshoots dominated Europe because Latin was the language of the Church. The invaders who replenished the depopulated territories of the ruined Roman Empire—Goths, Vandals, and Celts—learned in large measure dialects of Latin because Christianity made them into Europeans. European civilization arose by stamping out the kind of authenticity that characterizes primitive peoples. It is a construct, not a "natural" development. It is arbitrary in the sense that it could have been otherwise.

Guiding the warlike inclinations of primitive peoples is genetic kinship and the microcultures (such as dialect) that attend it. Christianity called out individuals from the nations and gave them a new birth through baptism in a new people, whose earthly pilgrimage led to the Kingdom of God. Christians began with contempt for the flesh of their own origins; the post-Christian envies the "authenticity" of the peoples who never were called out from the nations, for he has left the pilgrimage in mid-passage and does not know where he is or where he should go.

It is difficult to be a Christian, for the faith that points to the Kingdom of God conflicts with the Gentile flesh whence Christians come, but it is oppressive, indeed intolerable, to be an ex-Christian, for it is all the harder to trace one's way back. Europeans have less difficulty, for the Italians never quite gave up their pagan gods whom the Church admitted as saints, and the Germans never quite gave up their heathen religion, which lived on as a substratum of myth and magic beneath the veneer of Christianity. If the United States of America is the Christian nation par excellence, then the predicament of an American ex-Christian is especially miserable and, hence, most acute. Americans have close at hand neither the saints' days of Italian villages incorporating heathen practice predating Rome nor the elf-ridden forest of the German north celebrated in Romantic poetry. They have suburban housing developments and strip malls, urban forests of steel and glass, Hollywood and Graceland, but nothing "authentic."

An overpowering nostalgia afflicts the American post-Christian, for whom the American journey has neither goal nor purpose. He seeks authenticity in nature and in the dead customs of peoples who were subject to nature—that is, peoples who never learned from the Book of Genesis that the heavenly bodies were lamps and clocks hung in the sky for the benefit of man. Even more: In their mortality, the post-Christian senses his own mortality, for, without the Kingdom of God as a goal, American life offers only addictive diversions interrupted by ever sharper episodes of anxiety. With 90 percent of the world's more than six thousand languages likely to disappear during the next hundred years, the search for authenticity will turn from an exercise in frustration into a source of horror. For those upon whom mortality weighs heavily, the object lessons in mortality from the disappearing peoples of the world will be a terrifying form of instruction indeed.

CHAPTER 8

Why Sex Objects Object to Sex

The psychiatric profession observed the 150th anniversary of Sigmund Freud's birth on May 6, 2006. My modest proposal for the event was to exhume his body and put a stake through his heart. Freud's Viennese contemporary, the poet and writer Karl Kraus, quipped that psychoanalysis was "a disease posing as a cure." Time has proven him right.

No one did more than Freud to reduce women to sexual objects, a condition against which women rebel by seeking to destroy the objectified body. Epidemic self-destructiveness has reached proportions that are difficult to grasp. Eating disorders reportedly threaten the lives of ten million American women. "Anorexia or bulimia in florid or subclinical form now afflicts 40 percent of women at some time in their college career," wrote Hara Estroff Marano in *Psychology Today*. Self-harm often accompanies self-starvation, and millions of these women also mutilate themselves. One study claims that up to one in seven British adolescents self-harms, but up to half of those enmeshed in the Goth subculture do so. In the United States, a recent survey of one thousand pupils at one secondary school found that one-quarter had deliberately harmed themselves. Some British hospitals dispense "self-harm kits," including razors and antiseptics, apparently on the health-and-safety principle that causes them to dispense needles to drug users (they're going to do it anyway, why not now "safe and sterile"?). Eating disorders have the highest mortality rate of any mental condition: 20 percent of anorexics eventually kill themselves.

What impels so many young people in Anglo-Saxon countries toward slow-motion suicide? Often the undernourished wraiths who haunt the runways of the fashion industry are blamed for disseminating a twisted ideal of beauty that lures young women into anorexia. But that cannot be a complete explanation, because anorexics starve themselves into extreme ugliness and in many cases mutilate themselves as well. These women are not enhancing their bodies but rejecting them altogether.

What were Freud's crimes against humanity? Freud claimed to have discovered the source of all neurosis in the repression of the sexual impulse, or libido. In fairness, Freud did not think repression was a bad thing, for without it society would disintegrate. The object of psychoanalysis was not to spread universal joy but to proceed "from hysterical misery to ordinary unhappiness." He could never have anticipated the adolescent narcissism of the 1960s, when the complacent and affluent youth of the industrial world demanded something better than ordinary unhappiness. Freud unwittingly provided the ideological foundation for the so-called sexual revolution of the 1960s, and popularized versions of his theory dominated popular culture.

All the major religions of the world attempt to sanctify the family; Freud sought to expose it as a hypocritical viper's nest of neurosis. Religion, he taught, totemized power relations; God was the projected form of the castrating father. The mother provides sexual pleasure to the infant she nurses, whose initial polymorphously perverse sexuality focuses on the mother; the authority of the father then represses the son's sexual fixation on the mother through the threat of castration, while little sister laments the lack of a penis. Such a chamber of horrors cannot be entrusted with the upbringing of children, or so the left interpreted Freud. Sexuality must be severed from reproduction, through abortion and equal status for homosexuality, for example.

Few psychiatrists today defend his sexual derivation of neurosis. But the damage was done. Sexual liberation remains the core of the social agenda of the left. In U.S. politics, the most embittered battles are fought over gay marriage and abortion, not war and taxes. For adolescents in the industrial world, however, the battle was lost a generation ago. Among American adolescents, seeking a sexual outlet in the companionship of one's peers now is more common than the search for romantic attachments. The *New York Times* journalist Benoit Denizet-Lewis reported in a 2004 feature: "Over the course of several months spent hanging out and communicating online with nearly 100 high-school students (mostly white, middle- and upper-middle-class suburban and exurban teenagers from the northeast and Midwest), I heard the same thing: hooking up is more common than dating."

A 2001 survey conducted by Bowling Green State University in Ohio found that, of the 55 percent of local eleventh-graders who engaged in intercourse, 60 percent said they'd had sex with a partner who was no more than a friend. That number would perhaps be higher if the study asked about oral sex. While the teen intercourse rate has declined—from 54 percent in 1991 to 47 percent in 2003—this may be partly because teenagers have simply replaced intercourse with oral sex. To a generation raised on MTV, AIDS, Britney Spears, Internet porn, Monica Lewinsky, and *Sex and the City*, oral sex is definitely not sex (it's just "oral"), and hooking up is definitely not a big deal.

Women enter adolescence with the expectation that they will be used but not loved. Men no longer need to feign affection to receive sexual favors; they merely need ask. But human beings are not beasts content with daily fodder and rutting in season. To be sentient is to be sentient of one's mortality. Sexual objectification leaves women with a foretaste of death, and it should be no surprise that Freud's program drives women into deadly behavior.

Women can expect only a brief flowering of beauty before age and childbearing attenuate their sexual attraction. The love of a husband, the shared love of their children, the honor of the community, and the knowledge that the human life cycle is linked to something eternal are the consolations to women for the loss of their beauty. The status of wife and mother in a family within a community also offers women an honored position and a link to the eternal.

Freud admitted he was baffled by the question "What do women want?" That only goes to show how thick he was. There is no mystery in the feminine mystique. The feminine point of view amounts to what we otherwise call paranoia. No one displays more sensitivity or depends more on intuition than paranoids, who construct a worldview in the absence of or despite the relevant facts. Paranoia, to be precise, assigns meaning to utterly random events. Why did that fellow on the far side of the restaurant fold his newspaper? Was that a signal? Why is the newscaster wearing a green tie? Does he know something? Why are you reading this essay? Are you out to get me? What women want is what all people want—that is, to be unique. Every woman wants to be loved uniquely. The spontaneous attraction that women have for men, however, is not unique but generic. Men (or at least most men) are attracted to women, and under some circumstances, for example, after they have disembarked at port after a long stretch at sea, any instantiation of the gender will do. The women's magazines instruct women as to how to use generic sexuality to attract men. But if a woman succeeds in manipulating a man on the strength of her value as a sexual object, she never can be sure that another woman will not (or has not already done) the same thing with greater success. The most attractive woman in the world is a miserable creature, as Giuseppe Verdi's Princess Eboli lamented, because her physical presence will overwhelm any other perception of her in the eyes of men. Men as a general rule cannot have a sensible conversation with an extremely beautiful woman. They do not listen, but stare, and drool. When age eventually destroys her beauty, she will be left with nothing at all. Whether this is a cultural quirk subject to eventual remedy or a characteristic of humankind since the Fall is a different matter. Adolescent girls suffer the most. The therapists talk of "low self-esteem," but this amounts to uncertainty as to what features of a developing form will attract the opposite sex.

Having cured society of repression by making sexual pleasure a commodity, enlightened opinion is shocked, shocked to discover an epidemic of depression. In consequence, some seventy million Americans have taken antidepressants. Psychotropic drugs, I hasten to add, work miracles for many who suffer from imbalances of brain chemistry, and I mean no criticism of psychopharmacology in general. But the vast numbers and high percentage involved suggest that a spiritual ailment is epidemic for which antidepressants cannot be the solution.

To whom do families turn when a child starves or mutilates herself? There is nowhere to turn but to the psychiatric profession, the "disease posing as a cure." That is not only an exaggeration; it is also thoroughly unfair: Thousands of well-meaning therapists, including many with strong religious convictions, seek daily to keep children from destroying themselves, and I do not mean to diminish their contributions. But the prevalent notion that self-destructive behavior stems from a malfunction in adolescent brain chemistry or an idiosyncratic neurotic disorder does not square with the epidemic manifestation of symptoms.

The therapeutic community has perfectly valid explanations for anorexia and self-harm at the individual level. But it reminds me of a doctor who explains with great precision how a metal object has passed through your body, wreaking damage on various organs, without also mentioning that the city in which you live is subject to aerial bombardment. Without addressing the cultural catastrophe, the therapeutic profession will be hard put to save many of the individuals.

If Freud were allowed a rejoinder, doubtless he would remind us of the "death drive" that he purported to discover in the human psyche in the aftermath of the First World War. Perhaps he would blame the "death drive" for the morbid refusal to reproduce that condemns most of the industrial world to depopulation and even eventual extinction, not to mention the epidemic of suicide attacks in Iraq and elsewhere in the Muslim world. The trouble with the "death drive" is that some people seem to have one and others don't. With a sexual "life force" and a "death drive" (which Freud attributed to a desire to return to mother's womb), you can explain everything and nothing.

It is no surprise that young women have come to despise their bodies, some to the point of destroying them. Nor should it surprise us that they are paranoid and reject false cures to misdiagnosed neuroses. It will take long and painful efforts to repair the damage, but putting a stake through Freud's heart is not a bad way to begin.

But what about the effects on sex itself? How has objectifying the body affected desire and pleasure, especially in women? Across the ages, according to tradition in all cultures, the female sex drive vastly exceeds that of men. The Greek seer Tiresias, who had been both male and female, told the Roman gods (in Ovid's *Metamorphoses*) that women enjoy sex far more than men. In *The Arabian Nights*, the Persian shah Shahryar observes his new bride comporting with a whole troop of slaves. Giovanni Boccaccio famously stated in *The Decameron*, "While farmers generally allow one rooster for ten hens, ten men are scarcely sufficient to service one woman." The matriarch Sarah's first reaction to the angelic annunciation of the birth of Isaac was, "After I am waxed old shall I have pleasure, my lord being old also?"

Women universally are said to be more libidinous than men. I can find no ancient report to the contrary. Women get most of the pain in the propagation of the species, so they should get most of the pleasure. With the plunging birth rate in the industrial world, one suspects that something has changed in this equation—on both the libido side and the pleasure side.

A case in point is Joan Sewell's book *I'd Rather Eat Chocolate*, a middle-aged woman's account of sexual ennui. It is customary to find salacious material on the bestseller lists, but this to my knowledge is the first time that the absence of desire has attracted mass attention. Think of it as a companion volume to *Sex and the City*. American women are purchasing Sewell's volume, perhaps to leave as a hint on their husband's pillow. Mrs. Sewell "slathers her husband, Kip, in chocolate frosting," reports Sandra Tsing Loh, who interviewed the authoress in the *Atlantic Monthly*. "She whispers naughty nothings in his ear. She lights candles, dons a bustier and fishnets, and massages him with scented oil. Ho-hum. She would still prefer a brownie, a book—anything to sex. And she says most women, unless they're fooling themselves, consider the deed a chore."

No wonder. Mrs. Sewell dresses like a prostitute with her husband. Sex is a chore rather than a pleasure for prostitutes, and it is fair to assume that the same is true for women who act like prostitutes. Women do not like to be sex objects. Yet Mrs. Sewell's complaint is epidemic among American women. The supposed sexual freedom of modern secular culture objectifies women and eventually disgusts them. Nothing is more likely to kill desire than the life depicted in *Sex and the City*. Above I argued that sexual objectification makes women paranoid. It also makes them squeamish. Americans seem to suffer disproportionately from this problem, but they are not the only ones. One survey by Japan's Ministry of Health and Welfare concludes that two out of five married couples in Japan do not have sexual relations. Unfortunately the survey did not ask couples why this should be the case. I do not think it is because Japanese women dislike sex as a rule.

As noted, women in the modern world want what everyone wants, to be recognized as an individual unique upon the earth. One does not have to accept the religious view that God made every soul uniquely and for a unique purpose. Individuality is the marketing pitch of modern shopping-mall culture. Women wander through a labyrinth of chain stores that sell the same products in a thousand locations, to pay them to bolster their sense of individuality—which is to say, to become a better sex object, the generic object of male desire. Prior to our epoch of sexual liberation, men had to court women—or a culturally similar practice—to mate with them. The desired woman was a princess, the sovereign of the man's heart: That was the point of the ritual of kneeling and presenting a ring, a holdover of feudal obligation and etiquette. Women want to be loved for themselves, that is, for their unique and individual souls. Sex is part of it, but as the culmination, the consummation in old-fashioned terms—rather than the beginning. Sexual objectification diminishes their interest in sex. There is a story about a rabbi who is asked whether sex on the Sabbath is pleasure or work. "If it were work," the rabbi responds, "my wife would have the maid do it." Being a sexual object is work, not pleasure; it is something one does not for oneself but for someone else, and it must become tedious.

A woman expects a man to love her uniquely and in isolation from the rest of her sex, and she wants a man who actually and in fact loves her because there is something about her uniquely created soul that fulfills him. Love and libido, according to scientific studies, affect different parts of the brain. Helen Fisher of Rutgers University suspects that low sex drive in women is due to the absence of love. She told the *New York Times*: "I'm not so sure that sex drive diminishes when most people believe it does. Show me a middle-aged woman who says she's lost her sex drive, and I'll bet if she got a new partner, who excited her, her neurochemical levels for lust and romantic love would shoot back up." That may explain why the culmination of an epoch that offers free access to generic sexuality is a tendency to become asexual. According to the National Survey of Family Growth, released in March 2011, almost 30 percent of all Americans aged 15 to 24 never have had a sexual encounter.

No matter how hard we try, generic sexuality cannot be banished from human culture. It is human to want to be completed by another person, like Aristophanes' four-legged creatures in Plato's *Symposium*. The trouble is that, if all of us waited around to be quite certain that we were marrying the one individual on earth whom God had apportioned to us, the species would die out rather quickly. We do not have time to find our one true love among the other six billion or so inhabitants of the planet, but we (and women especially) need to believe that we are close to the mark. That is why God lies to us or, rather, induces us to lie to ourselves. That particular lie is the euphoria associated with falling in love. We cannot be sure that the person with whom we fall in love is uniquely apportioned to us by destiny or divine decree, yet that is the way it seems to us when love takes hold of us.

I say that "God lies" because of an extraordinary precedent in Genesis 18, the annunciation of the forthcoming miraculous birth of Isaac. Three angels appear at Abraham's tent and inform the centenarian that Abraham's elderly wife Sarah will bear him a son and heir. As noted, Sarah bursts out laughing at the idea that her elderly husband might give her pleasure, and God lies to Abraham to protect his feelings. The text reads:

> And [the angels] said unto [Abraham], Where is Sarah thy wife? And he said, Behold, in the tent. And he said, I will certainly return unto thee according to the time of life; and, lo, Sarah thy wife shall have a son. And Sarah heard it in the tent door, which was behind him. Now Abraham and Sarah were old and well stricken in age; and it ceased to be with Sarah after the manner of women. Therefore Sarah laughed within herself, saying, "After I am waxed old shall I have pleasure, my lord being old also?" And the Lord said unto Abraham, "Wherefore did Sarah laugh, saying, Shall I of a surety bear a child, which am old? Is any thing

too hard for the Lord?" At the time appointed I will return unto thee, according to the time of life, and Sarah shall have a son. Then Sarah denied, saying, I laughed not; for she was afraid. And he said, Nay; but thou didst laugh.

Perhaps Abraham did not quite believe God's explanation, for he growls at Sarah in verse 15, "What are you laughing at?" Or perhaps we are to understand that Abraham's outburst at Sarah preceded God's explanation. In either case, the medieval Jewish commentators observed that God lied to Abraham to preserve domestic harmony.

It is not always the case that the truth shall set you free. Sometimes the truth will make you crazy. That applies in the case of decisions we must make on earth that affect our sense of immortality. The choice of marital partner and parent to our children is the most important and intimate of these, and its implications are too sensitive to let truth get in the way. Of course, women discover in time that Prince Charming is neither a prince nor particularly charming, and men discover that the woman who once seemed to distill the energies of the universe into a single draft is not much different from a range of other women. Even God cannot keep the truth from us forever. If things work out, of course, by the time we come to our senses, it is time to fall in love once again, with our children.

But what about the men—who, of course, play a significant part in the culture of objectification? Not only do men also suffer from objectification, but the same principle, "Spengler's Universal Law of Gender Parity," which has been valid in every corner of the world and in every epoch of history, applies here: The men and women of any particular culture deserve one another. Where men subjugate women physically, women ravage them psychologically. That may explain why violence toward women and secret homosexuality so often are endemic in the same cultures.

In the most successful cultures, wives order their husbands about; exemplary are the Chinese and the Jews, whose husbands have been henpecked since the time of the Three Kingdoms and the Patriarchs. On the contrary, the evidence suggests that, where women are badly off, so are the men. For every Bill Clinton, nature avenges itself by bringing forth a Hillary.

Outside the American mainstream, gender parity produces some bizarre results. African Americans, for example, occupy an extreme position in the machismo spectrum. Not only have they succeeded through professional sports more than any other avenue, punctuated by many scandals of misbehavior toward women, but hip-hop now represents the most visible black contribution to popular culture, with repugnant expressions of misogyny and explicit descriptions of sexual violence toward women.

Rapper bravado belies the reality of the African American predicament. Fifty-three percent of black children lived in single-parent households as of the 2000 U.S. census, compared with only 22 percent in 1960. White American women may copy some of the lifestyles and careers of American men, but black women ever more shoulder the lion's share of family burdens. Black American males, for that matter, are not quite as macho as they seem. While young black men may rap about sexual violence toward women, a fair number of them are engaged in sexual violence and/or relations to each other. Being "on the down-low" appears to be a ritualized expression of power and submission. Several studies in the past years have shown a dramatic increase in HIV infection occurring among African American men who have sex with men. Homosexual behavior also appears common in Arab culture, although the available literature on homosexuality in the Muslim world is argumentative and anecdotal. A great deal of the anecdotal evidence does suggest that endemic homosexual behavior is the antipode of violence toward and ill-treatment of women. If men treat women brutally, it is because they are brutal to begin with and will treat other men with the same sort of brutality. Women brought up in a brutal culture will raise brutal sons.

A case in point is one of the most brutal cultures of present concern to the West, that of Afghanistan's Pashtuns, who have been at war as long as we have known of their existence. Social scientists attached to the Second Marine Battalion in Afghanistan in 2010 circulated a startling report on Pashtun sociology, in the form of a "Human Terrain Report" on male sexuality among America's Afghan allies. Most Pashtun men, Human Terrain Team AF-6 reports, engage in sex with men—boys—and in fact the vast majority of their sexual contacts are with males.

> A culturally-contrived homosexuality [significantly not termed as such by its practitioners] appears to affect a far greater population base then some researchers would argue is attributable to natural inclination. Some of its root causes lie in the severe segregation of women, the prohibitive cost of marriage within Pashtun tribal codes, and the depressed economic situation into which young Pashtun men are placed.

The human terrain team responded to scandalous interactions between Pashtun fighters and North Atlantic Treaty Organization troops, some reported with hilarity by the media. An article in the *Scotsman* of May 24, 2002, reported, for example:

In Bagram, British marines returning from an operation deep in the Afghan mountains spoke last night of an alarming new threat—being propositioned by swarms of gay local farmers. An Arbroath marine, James Fletcher, said: "They were more terrifying than the al-Qaeda. One bloke who had painted toenails was offering to paint ours. They go about hand in hand, mincing around the village." While the marines failed to find any al-Qaeda during the seven-day Operation Condor, they were propositioned by dozens of men in villages the troops were ordered to search.

Another interviewee in the article, a marine in his twenties, stated, "It was hell. Every village we went into we got a group of men wearing makeup coming up, stroking our hair and cheeks and making kissing noises." The trouble, the researchers surmise, is "Pashtun society's extremely limited access to women," citing a *Los Angeles Times* interview with a young Pashtun identified as Daud. He has sex only with men, explaining: "I like boys, but I like girls better. It's just that we can't see the women to see if they are beautiful. But we can see the boys, and so we can tell which of them is beautiful." Many of the Pashtuns interviewed allow

that homosexuality is indeed prohibited within Islam, warranting great shame and condemnation. However, homosexuality is then narrowly and specifically defined as the love of another man. Loving a man would therefore be unacceptable and a major sin within this cultural interpretation of Islam, but using another man for sexual gratification would be regarded as a foible—undesirable but far preferable to sex with an ineligible woman, which in the context of Pashtun honor, would likely result in issues of revenge and honor killings.

How prevalent are homosexual relations among Pashtuns? The researchers note that

medics treated an outbreak of gonorrhea among the local national interpreters on their camp. Approximately 12 of the nearly 20 young male interpreters present in the camp had contracted the disease, and most had done so anally. This is a merely anecdotal observation and far too small of a sample size to make any generalizations regarding the actual prevalence of homosexual activity region-wide. However, given the difficulty in procuring such data, it may serve as some indicator.

Through Khaled Hosseini's novel *The Kite Runner* (2003), Western audiences caught a glimpse of what the military team calls

an openly celebrated cultural tradition. Kandahar's long artistic and poetic tradition idolizes the pre-pubescent 'beardless boy' as the icon of physical beauty. Further, even the newly re-emerging musical nightlife of southern Afghan cities idolizes pre-pubescent boy performers, whose star status lasts only as long as their voices remain immature.

Kandahar's Pashtuns have been notorious for their homosexuality for centuries, particularly their fondness for naive young boys. Before the Taliban arrived in 1994, the streets were filled with teenagers and their sugar daddies, flaunting their relationship. It is called the homosexual capital of South Asia. Such is the Pashtun obsession with sodomy—locals tell you that birds fly over the city using only one wing, the other covering their posterior—that the rape of young boys by warlords was one of the key factors in Mullah Omar mobilizing the Taliban.

Although the Taliban discouraged open display, it "should not be viewed as free of the culture and tradition of homosexuality of the Pashtun world of which it is a part," the authors add. "Men who take on a halekon [young male lover] often attempt to integrate the boy into their families by marrying him to a daughter when the boy is no longer young enough to play the 'beardless' role. This maintains the love relationship between the father and son-in-law which inevitably makes difficult the establishment of a normal relationship with the wife," the human terrain team explains.

The compelling point, rather, is that sexual relations are human relations. When sex ceases to be, for the reasons described above, humane, it becomes neurotic: a foretaste of death.

CHAPTER 9

Admit It, You Really Hate Modern Art

There are aesthetes who appreciate the cross-eyed cartoons of Pablo Picasso, the random dribbles of Jackson Pollock, and even the pickled pigs of Damien Hirst. Some of my best friends are modern artists. You detest the twentieth century's entire output in the plastic arts. As do I. "I don't know much about art," you aver, "but I know what I like." Actually, you don't. You have been browbeaten into feigning interest in so-called art that actually makes your skin crawl, and you are afraid to admit it for fear of seeming dull. This has gone on for so long that you have forgotten your own mind. Do not fear: In a few minutes I can break the spell and liberate you from this unseemly condition.

First of all, understand that you are not alone. Museums are bulging with visitors who come to view works they secretly abhor, and prices paid for modern art keep rising. One of Jackson Pollock's (1912–1956) drip paintings sold recently for $140 million, a striking result for a drunk who never learned to draw and who splattered paint at random on the canvas. Somewhat more modest are the prices paid for the work of the grandfather of abstract art, Wassily Kandinsky (1866–1944), whose top sale price was above $40 million. An undistinguished early Kandinsky such as *Weilheim-Marienplatz* (43 by 33 centimeters) will sell for $4 million or so by Sotheby's estimate. Kandinsky is a benchmark for your unrehearsed response to abstract art, for two reasons. First, he helped invent it, and second, he understood that nonfigurative art was one facet of an aesthetic movement that also included atonal music.

Kandinsky was the friend and collaborator of the grandfather of abstract music, the composer Arnold Schoenberg (1874–1951), who also painted. Schoenberg, like Kandinsky, is universally recognized as one of the founders of modernism. Kandinsky attended a performance of Schoenberg's music in 1911 and afterward wrote to him:

> Please excuse me for simply writing to you without having the pleasure of knowing you personally. I have just heard your concert here and it has given me real pleasure. You do not know me, of course—that is, my works—since I do not exhibit much in general, and have exhibited in Vienna only briefly once and that was years ago (at the Secession). However, what we are striving for and our whole manner of thought and feeling have so much in common that I feel completely justified in expressing my empathy. In your works, you have realized what I, albeit in uncertain form, have so greatly longed for in music.

The critical consensus supports Kandinsky's judgment. An enormous literature now exists on the relationship between abstract painting and atonal music, and the extensive Kandinsky–Schoenberg correspondence can be found on the Internet. Clement Greenberg, the critic who made Jackson Pollock's reputation in the *Partisan Review,* noted a parallel between abstract painting and Schoenberg's atonality: "The resemblance in aesthetic method between this new category of easel painting and Schoenberg's principles of composition is striking.... Just as Schoenberg makes every element, every voice and note in the composition of equal importance—different but equivalent (Mondrian's term)—so these painters render every part of the canvas equivalent." That is correct as far as it goes, although it might be added that things of no *particular* importance have no importance at all. The hierarchy of importance is the source of meaning. The tonic, or the starting point of the scale and chord of the home key, is the most important note in a musical composition, for all tonal music undertakes a journey towards the tonic. Just as home is the most important location on a traveler's map, the home key is the reference point for other keys, just as the central figure in a traditional painting subordinates the rest of the composition.

Recent research by neuroscientists confirms what impresarios have known for more than a century: Audiences hate atonal music. In his book *The Music Instinct* (2010), Philip Ball draws on recent research to conclude:

> The brain is a pattern seeking organ, so it looks for patterns in music to make sense of what we hear. The music of Bach, for example, embodies a lot of the pattern forming process. Some of the things that were done by those composers such as Schoenberg undermined this cognitive aid for making music easier to understand and follow. Schoenberg's music became fragmented which makes it harder for the brain to find structure.

The most striking difference between Schoenberg and Kandinsky, the two founding fathers of modernism, is pecuniary: The price of Kandinsky's smallest work probably exceeds the aggregate royalties paid for the performances of Schoenberg's music. Out of a sense of obligation, musicians perform Schoenberg from time to time but always in the middle and never at the end of a program, for audiences would come late or leave early. Schoenberg died a poor man in 1951—and his widow and three children barely survived on the copyright royalties from his music. His family remains poor, while the heirs of famous artists have become fabulously wealthy.

Modern art is ideological, as its proponents are the first to admit. It was the ideologues, namely the critics, who made the reputation of the abstract impressionists, the most famous example being Clement Greenberg's sponsorship of Pollock. It is deliberately not supposed to "please" the senses on first glance, after the manner of a Raphael or an Ingres, but to challenge the viewer to think and consider. Why is it that the audience for modern art is quite happy to take in the ideological message of modernism while strolling through an art gallery but loath to hear the same message in the concert hall? It is rather like communism, which once was fashionable among Western intellectuals. They were happy to admire communism from a distance, but very few chose to live under communism. When you view an abstract expressionist canvas, time is in your control. You may spend as much or as little time as you like, click your tongue, attempt to say something sensible and, if you are sufficiently pretentious, quote something from the Wikipedia entry on the artist that you consulted before arriving at the gallery. But when you listen to atonal music, you are stuck in your seat for as long as the composer wishes to keep you. It feels like many hours in a dentist's chair from which you cannot escape. You do not admire the abstraction from a distance. You are actually living inside it. You are in the position of the fashionably left-wing intellectual of the 1930s who made the mistake of actually moving to Moscow rather than admiring it at a safe distance.

That is why at least some modern artists come into very serious money but not a single one of the abstract composers can earn a living from his music. Nonabstract composers, to be sure, can become quite wealthy—for example, Baron Andrew Lloyd Webber and a number of film composers. The American Aaron Copland (1900–1990), who wrote mainly cheerful works filled with local color (e.g., the ballets *Billy the Kid* and *Appalachian Spring*), earned enough to endow scholarships for music students. The Viennese atonal composer Alban Berg (1885–1935) had a European hit in his 1925 opera *Wozzeck,* something of a compromise between Schoenberg's abstract style and conventional Romanticism. His biographers report that the opera gave him a "comfortable living."

After decades of philanthropic support for abstract (that is, atonal) music, symphony orchestras have to a great extent given up inflicting it on reluctant audiences and instead are commissioning works from composers who write in a more accessible style. According to a recent report in the *Wall Street Journal*, the shift back to tonal music "comes as large orchestras face declining attendance and an elderly base of subscribers. Nationwide symphony attendance fell 13% to 27.7 million in the 2003–2004 season from 1999–2000," according to the American Symphony Orchestra League. The ideological message is the same, yet the galleries are full, while the concert halls are empty. That is because you can keep it at a safe distance when it hangs on the wall, but you can't escape it when it crawls into your ears. In other words, your spontaneous, visceral hatred of atonal music reflects your true, healthy, normal reaction to abstract art. It is simply the case that you are able to suppress this reaction at the picture gallery.

There are, of course, people who truly appreciate abstract art. You aren't one of them; you are a decent, sensible sort of person without a chip on your shoulder against the world. The famous collector Charles Saatchi, the proprietor of an advertising firm, is an example of the few genuine admirers of this movement. When Damien Hirst arranged his first student exhibition at the London Docklands, reports Wikipedia, "Saatchi arrived at the second show in a green Rolls-Royce and stood open-mouthed with astonishment in front of (and then bought) Hirst's first major 'animal' installation, *A Thousand Years,* consisting of a large glass case containing maggots and flies feeding off a rotting cow's head."

The Lord of the Flies is an appropriate benchmark for the movement. Thomas Mann in his novel *Doktor Faustus* tells the story of a composer, based mainly on Arnold Schoenberg, whom resentment drives to make a pact with the devil. Mann's protagonist cannot create anything new, so out of rancor he sets out to "take back" Beethoven's Ninth Symphony, by writing an atonal cantata ("The Lament of Dr. Faustus"). The point of the lampoon is to destroy the listener's ability to hear the original. The critical consensus considers Picasso's painting originally named *Les Demoiselles d'Avignon* (The bordello at Avignon) to be the single most influential statement in modern art. Picasso lampooned El Greco's great work *The Vision of St. John,* portraying the opening of the Fifth Seal in the Book of Revelation, the resurrection of the martyrs. El Greco's naked, resurrected martyrs become a gaggle of whores, and the arms upraised in ecstasy in the earlier painting become a blend of seduction and threat. Picasso is trying to "take back" El Greco, by corrupting our capacity to see the original. By inflicting sufficient ugliness on us, the modern artists believe, they will wear down our capacity to see beauty. That, I think, is the point of putting dead animals into glass cases or tanks of formaldehyde. But I am open-minded; there might be some value to this artistic technique after all. If Damien Hirst were to undertake a self-portrait in formaldehyde, I would be the first to subscribe to a commission.

Yet, especially among the educated elites there are many who will go to their graves proclaiming their love for modern art, and I owe them an explanation of sorts. At the risk of alienating most of my few remaining friends, I will provide it. You pretend to like modern art because you want to be creative. At least, you want to reserve the possibility of being creative, or of knowing someone who is creative. The trouble is that you are not creative, not in the least. In all of human history we know of only a few hundred truly creative men and women. It saddens me to break the news, but you aren't one of them. By insisting that you are not creative, you think I am saying that you are not important. I do not mean that, but we will have to return to the topic later.

You have your heart set on being creative because you want to worship yourself, your children, or some pretentious impostor rather than the god of the Bible. Absence of faith has not made you more rational. On the contrary, it has made you ridiculous in your adoration of clownish little deities, of whom the silliest is yourself. You have stopped believing in God, and as a result you do not believe nothing, but you will believe in anything (to paraphrase Chesterton). For quite some time, conservative critics have attacked the conceit that every nursery-school child should be expected to be creative. Allan Bloom observed more than twenty years ago in *The Closing of the American Mind* that creativity until quite recently referred to an attribute of God, not of humans. To demand the attribute of creativity for every human being is the same as saying that everyone should be a little god.

But what should we mean by creativity? In science and mathematics, it should refer to discoveries that truly are singular, which could not possibly be derived from any preceding knowledge. We might ask: In the whole history of the arts and sciences, how many contributors truly are indispensable, such that history could not have been the same without their contribution? There is room for argument, but it is hard to come up with more than a few dozen names. Europe had not progressed much beyond Archimedes of Syracuse in mathematics until Isaac Newton and Gottfried Leibniz invented the calculus. Throw in Euler and the Bernoulli family, and we have the eighteenth century covered; Gauss, Riemann, Weierstrass, Frege, Cantor, and Klein give us most of the nineteenth. Until Nicolaus Copernicus and Johannes Kepler, Europe relied on the first-century work of Ptolemy for cosmology. After Kepler only Newton, and after Newton only Albert Einstein fundamentally changed our views on planetary motion. Scholars still argue over whether someone else would have discovered special relativity if Einstein had not, but they seem to agree that general relativity had no clear precedent. How many composers, for that matter, created Western classical music? If only twenty names are known to future generations, they still will know what is fundamental to this art form.

We can argue about the origin of scientific or artistic genius, but we must agree that it is extremely rare. Of the hundreds of composers employed as court or ecclesiastical musicians during Johann Sebastian Bach's lifetime, we hear the work of only a handful today. Eighteenth-century musicians strove not for genius but for solid craftsmanship; how it came to be that a Bach would emerge from this milieu has no consensus explanation. As for the rest, we can say with certainty that, if a Georg Phillip Telemann (a more successful contemporary of Bach) had not lived, someone else could have done his job without great loss to the art form. If we use the term *creative* to mean more or less the same thing as *irreplaceable*, then the number of truly creative individuals appears very small indeed. It is very unlikely that you are one of them. If you work hard at your discipline, you are very fortunate to be able to follow what the best people in the field are doing. And if you are extremely good, you might have the privilege of elaborating on points made by greater minds. Beneficial as such efforts might be, it is very unlikely that, if you did not do this, no one else would have done it. On the contrary, if you are at the cutting edge of research in any field, you take every possible measure to publish your work as soon as possible, so that you may get credit for it before someone else comes up with precisely the same thing. Even the very best minds in a field live in terror that they will be made dispensable by others who circulate their conclusions first. Many are the stories of simultaneous discovery for this very reason, as the famous one about Alexander Graham Bell and Elisha Gray filing with the patent office the very same day to register inventions that would become the telephone.

Bach inscribed each of his works with the motto "Glory belongs only to God" and insisted (wrongly) that anyone who worked as hard as he did could have achieved results just as good. He was content to be a diligent craftsman in the service of God and did not seek to be a genius; he simply was one. That is the starting point of the man of faith. One does not set out to be a genius but rather to be of service; extraordinary gifts are responsibility to be borne with humility. The search for genius began when the service of God no longer interested the artists and scientists. Mozart was one the first artists to be publically hailed a genius. A little after this time, Friedrich Nietzsche announced the death of God and the arrival of the artist as hero, taking as his model Richard Wagner, about whose artistic merits we can argue on a different equation. Whether Wagner was a genius is debatable, but it is beyond doubt that the devotees of Nietzsche were no Wagners, let alone Bachs. To be free of convention was to create one's own artistic world, in Nietzsche's vision, but very few artists are capable of creating their own artistic world. That puts everyone else in an unpleasant position.

To accommodate the ambitions of the artists, the twentieth century turned the invention of artistic worlds into a mass-manufacturing business. In place of the humble craftsmanship of Bach's world, the artistic world split into movements. To be taken seriously during the twentieth century, artists had to invent their own style and their own language. Critics heaped contempt on artists who simply reproduced the sort of products that had characterized the past, and they praised the founders of schools: Impressionism, Cubism, Primitivism, Abstract Expressionism, and so forth.

Without drawing on the patronage of the wealthy, modern art could not have succeeded. Very rich people like to flatter themselves that they are geniuses and that their skill or luck at marketing music or computer code qualifies them as arbiters of taste. So, each day we read of new record prices for twentieth-century paintings—for example, the estimated $140 million paid to the media mogul David Geffen for a Jackson Pollock. Successful businesspeople typically are extremely clever, but they tend to be idiot savants, with sharp insight into some detail of industry that produces great wealth, but lacking any concept whatever of issues outside their immediate field of expertise. As George Gilder once wrote, an entrepreneur is the sort of person who stays up all night studying garbage routes. Entrepreneurs, Gilder explained, immerse themselves in the annoying details of implementation that well-adjusted people rightly ignore. There is limited overlap between the sort of thought process that makes one rich and the kind of thinking that produces fine art. Because the world conspires to flatter the wealthy, rich people are more prone to think of themselves as universal geniuses than are ordinary people, and far more susceptible to the cult of creativity in art. In *Doktor Faustus*, Mann portrayed this as the work of the devil. The new Faust who makes a pact with Satan: He sells his soul in return for a system for composing music. A new class of critics served as midwives at the birth of these monsters. I marveled above over the fact that museumgoers gush over Pollock's random dribbles but never would willingly listen to Arnold Schoenberg's twelve-tone compositions at a concert hall. The conductor Sir Thomas Beecham famously said that people don't like music; they only like the way it sounds. In the case of Pollock, people like neither his work nor the way it looks; what they like is the idea that the artist in his arrogance can redefine the world on his own terms. To be an important person in this perverse scheme means to shake one's fist at God and define one's own little world, however dull, tawdry, and pathetic it might be. To lack creativity is to despair. Hence the attraction of the myriad ideological movements in art that gives the despairing artists the illusion of creativity.

If God is the Creator, then imitation of God is emulation of creation. But that is not quite true, for the Judeo-Christian god is more than a creator; God is a creator who loves his creatures. In the world of faith there is quite a different way to be indispensable, and that is through acts of kindness and service. A mother is indispensable to her child, as husbands and wives and friends are to each other. If one dispenses with the ambition to remake the world according one's whim and accepts rather that the world is God's creation, then *imitatio Dei* consists of acts of kindness. In their urge toward self-worship, the artists of the twentieth century descended to extreme levels of artlessness to persuade themselves that they were in fact creative. In their compulsion to worship themselves in the absence of God, they produced ideas far more ridiculous, and certainly a great deal uglier, than revealed religion in all its weaknesses ever contrived. The modern cult of individual self-expression is a poor substitute for the religion it strove to replace, and the delusion of personal creativity an even worse substitute for redemption.

CHAPTER 10

Sacred Music, Sacred Time —and How Wagner Destroyed It

Pearls grow in oysters to soothe irritation; the high art of the West grew pearl-like in Christendom around an abrasion it could not heal: the refusal of mere humans to place all their hopes on the promise of life after death. Christianity made Europe by offering the kingdom of heaven to barbarian invaders while allowing them to keep their tribal culture. The high art of the West gave these rude men a presentiment of the Kingdom of Heaven and formed an authentic Christian culture opposed to pagan holdovers. The Beautiful is not the Good. The Good is *sui generis*, independent of any beauty devised by human craft. But we willfully choose what is ugly over what is beautiful because we are ugly, and we prefer to worship our own ugliness rather than the beauty created by an inspired few. That is not merely execrable bad taste. Ultimately it is a form of idolatry.

The sacred music of the West is the one true innovation that European art brought forth. The Renaissance had the plastic art of the ancient Greeks as a model, and the tragedians and novelists of the West could build on Sophocles and Homer. What music the Greeks might have had, we do not know. The Renaissance conflated the Greek modes as described by ancient theorists with the Church modes, as Claude Palisca of Yale University has demonstrated. Western counterpoint is a *novum*, a new art form that no other culture approximated. The fact that the classical Western piano style is studied by 35 million young Chinese, along with millions of other Asians, measures the standing of Western music in world culture.

How is it possible, though, to specify just what is "sacred" in sacred music? If we simply mean music that assists liturgy or prayer, the category includes Protestant hymns, Christian rock, church chant, musical aids for the memorization of sacred texts, and countless other kinds of music. Much music provides indispensable assistance to divine service, but so do the pastor's trousers, which cannot be called sacred, indispensable though they may be. Music that carries an association with liturgy may evoke religious feelings, whatever its provenance. Musicologists have demonstrated that the reconstructed Gregorian chant promulgated in the nineteenth century by the Benedictine monks of Solesmes was a modern synthesis rather than a rediscovery of ancient practice, but its associations are no less compelling for many Catholics.

There is music, though, that seems inherently sacred in character. "Whether it is Bach or Mozart that we hear in church," wrote Benedict XVI in his book *The Spirit of the Liturgy* (2000), "we have a sense in either case of what *Gloria Dei*, the glory of God, means. The mystery of infinite beauty is there and enables us to experience the presence of God more truly and vividly than in many sermons." Simpler music can foster camaraderie among worshipers and even communal joy. Authentically sacred music does more: It inspires awe, even fear. The question, of course, is what makes it possible for music to convey a sense of the sacred in the way that Benedict avers. And the answer should be sought first in our perception of time. Because we are mortal, and because all religion responds to mortality, our intimations of the sacred arise from our experience of the tension between the mortal existence of humankind and the eternal life of God. In revealed religion, God's time stands in contrast to the earthly time of days and years and the corporeal time of pulse and respiration. A creator God who stands outside nature also stands outside time itself. Eternity is incommensurate with natural time. God made the world *ex nihilo* before time existed and he will bring it to an end. Eternity breaks into the temporal world through revelation. For Jews, the sanctification of the Sabbath introduces an element of eternity into natural time; for Christians, the eschaton breaks into the natural time of human history through Christ's birth, death, and resurrection. God's time, the time of salvation in the coming of the Messiah or the second coming of Christ, stands in contrast to the natural time of ordinary existence. Music unfolds in time. The rhythms of the music of all cultures arise from the natural rhythms of respiration and pulse. Unique to the tonal music of the West, however, is its capacity to create a perception of time on two distinct levels—the natural time of systole and diastole, and the plastic time of tonal events. The coincidence or conflict of durational and tonal rhythm, between metronome time and the pace of tonal motion, gives composers the tools to depict higher orders of time. That is what makes possible the sacred in music, for our perception of the sacred involves a transformation in our perception of time. Music begins with respiration and pulse, the inborn rhythms of human life. We may intensify these rhythms with percussive accents and electronic amplification and, through this intensification, achieve the momentary sort of exultation that seems to buoy the audience at rock concerts. As Benedict has written, this is the opposite of Christian worship:

> It is the expression of elemental passions, and at rock festivals it assumes a cultic character, a form of worship, in fact, in opposition to Christian worship. People are, so to speak, released from themselves by the experience of being part of a crowd and by the emotional shock of rhythm, noise, and special lighting effects. However, in the ecstasy of having all their defenses torn down, the participants sink, as it were, beneath the elemental force of the universe.

We know, no matter what we do, that the rhythms of respiration and pulse will cease at the moment of death. But we do not know what eternity is. At best we can say what it isn't, as in Psalm 90:4, through poetic hyperbole: "For a thousand years in thy sight are but as yesterday when it is past, and as a watch in the night." Eternity manifests itself to us as an irruption of the divine into the temporal world, as a singularity, a moment that interrupts the procession of years and days, of systole and diastole. Music can no more depict eternity than can ordinary language. The use of lengthy repetition in music or dance to empty our minds aims not at eternity but rather at timelessness. In Judeo-Christian terms, timelessness is the antithesis of eternity, for God's time is not an absence but rather a content so full that our minds cannot absorb it.

Music cannot represent eternity—no human artifice can—but it can direct the mind's ear to the borderline at which eternity breaks into temporality. This is the argument of St. Augustine, whose theory of time at the end of the *Confessions* is cited in textbooks as the precedent for the phenomenological and existential theories of time that flourished at the turn of the twentieth century. Music is one of the examples Augustine uses to expound his theory of time, but that theory reaches back to inform his account of music. His purpose was not to make time relative but to show how we perceive eternity's intrusion into mortal experience. Thus, in book 6 of his *De Musica*, the theory of time becomes a theory of music, for music is Augustine's laboratory for temporal investigation. Eternity, as the Psalmist taught, is beyond our capacity to conceive, but eternity lurks in the perception of time as such. Our time is not commensurable with God's time, Augustine writes: "Nor do you by time precede time: or else you should not precede all times. But you precede all things past, by the sublimity of an ever present eternity; and you surpass all future because they are future, and when they come, they will be past; but you are the same, and your years fail not." Augustine is not concerned with time in the abstract but rather with the possibility of communication between God and humankind. "Lord, since eternity is yours, are you ignorant of what I say to you? Or do you see, in time, what passes in time?"

Aristotle's Prime Mover has no need to communicate with humans and, for that matter, no means of doing so. Aristotle's static time can have no interaction with the eternity of the biblical God— which means that, if Aristotle's description of time as a sequence of moments were adequate, we could not hope to commune with an eternal being. But Aristotle's theory, in Augustine's view, leads to absurdities. To consider durations in time, we must measure what is past, for the moment as such has no duration. Events that have passed no longer exist, leaving us in the paradoxical position of seeking to measure what does not exist. Augustine's solution is that memory of events, rather than the events themselves, is what we compare. "It is in you, my mind, that I measure times," he concludes. If the measurement of small intervals of time occurs in the mind, then what can we say about our perception of distant past and future? If our perception of past events depends on memory, then our thoughts about future events depend on expectation, and what links both is "consideration." For "the mind expects, it considers, it remembers; so what it expects, through what it considers, passes into what it remembers." Expectation and memory, Augustine adds, determine our perception of distant past and future: "It is not then future time that is long, for as yet it is not: But a long future, is 'a long expectation of the future,' nor is it time past, which now is not, that is long; but a long past is 'a long memory of the past.'" This is the insight that allows Augustine to link perception of time to the remembrance of revelation and the expectation of redemption.

An extensive literature connects the *Confessions* to the relativizing theories of time in Edmund Husserl and Martin Heidegger. Husserl wrote extensively on music but missed Augustine's insight about long expectations. It is not the moment-to-moment meandering of music in Husserl's account that interests us but the way that music establishes a sense of the future. This future cannot be understood except in eschatological context. Augustine's "long memory" and "long expectation" are not relative, for they presume the ontological primacy of revelation. Memory and expectation arise as eternity breaks into mortal time. In Judeo-Christian teleology, revelation demarcates the "long memory of the past," and the eschaton informs the "long expectation of the future." As Franz Rosenzweig put the matter in *The Star of Redemption*: "Revelation is the first thing to set its mark firmly into the middle of time; only after Revelation do we have an immovable Before and Afterward. Then there is a reckoning of time independent of the reckoner and the place of reckoning, valid for all the places of the world." Our memory of redemption in the past, however distant, and our expectation of salvation in the future, however remote, are the fixed points by which we judge time. As individual moments flee past, we struggle to keep them in memory so that our faculty of "consideration" can order them and judge them. Superior to our perception of these fleeting moments is memory. Memory in turn is understood through the expectation of events in time, through our faculty of "consideration." I have found this stunning assertion regarding the dependence of time perception on Revelation in the work of no other writer, although it seems implicit in Augustine. Jewels of thought like this make one mourn Rosenzweig's early passing and wish that he had had time to elaborate thoughts mentioned as mere asides to the main argument of his *Star of Redemption*.

Augustine returns to the problem of time, memory, and expectation in *De Musica*. Although there is no consensus as to the date of *De Musica*, it seems likely that it was composed well after the *Confessions*, for Augustine weaves his earlier ideas about time into a better-developed theory of musical rhythm. In *De Musica*, Augustine seeks to portray "consideration" as a form of musical number—that is, *numeri iudiciales*, "numbers [or perhaps rhythms] of judgment." These "numbers of judgment" bridge eternity and mortal time; they are eternal in character and lie outside rhythm itself but act as an ordering principle for all other rhythms. They stand at the head of a hierarchy of numbers that begins with "sounding rhythms"—the sounds as such—which are in turn inferior to "memorized rhythms." Only the "numbers of judgment" are immortal, for the others pass away instantly as they sound, or fade gradually from memory over time. They are, moreover, a gift from God, for "from where should we believe that the soul is given what is eternal and unchangeable, if not from the one, eternal, and unchangeable God?" For that reason the "numbers of judgment," by which the lower-order rhythms are ordered, do not exist in time but order time itself and are superior in beauty; without them there could be no perception of time. Memory and expectation are linked by the "numbers of judgment," which themselves stand outside of time, are eternal, and come from God. Augustine here proposes not merely a psychology of music but also an ontology: He seems to think that the "numbers of judgment" with which we evaluate rhythm exist eternally and were given to us by God. A thousand years later, the Renaissance philosopher most influenced by Augustine's treatise, Nicholas of Cusa, put the matter somewhat differently: "Creative art, which the happy soul will attain, is not of its essence that art which is God, but rather participation and sharing in it."

The great composers never imagined that they were participating in creation, only imitating it. Sacred music is not revelation, just the next best thing. We know almost nothing about the music that so deeply moved Augustine in Milan, so much so that he feared that its beauty might distract him from devotion. But ideas that seem obscure—for example, his rhythmic hierarchy—do not suffer from transposition into the framework of modern music theory. On the contrary, they become clearer. Augustine's hierarchical theory of rhythm fits uncannily well into the musical world that emerged in the fifteenth-century West. Starting in Paris during the fourteenth century, and coming to full realization during the fifteenth, Western musicians found means to create tonal expectations so compelling that the hearer's perception of the flow of musical time is guided by a sense of the musical future. Tonality—the system in which the horizontal unfolding of melody in time integrates with vertical consonance—has the unique capacity to generate a sense of the future. Once musicians discovered how to link musical rhythm to the resolution of dissonance into consonance, Western music acquired a teleology. Every tonal work has a goal, the resolution of tonal tension in the return to the tonic by way of a final cadence from the dominant. The Austrian music theorist Heinrich Schenker identified a fundamental structure that underlies each movement of a classical composition and that guides a great passage away from and back to the tonic. All the elements of composition are there to fulfill this journey. Once the composer has created an expectation, it is possible to create tension by prolonging it, or to create surprise and even humor by leading in an unexpected direction. Deep expectations of the future act on memory through the judgment of our mind's ear. Thus, for instance, the Schenkerian theorist Carl Schachter introduced the distinction between durational and tonal and identified higher-order rhythms in tonal music—work consistent with Augustine's teaching in the *De Musica*. The two kinds of rhythm in Western music—durational and tonal—arise from a practice first described explicitly by the Flemish contrapuntalist Johannes Tinctoris in 1477, although (as the musicologist Sarah Fuller has shown) the embryo of the idea can be found in the treatise *De Mensurabili Musica*, attributed to John of Garland at Paris in the late thirteenth century. All Western theory had taught that music was founded on consonance, the intervals that nature had provided in simple proportions that created a sense of stability for the ear. To sound two melodies together in counterpoint, the pitches intoned simultaneously must be at consonant intervals. But the musicians of Paris learned that not all notes had to be sung in consonant relation, only those that sounded at points of rhythmic stability. Dissonances were permitted so long as they occurred at points of rhythmic instability and led to a consonance.

The resolution of dissonance into consonance in the context of rhythm gave music a powerful means to create deep expectations. From the rhythmic alternation of dissonance and consonance in the note-by-note progression of late-medieval counterpoint, fifteenth-century composers learned to prolong the tension and resolution of dissonance and consonance in longer musical forms. In late-medieval counterpoint, a single dissonant note could be accommodated at a point of rhythmic instability; by the sixteenth century, tonality made possible whole regions of relative instability within a longer form.

Western music sprang into life in full armor, once the musicians of the fifteenth century learned to integrate rhythmic and tonal emphasis on a broader scale than the note-by-note setting. Tinctoris remarked in 1470 that all the music worth listening to had been written in the preceding forty years—at the only moment in music history when a leading musician would have made that remark, and when it would have been true. This uniquely Western art came into full flower in the last third of the fifteenth century in the Flemish school of Dufay, Ockeghem, and Josquin and was adopted by the Catholic Church in the middle of the sixteenth century during the generation of Palestrina and Victoria.

The fundamentals of rhythmic and tonal emphasis are perceptible to anyone who can hum a tune. Even the simplest rhythm creates expectations; we assume that the pattern we hear will continue and that one verse will be like the next. We judge the time of individual syllables and feet within that rhythm according to our expectations. Just as Augustine argued, we do not grope our way blindly from beat to beat; on the contrary, we hear the individual beats with our mind's ear. Tonality allows the composer to create yet another level of expectations. Take a melody everyone knows: Stephen Foster's "Old Folks at Home." The first two strophes—"Way down upon the Swanee River / Far, far *away*"—occupy four measures and end on the dominant in the bass (supporting the second-scale step in the treble). We expect that another four measures will follow and bring us back to the tonic, or home key, and that is just what Foster does. Our mind's ear demands that the second-scale step on which we lingered at the word "away" descend to the tonic at "That's where the old folks *stay*." The ear also wants the fifth degree, or dominant, in the bass to descend back to the tonic. This garden-variety melodic structure is called antecedent–consequent and links a rhythmic expectation (a second four-bar phrase to follow the first four-bar phrase) to a tonal expectation (a move from the tonic to the dominant at the end of the first phrase sets up a cadence on the tonic at the end of the second eight-bar phrase). We know where each beat should fall and how the voice-leading should return us to the tonic, because our mind's ear forms a judgment about the structure of the song. The expectations evoked by the first eight bars of "Old Folks at Home" and countless other songs require no musical training to understand. But simple tunes as such do not evoke the sacred, whatever their sacred associations might be.

Fortunately for students as well as teachers of music, the most pedagogical of composers, J. S. Bach, left us more than 150 works of sacred music whose purpose is to show how a simple hymn-tune can be prolonged in a more complex structure in a way that evokes the sacred. These are the chorale preludes and related chorale settings, which embed church hymns in a longer work. By choosing hymns as raw material for transformation, Bach is making a programmatic statement as well as a musical one. Consider another melody in antecedent–consequent form, the Bach chorale "Jesus bleibet meine Freude" from Cantata 147. In the familiar work known in English as "Jesu, Joy of Man's Desiring," Bach embedded this hymn in an orchestral setting, extending the time frame in which the expectations of tonal and rhythmic resolution are realized. Our expectations work on two levels. On the simpler level, we have the same sort of antecedent—consequent we heard in the Foster song, and on the more complex, we have the expansion in time of the chorale through a florid accompaniment. The intrusion of a higher order of expectations on the hymn-tune is what evokes the sacred. Even more poignant is the celebrated setting of the chorale "Sleepers, Awake" in Cantata 140. In this case, what appears to be an accompanying counterpoint not only extends in time the musical and rhythmic expectations of the chorale melody but also alters these expectations. The expected resolution of the hymn-tune, with its four-square phrasing, is displaced in time by the florid counterpoint played by the strings. The quotidian sense of time associated with the hymn-tune encounters a second set of expectations that subsume the first.

The two interlocking themes transform each other, shifting the rhythmic placement of voice-leading resolution. Bach, in effect, has introduced a higher order of time, in which a second set of expectations breaks in on the first. The tension between the two sets of expectations, the simple hymn-tune and the overlaid counterpoint, generates a sense of the sacred. Bach cannot put the infinite into notes but, by transforming our perception of time, he can attune our mind's ear to a higher order of time. The sense of the sacred arises from the response of our mind's ear (Augustine's "consideration," or *numeris judicialis*) to the juxtaposition of two temporal frameworks. *Pace* Benedict, there really is nothing mysterious about it after the fact. Miraculous, maybe. It seems simple, but only a Bach could do it. The chorale prelude was a venue for Bach to spell out

J.S. Bach's *Wachet Auf* Choral Setting (Conclusion)

the prolongation of the hymn-tune in schoolmasterly fashion. Bach is not more *lawful* than other composers (he fudged to fit melodies together when convenient); what delights us in the chorale from Cantata 140 is not mathematical fit but rather artistic surprise. In fact, this method of transforming expectations informs all Western counterpoint starting in the mid-fifteenth century. It subordinates an individual melody to a voice-leading structure that also accommodates other melodies (or the same melody sung with displacement in time or pitch). Imitative counterpoint is not mathematical but rather programmatic. It begins with one set of expectations embodied in a single line of music and subsumes them in a larger voice-leading structure. The tonal music of the West began with a teleology learned from Christianity.

The ordering of musical time by tonal teleology broke down with the so-called new German music of Liszt and Wagner. Charles Baudelaire saw *Tannhäuser* in 1861 and gushed, "Listening to this impassioned, despotic music, painted upon the depths of darkness, riven by dreams, it seems like the vertiginous imaginings of opium." (Baudelaire, author of *The Flowers of Evil*, meant this as a compliment.) The twenty-three-year-old Gustav Mahler, after hearing *Parsifal*, wrote, "I understood that the greatest and most painful revelation had just been made to me, and that I would carry it unspoiled for the rest of my life." For the first time in history, a composer lent his name to a cultural movement with ramifications far beyond music. As Adolf Hitler observed in 1943, "At the beginning of this century there were people called Wagnerians. Other people had no special name."

Why did Wagner loom so large to his contemporaries? The answer is that he evoked, in the sensuous, intimate realm of musical experience, an apocalyptic vision of the Old World. Wagner's stage works declared that the time of the Old Regime was over—the world of covenants and customs had come to an end, and nothing could or should restrain the impassioned impulse of the empowered individual. Wagner's baton split the sea of European culture. It is hard to make sense of what has become of the West without engaging Wagner on his chosen terrain in the musical theater, for electronic media are a poor substitute for live performance. To engage Wagner on that chosen terrain is harder to do as directors bury him under supposedly creative interpretations. We have had Marxist, feminist, and minimalist versions of *The Nibelung's Ring* and a production of Wagner's last opera, *Parsifal*, dominated by a video image of a decomposing rabbit. A demythologized Wagner opera, much less a decomposing one, is not Wagner at all; as Thomas Mann said, Wagner's work "is the naturalism of the nineteenth century sanctified through myth." Without the myth, there is no sanctification, and Wagner's effort to substitute art for religion becomes incomprehensible. Wagner's power comes, first of all, from his music, but we have lost the capacity to hear it the way Baudelaire and Mahler did. And our inability to hear Wagner's music constitutes a lacuna in our understanding of the spiritual condition of the West. Despite Wagner's reputation for compositional complexity, his tricks can be made transparent to anyone with a rudimentary knowledge of music. In some ways, Wagner is simpler to analyze than the great classical composers. Because—as Nietzsche said—Wagner is a miniaturist who sets out to intensify the musical moment, his spells, at close inspection, can be isolated.

Popular literature and program notes describe Wagner's compositional technique in terms of the so-called leitmotif, or leading motive—a musical theme associated with a particular concept or character. This is true, but trivial. His use of leitmotifs is not what makes his music so fascinating.

Above, I have sought to show that goal-oriented tonal motion in Western music portrayed, within musical time, the salvific time of Christian eschatology. The musical moment served only to propel the composition toward a necessary conclusion. To Wagner, by contrast, time itself was nothingness. He wrote to Theodor Uhlig in 1850:

> Time is absolute Nothingness; only what makes us forget time, what destroys time, is Something. If you want a life of plain black and white, you can have it for as long as you want; but if you

want some real color in your life, its length no longer is any of your business. If I die young, I quite certainly have done and accomplished what I could do and accomplish, for I can accomplish only what is possible given my nature; if this nature ultimately is consumed to the last drop, she nonetheless has accomplished what it could, and what it never could have accomplished if it did not consume itself.

Time is what takes us toward death, Wagner argues, and salvation lies in the all-consuming moment. Thus Wagner set out to destroy musical teleology, which he abhorred as the "tyranny of form." As Nietzsche perceptively noted:

> If we wish to admire him, we should observe him at work here: how he separates and distinguishes, how he arrives at small unities, and how he galvanizes them, accentuates them, and brings them into preeminence. But in this way he exhausts his strength; the rest is worthless. How paltry, awkward, and amateurish is his manner of "developing," his attempt at combining incompatible parts.

That is what Rossini meant when he said that Wagner has beautiful moments and awful quarter-hours. Wagner had a gift, as well as an ideological purpose, for the intensification of the moment. If Goethe's Faust bets the devil that he can resist the impulse to hold onto the passing moment, Wagner dives headfirst into its black well. And if Faust argues that life itself depends on transcending the moment, Wagner's sensuous embrace of the musical moment conjures a dramatic trajectory toward death. Yet Wagner's move contains an inherent difficulty. I quoted Augustine's argument that the moment itself cannot be the object of perception, for it has no duration. "Endless melody" was Wagner's rubric for his own style, in contra-distinction to classical form. But if a melody has no end, it cannot have a middle—or, indeed, any inherent differentiation in time. It is like a picture without perspective, in which all objects hover in an undefined space. Nietzsche derided "endless melody" as "the complete degeneration of rhythmical feeling" and "chaos in the place of rhythm." Too often, "endless melody" in Wagner simply means "interminable recitatives." Wagner created the illusion of timeless-ness—that is, of a musical moment that transcends time—but he did so with the tools of classical composition, with the presumption that his listener *expects* to hear the long-term teleology of goal-oriented motion. Nietzsche called Wagner a "miniaturist," but *ironist* would be a better term. Popular accounts emphasize Wagner's harmonic daring. His musical impact, though, depends on the manipulation of time. Bob Dylan may have sung that the times were a-changin', but Wagner announced that time itself had changed. His manifes-to appears in *Das Rheingold*'s first five minutes, in the form of an E-flat major triad stretched over 140 measures. No previous com-poser ventured to elongate a single chord to the span of an operatic overture, allowing the musical moment to overswim its banks and drown our perception of harmonic change. Wagner's prolongation is programmatic: It evokes the eternal Rhine as nature's synecdoche. A profounder program, though, informs this stroke: The audience that heard the work's premier in 1869 well understood that Wagner undertook to overthrow the ordering of time through tonality, an ordering that Western composers had striven to create from the High Renaissance through Schumann and Brahms. This elongated musical moment prepares the entrance of the three daughters of the Rhine who guard the subterranean abode of the river's gold, a magical treasure that confers on its possessor the capacity for world domination.

Das Rheingold premiered in Munich in 1869 under the patronage of King Ludwig II of Bavaria, who worshipped Wagner. The First Vatican Council was in session. A year later, Italy's unification destroyed the Vatican's territorial power, completing what Napoleon began: the dissolution of the old regime of church and empire. That the old regime of throne and altar had fallen, Wagner's generation could have had no doubt. Wagner told them to celebrate rather than mourn its demise, for in the twilight of the gods their impulses would be freed from the fetters of the law. As Nietzsche explained:

> Whence arises all evil in the world, Wagner asked himself? From "old contracts," he replied, as all revolutionary ideologists have done. In plain English: from customs, laws, morals, institutions, from all those things on which the ancient world and ancient society rests. "How can one get rid of the evil in this world? How can one get rid of ancient society?" Only by declaring war against contracts (traditions, morality). This Siegfried does.

Considered in the context of the subsequent National Socialist embrace of Wagner's music and his family's friendship with Adolf Hitler, Wagner's use of pagan materials supports the common view that he was, like the Nazis, a neopagan. Wagner's influence on Adolf Hitler can be exaggerated. (Hitler preferred Bruckner to both Wagner and Beethoven and took the idea of a "Twilight of the Gods" rather personally.) Still, Wagner provided much of the Third Reich's background music, and not without an underlying affinity. Very little distinguishes Siegfried, who is too impulsive to pay attention to rules, from Parsifal—the protagonist of Wagner's last opera—who is too innocent to understand them. For Wagner, Siegfried—who will be murdered by a scheming Nibelung, with a spear thrust in the back—was as much a Christ figure as was Parsifal. If the Germans, in Franz Rosenzweig's *bon mot*, could not tell Christ from Siegfried, it is because Wagner deliberately conflated the two.

Wagner, to be sure, was no Christian; he saw Christian doctrine as an allegory of an "ineffable divine truth" that underlay its "allegory." As he wrote in his 1880 essay "Religion and Art":

> The very shape of the Divine had presented itself in anthropomorphic guise; it was the body of the quintessence of all-pitying Love, stretched out upon the cross of pain and suffering. A—symbol?—beckoning to the highest pity, to worship of suffering, to imitation of this breaking of all self-seeking Will…. In this, and in its effect upon the human heart, lies all the spell whereby the Church soon made the Greco-Roman world her own.

The trouble with Christianity, Wagner maintained, was its Jewish foundation:

> What was bound to prove [the Church's] ruin, and lead at last to the ever louder "Atheism" of our day, was the tyrant-prompted thought of tracing back this Godliness upon the cross to the Jewish "Creator of heaven and earth," a wrathful God of Punishment who seemed to promise greater power than the self-offering, all-loving Savior of the Poor.

And he repeated the canard that the "Galilean" Jesus was not Jewish to begin with. "The popes knew well what they were doing," he wrote, "when they withdrew the Bible from the Folk; for the Old

Testament in particular, so bound up with the New, might distort the pure idea of Christ to such a point that any nonsense and every deed of violence could claim its sanction.... We must view it as a grave misfortune that Luther had no other weapon of authority against the degenerate Roman Church, than just this Bible."

Wagner's native habitat is not Teutonic paganism so much as the murky medieval frontier through which the newly Christianized Germans passed during the High Middle Ages. His main sources are twelfth-to-fourteenth-century epics that blend Christian content and pagan legend: Wolfram von Eschenbach's thirteenth-century Grail poem *Parzifal*, which provided the material for both *Parsifal* and *Lohengrin*; the thirteenth-century minnesinger Tannhäuser; the twelfth-century legend (in several versions) of Tristan and Iseult; and the *Nibelungenlied* itself, a half-Christianized redaction in Middle High German of eighth-century pagan legends. If Wagner himself was not quite a premature Nazi, he remains a horrible affirmation of Franz Rosenzweig's claim that Christianity, once severed from its Jewish roots, would revert rapidly to paganism.

Wagner's first anti-Jewish screed, the 1850 essay "Jewishness in Music," claimed that Jews could imitate but never create. Given Wagner's debt to Jewish musicians and writers, this was particularly twisted. His notorious anti-Semitism had many sources, but the main one was theological: He was a radical antinomian who wanted to isolate the supposedly pure impulse of Christian love from the foundation of Jewish law. That, as he maintains in "Religion and Art," motivates his break from traditional form; that is, from the subordination of the local musical event to a teleological goal. Wagner's ideological and compositional aims appear consistent, at least in principle.

Wagner was no Mendelssohn, but he could write competently in traditional forms, as in *The Mastersingers of Nuremberg*. When it suited him, he could sustain long-range tonal motion. Wagner understood the tools of classical composition and parasitized them. He despised the spiritual purpose for which the classical composers first devised them, and he set out to subvert it. If classical composition ordered time in the spirit of Christian teleology, subordinating the individual moment to a long-range goal, Wagner set out to undermine the organic unity of classical form. "Endless melody" sets out to create the illusion of an endless moment, the musical embodiment of unrestrained impulse. On occasion, he brings it off.

A justly celebrated moment in the Ring cycle—Brünnhilde's wakening on Siegfried's kiss—illustrates Wagner's technique. A preliminary word of explanation is required. In Western music, the "leading tone," the seventh-scale step (the "si" in solfège), leads upward to the tonic by a half step. This upward resolution (typically in an inner voice) occurs in every full cadence. So basic is the seventh-to-eighth-step resolution in tonal music that any alteration of it has a musical meaning. Some striking examples are found in the appendix to Oswald Jonas's *Introduction to the Theory of Heinrich Schenker*. When, for example, we hear the tonic eighth step descend to the seventh instead, we sense a move away from home. This has become a stock musical device to evoke nostalgia and was first employed, to my knowledge, in Franz Schubert's 1826 song "Im Frühling" (In spring). Every American has heard this device countless times, in "Over the Rainbow," "Puff the Magic Dragon," "Both Sides Now," and other popular songs. In "Over the Rainbow," the word "somewhere" is sung on the tonic and descends a half step to the seventh on the words "over the rainbow." In the accompanying bass, the tonic chord shifts to the chord on the third-scale step, a minor chord that anchors, as it were, the poignant seventh and holds it back from rising naturally back to the tonic.

In the final act of the opera *Siegfried*, the third of the Ring series, the hero has broken his grandfather Wotan's spear and braved
the magic fire to find the sleeping Brünnhilde. He never has seen a
woman before, but he quickly determines that she is not a man and
vaguely recollects his mother, who died in childbirth. He kisses her,
and the orchestra wanders into a loud B-major seventh chord that
is announced in a grand crescendo over two measures in which the
tempo slows to a stop. The B-major seventh loudly resolves on what,
at first hearing, seems to be its tonic, in the form of an E-minor
chord that appears to be the harmonic goal of the whole passage
(although Wagner leaves room for doubt by sounding the E-minor
triad in the brass only, and in the middle register rather than the
bass). The E-minor triad diminishes in volume ("very slowly," according to the composer's instruction), and its upper tone B resolves
upward into C major. The tone B, which we first heard as an element
of E minor, turns out to be the leading tone, or seventh step, in C
major.

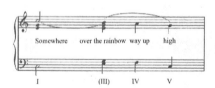

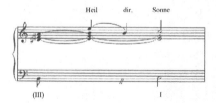

Siegfried, Act III, Scene III

Retrospectively, we reinterpret the B3 as a leading tone in C major, which resolves upward in the expected way; the grandly announced E-minor chord that so beguiled us was not really a chord at all but, rather, temporary support for the passing motion of the seventh to the eighth step. We thought we were in one place and, to our surprise, find ourselves in another—a purely musical evocation of the passage from a sleeping to a waking state. It is, both literally and figuratively, "somewhere over the rainbow" in reverse: As the leading tone rises to the tonic in its delayed resolution, we return from dream to reality.

Brünnhilde's awakening alters a well-worn compositional gesture to achieve a novel effect, which we might call retrospective reinterpretation. We hear backward from the eventual resolution to C major. Musical time has virtually stopped, for we stand transfixed at the juncture of two states: Brünnhilde's somnolent divinity and her awakening into mortality. It is a musical effect that breaks up the longer-range motion of the work rather than propelling it forward. The musical device has a programmatic meaning. Unlike Wotan, whose divine status paradoxically leaves him captive to destiny, the newly mortal Brünnhilde is in command of her own will. Her liberation from immortality sets in motion the events that, at the end of the final Ring opera, will burn Valhalla and destroy the gods. *The Twilight of the Gods* begins with a quotation from her awakening music—the E-minor chord revealed as passing motion to C major—and introduces the three Norns, the Fates of Teutonic myth, who spin a thread that breaks at the evocation of the heroic pair, Brünnhilde and Siegfried.

Wagner's most studied gesture is the so-called Tristan chord sounded in the first phrase of the prelude of *Tristan and Isolde*. Modernist criticism hailed it as a harbinger of the disintegration of tonal harmony—a step in the music's supposed progress toward the atonality of the twentieth century. That tendentious reading is still found in popular literature but has long since been rejected by music theorists. On the contrary, Wagner looks backward to the tonality of earlier generations, which he adapts for his own aesthetic purposes. The so-called Tristan chord appears in the music of the sixteenth-century composer Gesualdo da Venosa as well as in Bach, Mozart, Beethoven, and many others. William Rothstein has found precedents for the ambiguous statement at the outset of *Tristan* in the music of Purcell and Bach. In fact, in the reading of mainstream scholarship, the "Tristan chord" is not a chord to begin with but, rather, a metrical caesura on chromatic passing motion *between* chords. Example 2 below is adapted from the work of John Rothgeb and William Rothstein:

Tristan Prelude

Rothgeb/Rothstein Voice-Leading Analysis

The simultaneity F2, B2, D#3, G#3 that comprises the "Tristan chord" connects tonic and dominant, and its chromatic tones belong to an altered II chord. It is quite an ordinary progression. Two features of Wagner's move, though, produce an altered effect. The first is that he puts the ac-*cent* on the wrong syl-*la*-ble: That is, he places the metrical emphasis on passing motion rather than on the resolution. This presumably expresses longing and desire. The second is context: We do not immediately hear Wagner's voice-leading as a chromaticized I–II–V progression (from tonic through the second-scale step to the dominant) because its initial statement occurs with no evident harmonic direction. As with the apparent E-minor chord that prepares Brünnhilde's awakening, we must reinterpret what we have heard in retrospect. Together, the caesura on passing motion and the absence of context bring musical time to a dead stop. The intensified moment triumphs over musical teleology.

The novelty in Wagner's cleverest moments, therefore, does not stem from harmonic innovation—he resorts to well-worn devices of classical composition—but rather from temporal manipulation. Wagner takes for granted that his audience expects the classical resolution of voice-leading tension and will reinterpret his initially ambiguous material after the fact within the framework of classical expectations. But that raises a paradox: Wagner's shift away from goal-oriented motion to intensification of the moment deafens our ears to the expectations embedded in classical composition and ultimately ruins our ability to hear his manipulation of these expectations. In other words, Wagner's aesthetic purpose is at war with his methods. Once we are conditioned to hear music as a succession of moments rather than as a journey to a goal, we lose the capacity for retrospective reinterpretation, for such reinterpretation presumes a set of expectations conditioned by classical form in the first place. Despite his dependence on classical methods, Wagner's new temporal aesthetic weakened the capacity of later musical audiences to hear classical music.

This is as good as Wagner gets. But Wagner's best is very good indeed, evoking through the intensified musical moment the all-encompassing passion of pure impulse. He turns the instruments of classical music against their original purpose—that is, to recreate in the senses the eschatological time of Christian salvation—and uses them instead to create the illusion of a moment outside of time. Wagner was more than a musician. He was the prophet of a new artistic cult, a self-styled poet and dramatist who believed that his "totalizing work of art" (*Gesamtkunstwerk*) would replace Europe's enervated religion. His new temporal aesthetic served a larger goal: the liberation of impulse from the bonds of convention. Wagner's compositional approach coheres with his writings on music, which bristle with antinomian attacks on the tyranny of musical form. He associates classical form with the tyranny of convention and the despised biblical God.

"Wagner's heroines, once they have been divested of their heroic husks, are indistinguishable from Madame Bovary," Nietzsche sniffed. The impassioned impulse that breaks through convention sets a trajectory toward death. The soul burns out when it stakes everything on the impulse of a moment. Wagner's women are the mythological first cousins of Emma Bovary, Anna Karenina, Effi Briest, and their sisters in late-nineteenth-century literature. All of Wagner's women except *Mastersingers'* harmless Eva die for love. Senta in *The Flying Dutchman* flings herself from a cliff to prove herself "faithful unto death" to lift the curse. Elisabeth (*Tannhäuser*) dies of grief over her knight's obsession with Venus. Elsa drops dead when Lohengrin leaves her. Isolde sings the "Liebestod" and expires "in highest pleasure" over Tristan's corpse. Sieglinde dies in childbirth. Brünnhilde drives her horse onto Siegfried's funeral pyre to burn alongside him. Kundry falls lifeless when Parsifal lifts the curse that turned her into a satanic temptress. The opera's not over 'til the fat lady dies.

But Wagner gives us much more than Madame Bovary with a Hollywood score or, rather, the master template for the best scores Hollywood would invent. He gives us not Emma Bovary as provincial adulteress and spendthrift but Emma Bovary as co-redemptrix, dying not of poison but of an erotic elixir, not to please her vanity but to save humankind (or at least its male half) from the oppressive covenant of the Jewish God. Flaubert exposed Emma's shallowness and made her death grotesque; Tolstoy empathized with Anna Karenina as a sacrifice on the altar of tolerance. In their passion and death, by contrast, Wagner's women exalt erotic indulgence to the status of cosmic principle, buoyed by a music that purports to extend the supreme moment into an eternity—what the Wagnerite Baudelaire first named the "oceanic feeling." Unlike Flaubert or Tolstoy, Wagner flatters his audience with the conceit that their libidinous impulses resonate with the Will of the World and that their petty passions have the same cosmic significance as Isolde's or Kundry's. That was the debut of the culture of death. What made Wagner his century's most influential artist was not merely that he portrayed as inevitable and even desirable the fall of the old order but that through his music he turned the plunge into the abyss into an intimate, existential experience—a moment of unbounded bliss, a redemptive sacrifice that restores meaning to the alienated lives of the orphans of traditional society. On the ruins of the old religion of throne and altar he built a new religion of impulse: Brünnhilde becomes Siegfried's co-redemptrix in Wagner's heretical Christianity.

And that is why (as Bernard Shaw said) Wagner's music is better than it sounds. There really are a few moments worth the painful wait, when Wagner's application of classical technique yields the illusion of timelessness. Because we are mortal, and because our time on earth is limited, a transformation of our perception of the nature of time bears directly on our deepest emotions—those associated with the inevitability of our death. That, I think, is what Schopenhauer tried to get at when he argued that "music does not express this or that particular and definite pleasure, this or that affliction, pain, horror, sorrow, gaiety, merriment, or peace of mind, but joy, pain, horror, sorrow, gaiety, merriment, peace of mind themselves, to a certain extent in the abstract, their essential nature, without any accessories, and so also without the motives for them." Western composers altered the pace of musical time to depict the irruption of the sacred into the temporal realm. Wagner (as in the "Brünnhilde's awakening" example) performs this move in reverse, attempting to pack the sacred back into the temporal.

Writing in 1919, Franz Rosenzweig admonished the musicians to return to the Church and to the demarcation of time by revelation and redemption. In the chapter on Christianity ("The Eternal Rays") in *The Star of Redemption*, he wrote: "What is sacrilegious in music is idealized time, with which it subverts real time. If it is to be made clean of its willful sacrilege, it must be removed from the Beyond, and brought to this side of time, and its ideal time must be made real. For music, that would mean to make the transition from the concert hall to the church." Revelation, he continues, "makes fast its point of reference in the middle of time." Humanity can best understand in the Church year, particularly in "the festivals of revelation," which, "pointing backward toward the creation of revelation and forward toward revealed redemption, incorporate the immeasurable eternity of the day of God into the annual cycle of the Church year."

By integrating itself into these festivals and in the Church year as a whole, the individual piece of music alights from the artificial frame of its ideal time and becomes wholly alive.... He who joins in singing a chorale, or who listens to the Mass, the Christmas oratorio, the Passion...wants to make his soul stand with both feet in time, in the most real time of all, in the time of the one day of the world of which all individual days of the world are but a part. Music is supposed to escort him there.

Western composers abandoned teleology in music at the same time they turned away from Christianity. Tonality enabled music to create deep expectations about the future. With the abandonment of tonality, listeners lost their map of the musical future and found themselves trapped in a sort of Blind Man's Bluff of a perpetual musical present. Churchgoers shunned twentieth-century composers as resolutely as they had embraced Bach or Mozart. As in other venues, churchgoers turned to popular music, the last bastion of the old tonality. Classical music played a diminishing role in religious life. Not even Benedict XVI's advocacy has had much effect on church music. The music that attends worship of all Western denominations has little to do with the sacred in the sense that Benedict perceives it. But it is too early to relegate Western sacred music to the museum. More children are studying classical music than ever before, and more people are converting to Christianity. I do not know to what extent the estimated 140 million Christian converts in China overlap with the estimated 60 million students of classical music. But the potential surely exists for revival of sacred music on a scale that humanity never before has seen.

Part Three

The Home of the Brave

CHAPTER 11

What Is American Culture?

That American culture is an oxymoron has become a well-worn bon mot. But how do Americans look at the world? Is there a characteristic American way of thinking, an American culture? Through what filter does information reach their brain, and by what mechanism do they respond to it? Man thinks with his entire being, not with mere abstract powers of ratiocination. Tactile, gustatory, olfactory and sentimental habits bear on our view of the world more than do the philosophers we might have read in school. Writing of English culture, the poet and critic T. S. Eliot famously described it as follows: The reader must remind himself as the author has constantly to do, of how much is here embraced by the term culture. It includes all the characteristic activities and interests of a people: Derby Day, Henley Regatta, Cowes, the twelfth of August [the start of the grouse shooting season], a cup final, the dog races, the pin table, the dart board, Wensleydale cheese, boiled cabbage cut into sections, beetroot in vinegar, nineteenth-century Gothic churches, and the music of Elgar.

After the fashion of Eliot, I have compiled a list of characteristic features of American culture.

1. *Driving slowly in the fast lane.* Americans consider it their privilege to amble along in the fast (left-hand) lane, while swifter drivers overtake in the nearside lane (for which European policemen would arrest them straightaway). Clumps of slower drivers impede traffic and set the stage for pileups. This is the sad result of misguided egalitarianism. Americans believe that they should be able to drive wherever they wish, whereas class privilege rules the road in Europe. Faster cars belong in the fast lane and nudge slower-moving vehicles out of the way.

2. *Burnt coffee at exorbitant prices.* The most popular cafe chain, whose name decent people do not pronounce, burns its coffee beans to produce what Americans mistakenly believe is an authentic European taste. Proper coffee, by which of course I mean Italian coffee, is bittersweet, not burned. Americans evidently hate the wretched stuff because they drown its flavor in a flood of milk, in the so-called latte. If Americans do not like it, why do they buy it at exorbitant prices? They do so precisely because the high price makes it a luxury, but an affordable one for secretaries and shopgirls.

3. *Dishwater masquerading as tea.* Order tea from an American, and you will receive a cup of lukewarm water and a teabag. No beverage on earth is more revolting than this. This and the previous item bring to mind a riposte attributed to Abraham Lincoln: "Waiter, if this is coffee, then bring me tea. But if this is tea, then bring me coffee."

4. *Wood-flavored wine.* Americans know as little about wine as they do about coffee. California winemakers throw oak chips into vats of fermenting chardonnay to simulate the effect of aging in oak barrels. The American idea of a "big wine" is to suffuse cabernet sauvignon (properly used to produce a delicate wine) with the taste of oak. At best, American wines offer a soporific sort of smoothness but never achieve the quirkiness, eccentricity, and character that make European vineyards an enchanted realm.

5. *Shopping-mall architecture.* Most middle-sized American cities have disappeared into a suburban morass, while shopping malls have replaced the old town centers. Americans in most parts of the United States have no other place to congregate. Even churches are relocating to shopping malls in order to accommodate the habits of their congregations. Unlike European cities (and older American ones), the public aspect of cities is entirely absent: churches, public buildings, monuments, and so forth. The omnipresence of purely commercial architecture depresses the mind; Europeans accustomed to viewing well-proportioned buildings in their daily perambulations find it difficult to spend more than a day or two in such places.

6. *A consensus national restaurant menu* (Mexican-Italian-seafood-podge). One can count on finding pizza, tacos, fried shrimp, Caesar salad, and cheeseburgers in any American restaurant, as the American melting pot transforms various national cuisines into indistinguishable blobs of grease and dough. Unification of American cuisine is not much of a loss, as the local cuisine was wretched to begin with, but the result is nonetheless disheartening. Antiglobalists have made a target of the purveyors of fast food, but the chains have ho-

mogenized other cuisines, such as seafood, Italian, Mexican, steak, and so forth. Americans receive, in the place of texture and flavor, grease and quantity, which helps explain why they are so podgy.

7. *Chewing tobacco.* What more can one say? Heinrich Heine, the greatest poet of mid-nineteenth century Germany, wrote, "Sometimes I think of emigrating to America, but I am frightened by a country where human beings chew tobacco."

8. *Hand-me-down high culture.* The Pilgrim Fathers of New England rejected Western high culture as they found it, in favor of a radical return to ancient Israel. Americans once knew what high culture was, even if they had little high culture of their own. But, like Molière's bourgeois gentleman, in the nineteenth century they decided that a high culture of their own suited their new respectability. Modern-day Americans who would not recognize an allegory if it ate them alive by inches, and cannot read a line of Dante Alighieri or Johann Wolfgang von Goethe, gush over Herman Melville's confused and overwrought *Moby Dick.* American scholars who have not heard of the sixteenth-century *Lazarillo de Tormes* claim that Mark Twain's *Huckleberry Finn* is a work of originality. Harold Bloom, the defender of the "Western canon" against the barbarian hordes of deconstructionism, enthuses over Walt Whitman's onanistic (in the literal sense of the term) excuse for verse. Bloom dismisses the critics of the left as "resentniks," but is resentment not the other side of the coin of pretension? In any case, these are the embarrassing pretensions of two generations past, the putative classics beloved of American conservatives. University students today are more likely to wade through the works of black and feminist writers as a counterweight to the "elitist" high culture of Melville and

Whitman—that is, if they are not occupied with courses on film and comic books.

9. *Gullibility*. If Americans will buy chardonnay saturated with oak chips to the point of resembling turpentine, burnt coffee disguised by sweet hot milk, chain-restaurant parodies of Italian food, and hand-me-down literary classics, what will they not buy? Itinerant European academics turn up on their shores in emulation of the gypsy Melquíades in Gabriel Garcia Marquez's *One Hundred Years of Solitude*, from Paul de Man on the left to Leo Strauss on the right.

Perhaps the most poignant defining trait of American culture, however, is the regrettable fact that Americans cannot laugh at their own culture. Lampooning T. S. Eliot by compiling this short list of irritating features of American life as a *reductio ad absurdum* has made this clear, as many readers angrily demonstrated when I presented it as an essay online for *Asia Times*. I am grateful to the readers who denounced the list as "a disappointing screed," "classist piffle," "trash," "garbage," "condescending," "plain silly," "boorish," and so forth. They have proven that, in the matter of culture, Americans cannot take a joke. At first glance that seems out of character. As individuals, Americans will laugh at themselves all day long. So much do they love self-deprecating humor that few politicians attain high office without a knack for it. "I sure hope you guys are Republicans," Reagan told the surgeons as they wheeled him into the operating room after John Hinckley shot him. Nevertheless, they cannot laugh at their culture. Consider American humor in general: a telltale trait of it is the absence of "American" jokes, that is, jokes about Americans as such. Americans tell ethnic jokes, regional jokes, or generic jokes. But there are no characteristically American jokes, for the simple reason that there are no American characteristics.

By contrast, jokes that other nations tell about themselves refer to cultural characteristics the instant recognition of which makes them funny. For example, one may tell a joke about Spanish vengefulness: A dying Spaniard is asked by his confessors if he wishes to forgive his enemies. "I have no enemies," he replies, "for I killed them all." English diffidence: An Englishmen comes home and discovers his wife in bed with his best friend. "I have to do this, Nigel," says the cuckold, "but whatever possessed you?" Or about Scandinavian taciturnity: After drinking for hours in silence, Sven says to Ole, "Skol." Ole replies, "Did you come here to drink or to talk?" Or about Arabian megalomania: A man goes to the caliph and announces that he is God. "Careful what you say," warns the caliph, "A man came to me last year claiming to be a prophet and I put him to death." "It is well you did so," the lunatic replies, "for I did not send him." The French, to be sure, do not tell jokes about themselves.

To the contrary, *not* being American is the premise of the most characteristically "American" jokes. For example: The Lone Ranger (a Western sort of knight errant) and Tonto (his faithful American Indian companion) ride through a deep valley when suddenly an army of hostile Apaches appears on the ridges above them. "Kimosabe, looks like we're in trouble," says the Ranger. Tonto replies: "What do you mean 'we,' paleface?" Americans cannot laugh at their "culture" in this fashion because they do not quite know what it is. One cannot laugh at what one cannot define, and definition is the essence of humor; it is the flash of unexpected recognition that evokes laughter. In postmodern philosophical usage, we would say that humor is essentialist or, to say the same thing, postmodernism is humorless.

Trivial as these examples may seem, the same applies to Amer-

WHAT IS AMERICAN CULTURE?

ica's culture. Ask an Englishman who epitomizes his culture, and without hesitation he will reply, "Shakespeare." From other Europeans one will hear Goethe, Dante, Pushkin. The *Kulturnationen* often choose as their national poet the one who makes them laugh the best at their own culture. Cervantes, whose *Don Quixote* lampoons Spanish chivalry, is the clearest case. Dante Alighieri invented an *Inferno* full of the foibles of the Italians. One also might mention in this context Gilbert and Sullivan, the lampooners of English silliness. Heinrich Heine did the same for the Germans, Ibsen for the Scandinavians, and so forth. Among the Europeans, only the French cannot laugh at their high culture, for it was a political instrument from the time of Cardinal Richelieu, as I explain in chapter 3.

But who defines American culture? No one seems to agree. Is it Herman Melville and his white whale? England's cleverest writer of fiction, Martin Amis, has hailed the Nobel Prize winner Saul Bellow of Chicago as the "supreme American novelist," observing that "the American novel is dominated by the Jewish-American novel and everybody knows who dominated that: Saul Bellow." "It transpired," Amis wrote:

> that there was something uniquely riveting about the conflict between the Jewish sensibility and the temptations—the inevitabilities—of materialist America. As one Bellow narrator puts it, "At home, inside the house, an archaic rule; outside, the facts of life." The archaic rule is somber, blood-bound, guilt-torn, renunciatory, and transcendental; the facts of life are atomized, unreflecting, and unclean.

America is not the subject of Bellow's joke; America is the "atomized" and "unreflecting" melting pot into which Bellow's hapless heroes dissolve. There is no "there" there, as Gertrude Stein said of Oakland. The melting pot offers no solace. "What do you mean 'we,' paleface?" rejoined Tonto. Americans cannot laugh at themselves as a "we," because there is no "we" to laugh at. "American" jokes invert the problem; the punch line depends on recognition that there is no "we" to begin with. The outsider is the premise of the characteristically "American" joke—that is, the joke that requires an American setting: Tonto, Augie March, the Scandinavian residents of Lake Woebegon or Fargo, the Clintons of Arkansas. The same genetic trait defines the Lone-Ranger-and-Tonto joke and the Nobel Prize–winning novel. Americans cannot tell jokes about their own culture because there is no "there" there. It is "atomized," in Amis's word. There always are exceptions that prove the rule; one is the mystery writer Dashiell Hammett, whom we will discuss later, in chapter 18. His detectives are walking personifications of non-Being, poor cousins of Goethe's Mephistopheles, and his American cities are a "there" that is not there, for he sets out to destroy them.

That is why Americans make jokes about other cultures—in Bellow's case, Jewish culture. Not only are there no essentially American jokes, there also is very little American high culture. In fact, no other nation rejects the notion of a high culture with such vehemence, or celebrates the mediocre with such giddiness. Americans prefer to identify with what is like them rather than emulate what is better than them, as I'll explain below. The epitome of its popular culture is a national contest to choose a new singing star from among random entrants, the "American Idol."

Three or four generations ago, U.S. popular culture shared a porous boundary with classical culture. The most successful musical comedy of the 1920s, Jerome Kern's *Showboat*, contained classical elements requiring operatic voices. George Gershwin, the 1930s' most popular tunesmith, prided himself on an opera, *Porgy and Bess*. Benny Goodman, the decade's top jazz musician, recorded Mozart. The most successful singer of the 1930s, Bing Crosby, had a voice of classical quality. Never mind that what he sang was insipid; his listeners knew very well that they could not sing like Bing Crosby.

Americans of earlier generations, in short, listened to music that they admired but could not hope to imitate, because they looked up to a higher plane of culture and technique. Today, Americans favor performers with whom they can identify precisely because they have no more technique or culture than the average drunk bellowing into a karaoke machine. Taste descended by degrees. Frank Sinatra sounded more average than Bing Crosby, Elvis Presley more average than Sinatra, the Beatles more average than Elvis, and Bruce Springsteen (or Madonna) about as average as one can get, until *American Idol* came along to elevate what was certified to be average. The dominant popular style of the 1930s, swing, required in essence the same skills as did classical music. By the early 1950s, every adolescent with a newly acquired guitar could hope to follow in the acne-pitted footsteps of Bill Haley or Buddy Holly. This was "a voice that came from you and me," as Don McLean intoned in his mawkish ode to Holly, "American Pie" (1972). That was just the problem.

Stylistically, rock 'n' roll offered little novelty. It drew on the music of rural resentment, the country and hillbilly music that appealed to failing farmers at county fairs and honky-tonks. Rural America began its Depression a decade before the rest of the country, and country music developed as a parallel culture before Hollywood adopted singing cowboys such as Gene Autrey and Roy Rogers in the

1930s. Hard-time country audiences preferred the hard edge of a Hank Williams to the mellifluous crooners who charmed the urban audience.

What requires explanation is how the whining, nasal, querulous style of country music came to dominate national taste with the rock 'n' roll of the 1950s. The leap from the county fair to The Ed Sullivan Show occurred because the United States, for the first time in its history, had spawned a distinctive youth culture. That is, the postwar generation of American adolescents was the first with sufficient spending power to afford its own culture. Before the First World War, adolescents went to work. The years after the Second World War produced an unprecedented level of affluence, and teenagers for the first time had money to spend on records, instruments, and cars. Young people are as resentful as they are narcissistic, and the easily reproduced complaint of country music satisfied both criteria.

The resentful country folk who formed the first audience for the now dominant style in American music turn up in literature as noble, suffering peasants fighting for a traditional way of life, as in John Steinbeck's *The Grapes of Wrath*. Nothing could be further from the truth. American farmers were migratory entrepreneurs who did well during the First World War, when agricultural exports surged, and very badly during the 1920s, when exports fell, and even worse during the 1930s. As an American epic, Steinbeck's modern classic is a fraud, as Keith Windschuttle demonstrated in an essay in *The New Criterion* (June 2002):

> It is true that many people left Oklahoma for California in the 1930s. This was anything but a novel phenomenon, however. People had been doing the same since before World War I, as the

Southwestern states' economy failed to prosper and as better opportunities were available in other regions. Between 1910 and 1930,
1.3 million people migrated from the southwest to other parts
of the United States. In the 1920s, census data show that about
250,000 of them went to California, while in the 1930s this total
was about 315,000. The real mass migration of Okies to California
actually took place in the 1940s to take advantage of the boom in
manufacturing jobs during World War II and its aftermath. In this
period, about 630,000 of them went to the West Coast. It was not
the Depression of the 30's but the economic boom of the 40's that
caused an abnormal increase in Okie migration.

Country people were resentful because they were becoming
poorer. That was unfortunate, but feeling sorry for oneself is no
excuse to inflict the likes of Hank Williams on the world. The object
of high art is to lift the listener out of the misery of his personal cir-
cumstance by showing him a better world in which his petty troubles are beside the point. What is the point of music that assists the
listener in wallowing in his troubles? Some country-music fanciers
no doubt will find this callous, and I want to disclose that I do not
care one way or another whether their wife left them, their dog died,
or their truck broke down.

Wordplay aside, what does this have to do with idolatry? Resentment is simply an expression of envy, the first and deadliest of sins.
Adam and Eve envied God's knowledge of good and evil, Cain envied Abel, Ishmael envied Isaac, Esau envied Jacob, Joseph's brothers
envied the favorite son, and the Gentiles envied the nation of Israel.
Why reject what comes from on high to worship one's own image,
unless you resent the higher authority? Sadly, the self-pitying drone
of immiserated farmers, amplified by the petulant adolescents of the

1950s as a remonstration against parental authority, now dominates the musical life of American Christians. Not only Christian country but Christian rock and Christian heavy metal have become mainstream commercial genres. I agree with the minority of Christians who eschew Christian rock as "the music of the devil," although not for the same reasons: It is immaterial whether Christian rock substitutes "Jesus Christ" for "Peggy Sue," permitting its listeners to associate putatively Christian music with secular music with implied sexual content. It is diabolical because the style itself is born of resentment.

As Pope Benedict XVI said in 1985:

> Rock music seeks release through liberation from the personality and its responsibility.... [It is] among the anarchic ideas of freedom which today predominate more openly in the West than in the East. But that is precisely why rock music is so completely antithetical to the Christian concept of redemption and freedom, indeed its exact opposite. Hence music of this type must be excluded from the Church on principle, and not merely for aesthetic reasons, or because of restorative crankiness or historical inflexibility.

There are American Christians who had no choice but to invent their own music, namely, the African American Church, whose spirituals are gems of rough-hewn beauty. It is no coincidence that black church music maintains the closest ties to classical music and that the preeminence of African American singers on the operatic stage stems from the music training of church choirs. By and large, though, the evangelicals ought to know better. Americans, like the English, have George Frideric Handel's *Messiah* and other great classical works, and access to a musical tradition that is one of the supreme achievements of the human spirit. The evangelicals' inability to rise above the ambient culture is one of their great failings. This helps explain why Americans are so stupid. Listening to the repetition of three chords does not exercise the mind after the fashion of Mozart, to be sure, but that is not the main reason that stupidity attends the culture of resentment. One learns only by accepting a suitable authority. If one rejects authority in favor of one's own impulses, one cannot learn. Most Americans do accept an authority, to one extent or another—namely, the Bible. The Bible remains America's national epic, and the Protestant precept *sola scriptura* is alive and well in the United States. But the Bible is too difficult a text for the ordinary reader to absorb; it requires a level of culture inaccessible to all but a handful to read it properly. The culture of resentment tends to reduce Bible-reading to slogans and sound bites, with the result that side issues such as creationism sap the emotional energy of American Christians. Quite a shock will be required before any of this changes.

Perhaps we should be lenient toward Americans for their cultural poverty. After all, folk came to America precisely in order to shed their culture. More precisely, they fled the tragic destiny of their cultures. Immigrants to America were the poor or the rebels. Not the Milanese but the Calabrians, not the Berliners but the Bavarians, not the assimilated Jews of Germany but the persecuted Jews of Russia made their way westward. These had little stake in their own cultures and no connection to the high culture of the countries they abandoned. There are a few exceptions, such as the German political exiles of 1848, but these are few. What did the Irish immigrants care for Shakespeare, or Russian Jewish immigrants for Tolstoy? They shed their old culture almost as fast as their traveling clothes. America has little culture in the strict sense of the term. Culture—the transmittable experience of one's antecedents—is the stuff from which we weave the illusion of immortality. In the Old World one could not separate religion and culture. Myths of national origin, poetry and song, cuisine and geography fused into a shared experience, an experience shared by those who went before with those who come after.

America never, in my surmise, offered fertile soil for the propagation of Western civilization. The founders of Massachusetts came to America because they rejected Western civilization as hopelessly corrupt, and conceived of a New Jerusalem. The Virginians, with their mock-classic temples and slave-based culture of leisure, identified with the Greco-Roman classics. We know who won that argument. America, such as it is, is not really a continuation of Western civilization at all but a strange throwback to Hebraic rather than Greek origins. Not to possess a high culture of your own is both a curse and a blessing, however. Culture restricts our vision of the future to what we drag with us from the past. It is destiny, too often a tragic one: cultures and languages eventually die out. The highest expression of European high culture was classical music. Asian classical musicians now constitute more than half the student body at the great American conservatories. They bear the remnants of the high culture even while it falls into neglect in the lands of its origin. America has no high culture, but it has the capacity to reinvent itself. What America offers, by contrast, is redemption through a new beginning, as closely as anyone is likely to get to a realization of the original Christian project.

CHAPTER 12

Horror Movies and American Culture

The "horror" genre supplied one out of ten feature films released in the United States in 2009, according to the Internet Movie Database. During Universal Studios' heyday in the 1930s, the proportion was one in two hundred; at the turn of the millennium, it was one in twenty-five. Vampire teen heartthrobs meanwhile take first place on some lists of bestselling books.

By way of contrast, 716 horror features were released in 2009, compared to 39 Westerns, a ratio of almost twenty to one. During 1960–1964, Americans saw more Westerns than horror movies. The earlier date is pertinent because it includes two of the most fearful events in postwar American history, namely, the Cuban missile crisis and the assassination of President Kennedy. Westerns invariably portray a well-understood form of evil and contrast it to the courage to stand up to evil. Horror films involve an evil that is incomprehensible because it is supernatural and so potent that ordinary courage offers no remedy. Americans never were more frightened than during the

Cuban missile crisis, when nuclear war might have erupted, and never more affected by an act of violence than by the murder of a president. But in the 1960s Americans thought they understood what they most feared; today they appear to fear most what they cannot understand.

What has horrified them? The element of incomprehension, that is, of the supernatural, distinguishes the horror genre from mere gratuitous violence. It is not the spurting blood or mangled flesh that defines horror but the presentiment that the world itself is disordered: Demons abound in the absence of a beneficent God, who is somehow absent. There is nothing new in the monsters that infest popular culture, indeed, nothing particularly scary about them compared to the lurid products of the pagan imagination in antiquity. What is new is the unprecedented way in which they have proliferated in the American popular media.

In his essay *Religion and Philosophy in Germany* (1835), Heinrich Heine twitted the French for their incapacity to grasp the truly horrible:

> Your fairy Morgana would recoil in terror were she to meet by chance a German witch, naked, smeared with unction, riding a broomstick to the Brocken! This mountain is no merry Avalon, but a rendezvous for everything that is ruined and ugly. Satan squats on the summit in the shape of a black goat. Each witch approaches him bearing a lighted candle, and kisses him on the rear end. Then the whole depraved sisterhood dances round about him, singing Donderemus, Donderemus! The goat bleats, the infernal gang exults... and when the poor witch wakes in the morning from her intoxication, it is to find herself lying naked and exhausted among the ashes of the dying fire.

The monsters of legend, Heine explained, were nothing other than the remnants of the old Teutonic gods who lived on in the popular religion of Germany:

> These creatures did not originate directly in the Christian Church, though indirectly such was their origin; for, the Church had so cunningly inverted the old Teutonic religion, that the pantheistic cosmogony of the Germans was transformed into a pandemonic conception; the former popular divinities were changed into hideous fiends. But man does not willingly abandon that which has been dear to his forefathers, and his affections secretly cling firmly thereto, even when it has been mutilated and defaced. Hence popular superstitions, travestied as they have become, may in Germany outlive the official creed of our days, which is not, like them, rooted in the ancient nationality.

Heine was too ready to blame the brutal Germans for the archetypes of horror. Nothing, though, in the whole of modern Gothic literature approaches the revolting literary tastes of the imperial Romans. Hollywood probably is not ready for a character quite as revolting as Lucan's witch Erichto. The first-century Roman poet, an intimate of the Emperor Nero, sang of her feasting on corpses

> ...whose dried and mummied frames
> No longer know corruption, limb by limb
> Venting her rage she tears, the bloodless eyes
> Drags from their cavities, and mauls the nail
> Upon the withered hand: she gnaws the noose
> By which some wretch has died, and from the tree
> Drags down a pendent corpse, its members torn

Asunder to the winds: forth from the palms
Wrenches the iron, and from the unbending bond
Hangs by her teeth, and with her hands collects
The slimy gore which drips upon the limbs.

The Romans, who amused themselves with violent death in the public area, doubtless had a higher tolerance for imagined mayhem than do American teenagers.

In biblical terms, we may define horror as the presentiment that the forces of chaos have escaped their appointed bounds and that a good God no longer exercises mastery. Fear and awe of God differ radically from horror: We fear God's punishment and stand in awe of his presence, but we are horrified when we no longer believe that God will do justice. One might mention in this context Psalm 74:

O God, my king from of old,
Who brings deliverance throughout the land;
It was You who drove back the sea with Your might,
Who smashed the heads of the monsters in the water;
It was You who crushed the heads of Leviathan,
Who left him as food for the denizens of the desert.

As Jon Levenson of Harvard University observes (in *Creation and the Persistence of Evil*), these are unmistakable references to a Canaanite myth discovered in the excavation of Ugarith (fourteenth century BCE). "Each of these words occurs in some form in the passage just quoted. Without the Ugaritic literature, these allusions would remain tantalizing obscurities." In Levenson's reading, creation *ex nihilo* in the sense of an instantaneous change from nothing to something fails to capture the theological implication of the biblical creation story.

Two and a half millennia of Western theology have made it easy
to forget that throughout the ancient Near Eastern world, including Israel, the point of creation is not the production of matter
out of nothing, but rather the emergence of a stable community
in a benevolent and life-sustaining order. The defeat by yhwh
of the forces that have interrupted that order is intrinsically an
act of creation. The fact that order is being restored rather than
instituted was not a difference of great consequence in ancient
Hebrew culture. To call upon the arm of yhwh to awake as in
"days of old" is to acknowledge that these adversarial forces were
not annihilated in perpetuity in primordial times. Rising anew,
they have escaped their appointed bounds and thus flung a challenge at their divine vanquisher.

There is a radical difference, by the same token, between Christian apocalyptic literature and the corresponding subgenre of horror films: In the former, God manifests himself in the world and
his mastery over the fearful apparitions never is in doubt. But God
remains inexplicably absent while Hell rampages in *The Omen* or
Rosemary's Baby.

We make ourselves vulnerable to horror when we envision an
abstract God of order rather than a personal God of love and justice.
The postbiblical concept of creation ex nihilo can reduce to justify-
ing the created world (as did Leibniz in *Theodicy*) as the best of all
possible ones. If this is the best of all possible worlds, though, what
need is there for the Eschaton? More pertinently, Voltaire's riposte
to *Theodicy* in *Candide*—why would the Lisbon earthquake occur
in this best of all possible worlds—has no good answer. Everyone
reads *Candide* today, and no one reads *Theodicy*, so that Voltaire
emerges as the winner, by knockout, of that bout. Hitler and Stalin

said, in effect, "Why wait for an earthquake?" and used political means to inflict even greater horrors. Now that religion has been forced to the margins of European culture, it is hard to argue that they did not succeed.

Biblical faith has no need of theodicy (YHWH explicitly condemns the theodical arguments of Job's friends in 42:7). Jeremiah's famous accusation (Jer. 12–13) against YHWH is neither a philosophical judgment of God nor a cry of horrified despair but rather an indignant demand that God rise up and destroy the wicked:

> You will be in the right, O LORD, if I make claim against You,
> Yet I shall present charges against you:
> Why does the way of the wicked prosper? ...
> Drive them out like sheep to the slaughter,
> Prepare them for the day of slaying!

As Levenson comments:

> The answer—and please note that there is an answer here—is nothing like those rationalizations proposed by the philosophers: "Drive them out like sleep to the slaughter." The answer to the question of suffering of the innocent is a renewal of activity on the part of the God of Justice. In light of the answer, it becomes clear that the question is not an intellectual exercise but rather a taunt intended to goad the Just God into action.

Jeremiah recounts dreadful events, but he is outraged rather than horrified. That is the decisive difference. The faith of the West too easily devolves into philosophical rationalization about divine Justice rather than persisting as faith in the covenantal relationship with a just and loving God. We then become vulnerable to a neo-pagan foe that wielded horror as an instrument of policy. What produces monsters is not the sleep of reason but the absence of faith. God's creation metaphorically banished the monsters from the world in the biblical creation story. If we cease to believe that God will rise up as of old and fight our fight, then we will reify the world's evil in the guise of fictional monsters. That is the secret of our morbid fascination with the horror genre.

Why do Americans pay to watch images as revolting as the cinematic imagination can discover? Many things might explain the vast new market for uncanny evil. If you do not believe in God, you will believe in anything, to misquote G. K. Chesterton, and, one might add, if you do not feel God's presence, you will become desperate to feel anything at all. Terror and horror are at least some kind of feeling. After pornography has jaded the capacity to feel pleasure, what remains is the capacity to feel fear and pain.

But there is to the horror genre a pattern, of highs and lows, that may reflect something specific about Hollywood's feeding of the mood of the United States—something about America's encounter with truly horrible events, from the Second World War through Vietnam and down to the attacks of September 11, 2001, and the lingering conflict in Iraq. Terror loiters in dark corners just off the public square.

Among all the film genres, horror began as the most alien to America. The iconic examples of the genre in the 1930s required European actors and exotic locales—vampires from central Europe, for example, and zombies from Haiti. The films were noteworthy precisely because they were so unlike the cinematic mainstream: In 1931, the year that Frankenstein and Dracula first appeared, the worldwide film industry managed to make and release 1,054 features, of which only seven could be called supernatural thrillers. After retreading the same material for twenty years, Hollywood finally put a stake through the genre's heart. By 1948, the few horror films being made were the likes of Abbott and Costello encountering Dracula, the Wolfman, and Frankenstein's monster. Laughing at monsters was emblematically American—and remained so, as when Mel Brooks and Gene Wilder did it, perhaps best of all, in 1974 with *Young Frankenstein.*

In other words, Hollywood gave us a small run of exotic-origin horror films in the 1930s, all drawn from European fiction: *Dracula, Frankenstein, Dr. Jekyll and Mr. Hyde, The Portrait of Dorian Grey.* After the Second World War, however, these nightmares of tormented Europeans were mostly naturalized as sight gags for American adolescents.

And that was how it was supposed to be. The monsters had a different meaning in their Old World provenance. The pagan sees nature as arbitrary and cruel, and the monsters that breed in the pagan imagination personify this cruelty. Removed from their pagan roots and transplanted to America, they became comic rather than uncanny. America was the land of new beginnings and happy endings. The monsters didn't belong.

Making fun of foreign monsters fit the national mood after the war—a war, after all, in which Americans had encountered for the first time a neopagan foe that wielded horror as an instrument of policy. The existence of horror is, generally, a weakness of Christian civilization, for such civilization stands, finally, as the rejection of the horrors that paganism always accepts and often embraces. How can a good God permit terrible things to happen? Voltaire used the most horrific event of the eighteenth century, the 1755 Lisbon earthquake, to ridicule the idea of a loving God. The neopagans of the twentieth century went Voltaire one better. Rather than wait for natural disaster, they staged scenes of horror greater than the civilized mind could fathom—as though the most effective assault on faith were to commit crimes beyond the imagination of the observer. As Goebbels bragged in a 1943 broadcast, "We will either go down in history as the greatest statesmen of all time, or the greatest criminals."

The United States would have none of it. After 1946, Hitler had been crushed, and that was that. Americans did not want to think about it anymore. And at the height of the national self-confidence that followed, the horror genre almost disappeared from American film. In 1950, for example, Hollywood managed only four films in the genre, all B-movie filler.

Horror recolonized American culture during late 1960s. The genre jumped from 2 percent of all films to 6 percent between 1968 and 1972. The homegrown American horror film, moreover, evolved from summer-camp slashers to truly disturbing portrayals of torture and madness. As the online commentator Marco Lanzagorta notes, "a renewed interest in the horror genre" arrived "in the late 1960s, most probably due to the success of sophisticated and revolutionary horror films" in the vein of *Night of the Living Dead* (George Romero's 1968 surprise B-movie hit) and *Rosemary's Baby* (Roman Polanski's 1968 major-studio release).

What motivated so many Americans to subject themselves to such torment? Perhaps the explanation is that, with Vietnam, horror had returned as a subject in American life. U.S. troops were engaged with an enemy that made civilian populations the primary theater of battle, fighting a different and terrible sort of war. The images of civilians burnt by napalm transformed my generation. Until our adolescence—I was already twelve when John F. Kennedy was killed—America's civic religion was taken for granted. In 1963, my peers and I put our right hands over our hearts when the flag passed; by 1967 we did not flinch at flag burning. Horror over a war in which civilians could not be distinguished from combatants destroyed America's civic religion, and it was, I suspect, also the beginning of the end of mainline Protestantism.

Long after the fact, Francis Ford Coppola took Joseph Conrad's tale of horror in the jungle and transplanted it to Vietnam. Compared to what we had seen on television, the *Apocalypse Now* of 1979 seemed trivial, but it gave permanent images to the post-Vietnam national mood: the sense of being lost in a nightmare of pointless and pervasive cruelty.

As data drawn from the Internet Movie Database shows, the horror genre grew from insignificance during the 1950s to 6 percent of all releases by 1972, in the last phase of the Vietnam War. A second spike came in 1988, driven by a bumper crop of sequels to established series (*Halloween, A Nightmare on Elm Street, Critters, Friday the 13th*, and so on).

But what accounts for the six-fold increase in the total number of horror films released since 1999? Subgenres such as erotic horror (mainly centered on vampires) and torture (the *Saw* series, for example) dig deep into the vulnerabilities of the adolescent psyche. Given the success of these films over the past ten years, the number of Americans traumatizing themselves voluntarily is larger by an order of magnitude than it has ever been before.

There are any number of possible explanations for this phenomenon. What the bare facts show, however, is that moviegoers are now evincing a susceptibility to horror. People watch something in the theater because it resonates with something outside the theater. To see the cinematic representation of horrible things may be frightening, but the viewer knows that it is safe. And the sense of safety we derive from watching make-believe things helps us tolerate the prospect of real things. What in the world today horrifies us the most? The horror that attended the Vietnam War had far-reaching cultural effects even though not a single shot was fired on American territory. All the more so should we expect the attack on the World Trade Center and its aftermath to have such consequences.

Random acts of terror against civilians seem a new and nearly incomprehensible instrument of war to most Americans. That is why they have such military value: The theater of horror has a devastating effect on our morale. The same is true for suicide attacks, which continue on a scale that has no historical precedent. The enemy's contempt for his own life is, in a sense, even more disturbing than his disregard for ours. Nor should we underestimate the cultural impact of the torture debate. Not only has America considered regularizing an abhorrent practice, but our armed forces have became entangled in countries where torture is a routine and daily matter. Americans do not need to imagine what might be going on in Afghanistan. On YouTube they can see videos of young Muslim women being tortured for minor infractions.

Starting on September 11, 2001, Americans were exposed to an enemy that uses horror as a weapon, as did the Nazis—who never succeeded in perpetrating violence on American soil. In its attempt to engage the countries whence the terrorists issued, America has exposed its young people to cultures in which acts of horror (suicide bombing, torture, and mutilation) have become routine. As long as we insist that there is no fundamental difference between our outlook and theirs—and as long as we make only weak attempts to take responsibility for the civic outcome in such cultures—their horror becomes ours. In the Second World War, America portrayed its cause as a crusade against the forces of evil. Today we send female soldiers wearing headscarves under their helmets to show cultural sensitivity to the Afghans.

How much damage the souls of Americans have incurred in consequence of this exposure to real horror, we cannot say. But the growing morbidity of America's imagination as shown in the consumption of cinematic horror suggests we might heed the tagline of Jeff Goldblum's 1986 remake of Vincent Price's *The Fly*, made famous by Christina Ricci in the 1993 spoof *Addams Family Values*: Be afraid—be very afraid.

CHAPTER 13

America's Special Grace

The *Kulturnationen* have chosen extinction: By killing the Jews, Europe killed itself, because Christianity cannot thrive except as a graft on the good olive tree of Israel. Only in a new nation free of the taint of pagan birth, conceived in spirit, could Christianity truly flourish. As the last remaining Christian country in the industrial world and, together with Israel, the only country with a healthy birthrate, America stands as an exception to the great extinction of the nations. She seems endowed with a special grace.

To ascribe a special grace to America is outrageous, as outrageous as the idea of special grace itself. Why shouldn't everyone be saved? Why aren't all individuals, nations, peoples, and cultures equally deserving? History seems awfully unfair: as I have discussed in part 1, half or more of the world's seven thousand or so languages will be lost by 2100, linguists warn, and, given present fertility rates, Italian, German, Ukrainian, Hungarian, and a dozen other major languages will die a century or so later. The agony of dying nations rises in reproach to America's unheeding prosperity. An old joke divides the world into two kinds of people: those who divide the world into two kinds of people, and those who don't. America is one of the things that sorts the world into polar opposites. To much of the world, America is the Great Satan, the source of the plague of globalization, the bane of the environment, the Grim Reaper of indigenous cultures, the carrier of soulless industrialism, and the perpetrator of imperial adventures. To hundreds of millions of others it is an object of special grace. Whether one subscribes to the concept or not, America's grace defines one of the world's great dividing lines, perhaps its most important. Violent antipathy to America measures the triumph of the American principle and the ascendance of America's influence in the world. America's influence leapt as result of her victory in three world wars, including the fall of communism in 1989. It may be outrageous, but it is not far-fetched, to speak of a special grace for America, because hundreds of millions of people around the world look toward such a special grace, in the precise sense of the word. There are nearly a billion more Christians in the world today than in 1970, including a hundred million Chinese, most of whom adhere to the house-church movement on the American evangelical model. Denominations of American origin, notably Pentecostals, led the evangelization of a quarter of a billion Africans in the past generation. There are nearly 100 million additional Latin American Christians, of whom perhaps 40 million belong to Pentecostal or other Protestant denominations centered in the United States. No one is more keenly aware that all will not be saved than the fragile peoples of the Global South. Christianity, it might be argued, is garnering in a greater proportion of the world's population than at any time since late antiquity precisely because conditions in so many parts of the world resemble late antiquity.

The Great Extinction of the peoples makes short work of the hope that all shall be saved, for those who cling to blood, soil, ethnicity, and hearth gods will perish under the onslaught of modernity.

Special grace, according to the standard definition, is the grace by which God redeems, sanctifies, and glorifies his people. The fate of individuals cannot be abstracted from the fate of nations. We derive our notion of salvation from the concept of Israel's special grace, God's eruption into human history to redeem his people from Egyptian bondage. From the Jewish idea of national redemption comes the Judeo-Christian hope of resurrection. Individual salvation means to participate in the salvation of the People of God, as Benedict XVI emphasized in his encyclical *Spe Salvi* (2007). What is this special grace for America that, if it is not the Desire of the Nations of which Isaiah wrote, nonetheless has become the desire of so many nations?

For all its flaws and fecklessness, America remains in the eyes of its people an attempt to order a nation according to divine law rather than human custom, such that all who wish to live under divine law may abandon their ethnicity and make themselves Americans. The rights of Americans are held to be inalienable precisely because they are a grant from God, not the consensus of the sociologists or the shifting custom of a particular historical period. They are not a discovery on the part of the political philosophers, in the way that Jupiter's moons were a discovery by Galileo, but an artifact of faith. Ridiculous as this appears to the secular world, it is embraced by Americans as fervently as it was during the Founding, and in the Global South has raised a following in the hundreds of millions among people who also would rather be ruled by the divine law that holds their dignity to be sacred than by the inherited tyranny of traditional society. Americans themselves may not love their country more than other peoples love their own, but they love it in a different way. This love is visible at any small-town celebration of Independence Day, in the tearful eyes of older people. They have not forgotten the humiliations that drove their antecedents out of their countries of origin. European states always have been the instruments of an elite; Americans believe their government is there to defend them against the predation of the powerful. If America has been given a special grace, it is because its founders as well as every generation of its people have taken as the basis of America's legitimacy the Judeo-Christian belief that God loves every individual, and most of all the humblest. Rights under law, from the American vantage point, are sacred, not utilitarian, convenient, or consensual. America does not of course honor the sanctity of individual rights at all times and in all circumstances, but the belief that rights are sacred rather than customary or constructed never has been abandoned.

Modern (as opposed to ancient Greek or Roman) democracy stems from the Protestant motto *sola scriptura*, "only the Bible," and the attendant idea that every man must interpret scripture for himself. In such a world, congregations must elect their church elders (Presbyterians) or even their pastors (Congregationalists) rather than accept church hierarchy. If democracy rules ecclesiastical affairs, why not then secular affairs as well? American democracy grew from a seed-crystal of representative institutions, beginning, as noted, with the election of church officials. Americans are used to governing their own affairs through a vast number of institutions at the capillary level of society. The election of local school boards in American towns can excite more partisan passion than a presidential election. Unlike Europe, where education ministries dispense a centralized budget, American towns tax themselves for elementary and secondary education. Towns with better schools attract higher-income residents who can afford to pay for better education, in a virtuous cycle. Hospitals, public libraries, and even the fire brigade draw on private resources and volunteer labor.

It is a commonplace that Bible translation was a cornerstone of modern democracy and, therefore, of the founding of America. However, iconoclasm, the destruction of sacred images, was no less essential. The Protestant reformers—John Wycliffe in England, Jan Hus in Bohemia, and then Martin Luther in Germany, Huldreich Zwingli in Zurich, and John Calvin in Geneva—set out to rid Christianity of the pagan baggage it had carried since the time of Constantine. As Rodney Stark has observed, in uniting the empire, ancient Rome had created economic and political unity at the cost of cultural chaos. Out of the Roman Empire's tribal chaos Christianity proposed to form a single people of Christ, a people stripped of ethnicity. As a Roman state religion and later as a missionary movement in barbarian Europe, however, Christendom failed to transcend the Roman welter of contending ethnicities. The Catholic empire failed as a political model for the new people. In Catholic Europe, the anguished soul of the sinner shriveled before the imposing edifice of the Church, and the sinners sought refuge in a quasi-pagan religion in which Jesus and his saints bore the visage of each tribe. Through syncretism—that is, adoption of pagan customs as an aid to conversion—the Church encouraged the practice. The protestant reformers banished the worship of saints, the adopted tribal gods in Christian garb; the adoration of the ancient Queen of Heaven in the guise of the Virgin Mary; and the consumption of the blood and body of the sacrificed god taken from the cult of Dionysus.

The more radical of the Protestants—for example, Zwingli— fired up mobs to rip down from church walls the representations of God, including his Son. Good, bad, or indifferent as works of art,

the bloodied Jesuses and weeping Virgins had to go. Christians secure their sense of immortality from the death and rebirth of Jesus
Christ. But eternal life is never entirely one's own; rather, it is the life
of one's people and the culture of that people. However strongly we
believe that we shall sit beside Jesus singing psalms for eternity, we
assume that the psalms will be written in a language we know and
that our fellow singers will employ a musical system that speaks to
us. That is why a fragile barrier separates the Christian's rebirth into
the People of Christ from a cryptopagan revival of pre-Christian pagan death-and-resurrection cults, such as those of Dionysus, Tam-
muz, Osiris, Mithra, and Adonis, with Jesus, Mary, and the saints
recast as tribal gods. The converted tribes of the post-Roman world
found it hard to tell the difference between resurrection in the flesh
and the perpetuation of their tribal skin. At the extreme of such
backsliding, we encounter the "Aryan Christianity" of the twentieth
century, through Hitlerian Christians who denied that Jesus was
a Jew to begin with. That is why the Reformers insisted that it is
no more possible to depict the Son of God than God the Father,
the incorporeal author of Creation whose existence lies outside the
physical universe.

The Reformers failed on their home ground, as the national con-
stituents of European Christianity came to worship its own ethnicity under the guise of a Savior recast in its own ethnic image. But
thanks in large part to the colonization of America, Anglo-Saxon
Protestantism had the opportunity to take on a political form.
America's so-called revolution was in fact a second English civil
war, in which the Whigs supported the American rebels against the
Tory government. England's democratic impulse came from the
extreme wing of its Protestants, from such sects as the Separatists
who founded the Massachusetts Bay Colony, or the Quakers who

founded Pennsylvania. Only on American soil did radical Protestantism flourish unimpeded by monarchy, established church, and ethnopagan historical baggage. America's founders set forth with messianic ambitions.

The Puritans tolerated none of the old pagan devices to pad the Kingdom of God with corporeal consolations, but they did not abjure the world this side of the grave. Instead of the old pagan devices, the Puritans instead adopted a Hebrew one—a temporal order in emulation of Israel. New Israel—those called to the Cross from among the nations—has no kingdom of this earth. Old Israel, by contrast, is quite at home in this world. To the Christian these are promises of things to come; to the Jews this is mere family history. To stretch the point, one might say that that the United States is founded on a Judaizing heresy. In this sense, anti-Semites such as the Malaysian prime minister Mahathir Mohamad was right when he alleged that the "Jews rule this world by proxy." Jews played a small role in the creation of the American colonies and a marginal role in the revolution, but American democracy stemmed from Jewish ideas. The founders of the Massachusetts Bay Colony undertook one of the boldest acts of will in human history—namely, to seek redemption by becoming a new People in a new Land. They saw themselves as a new Israel setting out to found a new Jerusalem, as in John Winthrop's famous sermon "On Christian Charity":

> We shall find that the God of Israel is among us, when ten of us shall be able to resist a thousand of our enemies, when He shall make us a praise and glory, that men shall say of succeeding plantations, the Lord make it like that of New England. For we must consider that we shall be as a city upon a hill, the eyes of all people are upon us.

America became the New Israel, the only approximation of a Christian nation, because it called individuals out of the cultures of the Old World and from them formed a new people. Rather than the atomized, anguished rabble of sinners cringing before the Seat of St. Peter, Americans from the outset elected their own pastors and read their own scripture. That explains why New England farmers would fall into line against British regulars at Lexington in 1775. Self-governance was to them a matter of life and death.

America's founders did not anticipate that all would be saved. On the contrary: When the Pilgrim Fathers sailed from Delfshaven in 1620, they fled a Europe already two years into a war that would last for thirty years and kill off a third of the population of central Europe. America was at its first settlement. As the only nation with no ethnicity, America is the most Christian, and indeed the last Christian nation in the industrial world as a practical matter. Thus it became a refuge and a beacon for those who seek special grace— that is, to place God's law above custom.

Only a small minority of American Protestants can point to a direct link to spiritual ancestors a century ago, because little remains of the membership of the traditional Protestant denominations who a century ago formed what Samuel P. Huntington calls "Anglo-Protestant culture," and virtually nothing remains of their religious doctrines. More than any other people in the industrial world, Americans change denominations freely. What makes American Christianity so baffling to outsiders is its discontinuity. America never has had a dominant religion. On the contrary: America has had to rediscover Christianity every few generations, in the form of new "Great Awakenings."

By the turn of the nineteenth century, most of the descendants of the Puritans who colonized New England had become Unitarians.

Harvard College became Unitarian in 1805, and all but one major church in Boston had embraced Unitarianism, a quasi-Christian doctrine that denies the Christian Trinity. The remnants of Puritan "Congregationalism" now find themselves in the vanguard of permissiveness. With good reason, the American critic Harold Bloom characterized this peculiar variety of American religion as Gnostic. The Unitarian path, which stretches from the sixteenth-century Spanish theologian Servetus to Emerson, leads to doubt and agnosticism, for once one throws out original sin, the personal God who died on the cross for man's sins becomes nothing more than another rabbi with a knack for parables. Ralph Waldo Emerson, a Unitarian minister, abandoned the pulpit in 1831 for a career as a "Transcendentalist" philosopher, admixing Eastern religion and German philosophy with scripture. As Christianity melted away into a mushy Unitarianism, however, another group of Americans, largely Westerners, joined the Second Great Awakening during the nineteenth century. John Winthrop's descendants found themselves redeemed from earthly tyranny and promptly became the Brahmins of Boston, a byword for the arrogance of inherited wealth. Without the benefit of the Puritans' accumulated wisdom and with no help from the faculty of Harvard, Americans of the frontier revived Christianity, making Methodists and Baptists the dominant U.S. denominations by the fourth decade of the nineteenth century. Not the American Puritan religion but the transplanted denominations of the English working class prevailed. This grassroots revival made Methodism the largest American sect by 1844. From this milieu (the "Second Great Awakening") came Abraham Lincoln, the self-educated frontiersman who would join no church yet spoke in near-prophetic tones of the mingling of divine will in the affairs of men. Just as the First Great Awakening a century earlier gave impetus to the American Revolution, evangelicals led the movement to abolish slavery.

Again during the past generation, the ten largest born-again denominations have doubled their membership, while the six largest mainstream Protestant denominations have lost 30 percent. This suggests an enormous rate of defection from the mainstream denominations, whose history dates back to the sixteenth century (in the case of Episcopalians, Lutherans, and Presbyterians) or the eighteenth century (in the case of Methodists), in favor of evangelical churches that existed in seed-crystal form at best at the beginning of the twentieth century. If the rapid growth of born-again denominations constitutes yet another Great Awakening, as some historians suppose, the United States is repeating a pattern of behavior that is all the more remarkable for its discontinuity. Today's evangelical Great Awakening well may spill out of its American confines and change the course of the world. Few of the Americans who joined the Second Great Awakening knew much about the first; even fewer of today's evangelical Christians have heard of Jonathan Edwards, the fiery sermonist of the 1740s. Without organizational continuity, doctrinal cohesion, popular memory, or any evident connection to the past, Americans are repeating the behavior of preceding generations—not of their forebears, for many of the Americans engaged in today's evangelical movement descend from immigrants who arrived well after the preceding Great Awakenings.

This sort of thing confounds the Europeans, whose clerics are conversant with centuries of doctrine. They should be, for the state has paid them to be clerics. For example, the English monarch is still head of the Church, as the Danish queen heads the Danish Lutheran Church—with the minister of ecclesiastical affairs as its highest administrative authority. The Germans pay a church tax to the state but it is pocketed by the churches. Americans, on the other hand, leave a church when it suits them, build a new one when the whim strikes them, and reach into their own pockets to pay for it.

Two combustible elements unite every century or so to re-create American Christianity from its ashes. The first is America's peculiar sociology: It has no culture of its own, no set of purely terrestrial associations with places, ghosts, and traditions passed from generation to generation as a popular heritage. Americans leave their cultures behind on the pier when they make the decision to immigrate. The second is the quality that unites Wycliffe with Tyndale, Tyndale with the pilgrim leader John Winthrop, and Winthrop with the leaders of all the Great Awakenings—and that is the Bible itself. The startling assertion that the Creator of Heaven and Earth loves mankind and suffers with it, and hears the cry of innocent blood and the complaint of the poor and downtrodden, is a seed that falls on prepared ground in the United States. Within the European frame of reference, there is no such thing as American Christendom—no centuries-old schools of theology, no tithes, no livings, no church taxes, no establishment—there is only Christianity, which revives itself with terrible force in unknowing reenactment of the past. It does not resemble what Europeans refer to by the word "religion." American Christianity is much closer to what the German pastor Dietrich Bonhoeffer, writing in 1944 from his cell in Adolf Hitler's prison, called "religionless Christianity." Søren Kierkegaard, I think, would have been pleased. Despite my boundless admiration for Bonhoffer, his later vision of "religionless Christianity" in a new "Johannine epoch" of spiritual uplift seems quite inadequate. Without organized faith communities founded in some theological tradition, it is very hard to imagine what entity might oppose the arbitrary sovereignty of the individual.

CHAPTER 14

America's Holy War

The first Great Awakening of American Christianity made the Revolution, the second made the Civil War. February 12 is the birthday of a grim-handed killer who inflicted more casualties on his foes than anything the Russians did in Chechnya. Of course I refer to Abraham Lincoln, whom the Americans have reinvented as a kindly national paterfamilias. War ranks among the strangest forms of willful self-destruction, and America's Civil War of 1861–1865 in turn ranks among the strangest of wars. Three-quarters of Southern men of military age served in the Confederate ranks, and of these almost 40 percent fell. What prompted these men to cast away their lives with such abandon, and what motivated their enemies to slaughter them? In fact, the North and South of the United States have agreed to perpetuate two sets of self-consoling lies about each other:

(1) Southerners were simple patriots fighting for love of their home states.

(2) Kindly Abe Lincoln went to war only when the rebel Confederacy left him no choice.

The first lie addresses a glaring question: If the South fought the war to preserve chattel slavery, what possessed the 80 to 90 percent of Southerners who owned no slaves to die for a practice from which they drew no immediate benefit? In his book *The Confederate War* (1997), Gary W. Gallagher represents the scholarly side of this myth, while popular fiction and films such as *Gods and Generals* dish it out to the broad public. That does not wash; one does not register 40 percent casualty rates for sentimental reasons. Catastrophic casualties pile up when a conqueror rallies greedy men to his banner. Ask the half million men who marched to Moscow in 1812 under Napoleon Bonaparte's banner why they fought for an emperor, although they had no empire of their own. Napoleon said it best: Every soldier carried a field marshal's baton in his rucksack. The same applies to Alexander of Macedonia, Mohammed and his successors, General Albrecht von Wallenstein (1583–1634) of the Thirty Years' War, Francisco Villa during the Mexican civil war of 1910–1918, the Germans during the Second World War, and so forth. The unpleasant fact is that Southerners who had no slaves hoped eventually to get some, and fought for the Confederacy for the same reason that Napoleon's freebooters fought for the emperor. The poor whites of the U.S. South fought for a dream of an empire in which they, too, would have land and slaves. In fact, for a generation before the outbreak of war, Southerners had been fighting for the right to bring slaves to new territories in Kansas and elsewhere. Cotton, their principal cash crop, exhausted the soil in a decade's planting, and the planter took his slaves and moved on. Slavery and the Southern economic system would choke to death without expansion. Had the

South formed an independent state, it would have embarked on a campaign of conquest and imposed slavery on the whole southern half of the Western Hemisphere. Professor Robert E. May demonstrated this in *The Southern Dream of a Caribbean Empire* (1973). Of hundreds of newspaper citations in May's book, here is one:

> The *Memphis Daily Appeal*, December 30, 1860, wrote that a slave "empire" would arise "from San Diego, on the Pacific Ocean, thence southward, along the shore line of Mexico and Central America, at low tide, to the Isthmus of Panama; thence South— still South!—along the western shore line of New Granada and Ecuador, to where the southern boundary of the latter strikes the ocean; thence east over the Andes to the head springs of the Amazon; thence down the mightiest of inland seas, through the teeming bosom of the broadest and richest delta in the world, to the Atlantic Ocean."

No pipe dream was this plan. That is what Southerners read day in and day out during the ten years that preceded the Civil War. The slaveholding interest had engaged in land grabs for a generation before the outbreak of civil war, including a brief takeover of Nicaragua by American adventurers.

As for the second self-consoling lie, it suffices to observe that Lincoln easily could have averted the war by agreeing to let the South acquire slave territories outside of the continental United States. His 1860 election victory (by a minority of votes in a four-way race) provoked a crisis. Future Confederate president Jefferson Davis supported a compromise that would have allowed the South to acquire slave territories to the south. Georgia senator Robert Toombs, along with Davis, the South's main spokesman, pleaded for the compromise that would have given the North "the whole continent to the North Pole" and the South "the whole continent to the South Pole," as May reports. It was Lincoln, not the Southerners, who shot down the compromise. "A year will not pass, till we shall have to take Cuba as a condition upon which they will stay in the Union.... There is in my judgment, but one compromise which would really settle the slavery question, and that would be a prohibition against acquiring any more territory," he wrote (cited by May). Republicans preferred to fight. Said congressman Orris Ferry of Connecticut:

> Let but the ties which bind the states to the federal government be broken and the leaders of the rebellion see glittering before them the prizes of a slaveholding empire which, grasping Cuba with one hand, and Mexico with the other, shall distribute titles, fame and fortune to the foremost in the strife. Such, in my opinion, is the real origin of the present revolt, and such are the motives which inspire its leaders.

For those who do not know the Americans well, it is much easier to understand why the Southerners should have taken up arms in the pursuit of wealth and status than to understand why the North should have expended so much blood and treasure to stop them. What was the fate of an African slave in Cuba to a farm boy from Wisconsin? Yet Lincoln's Republicans found the prospect of a slave empire to the south sufficiently repugnant as to merit a terrible war. Lincoln sustained a biblical scale of slaughter to stop men from "wringing their bread from the sweat of other men's faces."

A cloud of myth protects Americans from the truth about bloody Abe Lincoln. His statue sits in a mock-Greek temple like the statue of Zeus at Olympus. Chiseled into the marble are Lincoln's words to the nation weeks before the war's end, an abiding source of horror for European tourists:

> Fondly do we hope—fervently do we pray—that this mighty scourge of war may speedily pass away. Yet, if God wills that it continue, until all the wealth piled by the bond-man's two hundred and fifty years of unrequited toil shall be sunk, and until every drop of blood drawn with the lash, shall be paid by another drawn with the sword, as was said three thousand years ago, so still it must be said, the judgments of the Lord are true and righteous altogether.

It sounds like a sort of religious fanaticism that would make the mild Methodist George W. Bush hide under the bedcovers. Yet that is how the Northerners sang as off to war they marched: "He has sounded forth the trumpet that shall never call retreat / He is sifting out the souls of men before his judgment seat / O be swift my soul to answer Him, be jubilant my feet!" A noteworthy conclusion is that America fought the bloodiest war in its history (and a bloodier war than any in Western Europe since 1648) in order to prevent an imperialist war—that is, out of fanatical religious principle. Should they by some means reestablish the frame of mind of 1860, may God help their enemies.

During the past century the people of the U.S. South have won deserved fame for industriousness and self-reliance. That is no surprise, for the Civil War killed off all the Southerners who preferred to hunt, gamble, and duel. Still, pour a few bourbons into the average white citizen of the U.S. state of Georgia, and the same irredentist fantasy will still bubble up: "The South shall rise again!" In defeat, they did not even have the consolation of fighters for a lost but noble cause, only the self-reproach of the frustrated freebooter who got what he deserved. White Southerners who dwell on the subject of forgiveness and reconciliation can evince a unique sort of self-serving hypocrisy. They would rather wallow in sentimental memories of Southern gallantry than to admit that their ancestors died for sordid imperialistic ambitions. They cannot come to terms with the evil of the ancestors whom they portray as gallant, aristocratic warriors. It is not the descendants of African slaves whom they pity as an oppressed class but rather themselves. This also serves to explain the behavior of President Jimmy Carter, whose sanctimonious ineptitude and see-and-hear-no-evil view of the world made him the least successful president in U.S. history. This form of obsessive self-pity produces the unctuous forms of expression that make it so painful to listen to a Jimmy Carter or a Bill Clinton talk about political morality, with a lip-sucking, voice-throbbing, eye-tearing, fixed-staring, self-pitying, and downright creepy form of bathos. The difference, of course, is that Bill Clinton is an utter hypocrite, while Jimmy Carter is quite sincere—which makes him all the more nauseating. The U.S. South chafes in anger and shame at its defeat, and the North recoils in horror from its own victory.

Amid a great extinction of nations, in an era when whole peoples seem to hold their lives cheap, what can we learn from these events? Some wars end not when they are won but when those who want to fight to the death find their wish has been granted.

When brave men are convinced that conquering others is the best way to make their fortune, it may be necessary to keep on killing until not enough are left to fight. Across epochs and cultures, blood has flown in proportion inverse to the hope of victory. *Mut der Verzweiflung,* as the Germans call it, courage borne of desperation, arises not from the delusion that victory is possible but rather from the conviction that death is preferable to surrender. Wars of this sort end long after one side has been defeated. The Southern cause was lost after Major General Ulysses S. Grant took Vicksburg and General George G. Meade repelled General Robert E. Lee at Gettysburg in July 1863. With Union forces in control of the Mississippi River, the main artery of Southern commerce, and without the prospect of a breakout to the North, the Confederacy of slaveholding states faced inevitable strangulation by the vastly superior forces of the North. Nonetheless, the South fought on for another eighteen months. Between Gettysburg and Vicksburg, the two decisive battles of the war fought within the same week, 100,000 men had died, bringing the total number of deaths in major battles to more than a quarter of a million. Another 200,000 soldiers would die before Lee surrendered to Grant at Appomattox in April 1865. The chart below shows the cumulative number of Civil War casualties as the major battles of the war proceeded.

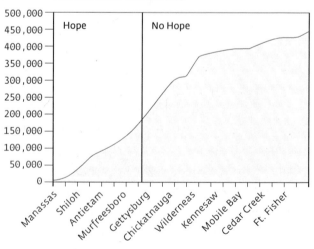

The chart is demarcated into sections labeled "Hope" (prior to Gettysburg and Vicksburg) and "No Hope." Geometers will recognize a so-called S-curve in which the pace of killing accelerates immediately after Gettysburg and Vickburg and remains steep through the Battle of Cold Harbor, before leveling off in the last months of the war. Not only did half the casualties occur after the war was lost by the South, but the speed at which casualties occurred sharply accelerated. The killing slowed after the South had bled nearly to death, with many regiments unable to field more than a handful of men. Nonetheless, Lee barely could persuade his men to surrender in April 1865. The Confederate president, Jefferson Davis, called for guerilla war to continue, and Lee's staff wanted to keep fighting. Lee barely avoided a drawn-out irregular war. In all, one-quarter of military-age Southern manhood died in the field.

Americans invented the war of extermination in the modern world—the total war that can be won only by killing so many of the enemy that not enough young men are left to be put into the line. Modern Americans fail to grasp decisive strategic issues not only because they misunderstand other cultures but because they avert their gaze from the painful episodes of their own history. In his book *The Metaphysical Club*, Louis Menand observes that the horrors of the Civil War discredited the idealism of young New Englanders (his case study is Oliver Wendell Holmes Jr.), producing the vapid pragmatism that has reigned since then in American culture. Americans suffer from a form of traumatic amnesia, such that every generation of Americans must learn the hard way.

An uncanny parallel links the fate of young African Americans today and that of the young white men of the slaveholding South in 1865. Both cohorts have lost a terrifying proportion of their number to violence. One-third of black Americans between the ages of twenty and thirty passed through the criminal-justice system in 1995, according to the Sentencing Project, a prisoners' advocacy group. According to the Sentencing Project, "More than 60 percent of the people in prison are now racial and ethnic minorities. For black males in their twenties, one in every eight is in prison or jail on any given day. These trends have been intensified by the disproportionate impact of the 'war on drugs,' in which three-fourths of all persons in prison for drug offenses are people of color." A generation of African Americans has been decimated. Murder is the leading cause of death among young African American men; an American black has a 5 percent lifetime probability of becoming a murder victim (against a 0.7 percent probability for a white American).

As noted, nearly a third of Southern men of military age were killed or wounded during the Civil War. It is a measure of the inherent goodheartedness of Americans that they evince a low threshold of horror. Three hundred thousand Confederate dead and millions of ruined African American lives are too awful to contemplate. Some part of Senator Barack Obama's appeal derives from America's revulsion over the destruction of a generation of young black men; electing an African American president would assuage part of the guilt.

From this great suffering arise two genres of American popular culture, the *Gone with the Wind* ilk of Civil War epic and the *Get Rich or Die Tryin'* brand of gangsta tale. Both try to take the edge off the revulsion and placate the dishonored dead by turning them into folk heroes. That is understandable, but also unfortunate, for America still has a great deal of killing left to do around the world and might as well get used to it. "Get Rich or Die Tryin'" would have been a good epitaph for the Confederate dead, who fought for land and slaves, not for "states' rights" or the sanctity of their soil. Slave owners along with want-to-be slave owners had it coming.

The Union general William Tecumseh Sherman said after he burned Atlanta, "I fear the world will jump to the wrong conclusion that because I am in Atlanta the work is done. Far from it. We must kill three hundred thousand, I have told you of so often, and the further they run the harder for us to get them." There existed three hundred thousand fanatics in the South who knew nothing but hunting, drinking, gambling, and dueling, a class who benefited from slavery and would rather die than work for a living.

Given the sad history of racial oppression in the South for a century after the Civil War, the only thing to regret is that Sherman didn't finish the job. I stopped watching the film version of *Gone with the Wind* after Scarlett O'Hara saved her plantation from the tax collector. I wanted her to pick cotton until her back broke. It is appalling that the criminal-justice system has devoured one out of three young African Americans, to be sure, but the number must be too small, because the police will have failed to apprehend some who still commit crimes. I did not attempt to watch the film *Get Rich or Die Tryin'*. I want the police to incarcerate such people before they commit enough crimes to fill a screenplay.

Europeans are far more attuned to horror. They have had the opportunity to get used to it. Cannibalism was rampant in seventeenth-century Germany during the Thirty Years' War and in the Ukraine during Joseph Stalin's 1931 starvation. Americans abandoned the horrors of the Old World. Terrible as the Civil War may have been, it spared civilians. Sherman burned his way from Atlanta to the sea in 1864, but the number of rapes and murders committed by his soldiers can be counted on one's fingers. Nonetheless, there is no market for Hollywood epics about Sherman's March to the Sea, arguably the most brilliant military campaign in the history of

American arms, while the film industry still grinds out kitsch about the supposedly gallant losers.

The embittered fighters of the South sacrificed themselves in proportions unsurpassed in modern history, excepting the Serbs in the First World War. But there was no honor, no gallantry, and no nobility in the bloodletting. They fought for empire and advancement, like Albrecht von Wallenstein's freebooters of the Thirty Years' War or Napoleon's ambitious Grande Armée. Sherman's belief that the war objective was not to occupy this or that piece of territory, but to kill 300,000 men, was almost exactly correct: The final total of Confederate dead was 289,000, just 11,000 short of his estimate. Perhaps the 11,000 men Sherman failed to kill were the founders of the Klu Klux Klan. In fact, Sherman's superior, General Ulysses S. Grant, did far more of the killing. Sherman burnt property and humiliated the South on their home soil. But a people that has given its all for a defeat that is too terrible to recall with clarity has nothing left but pride, and the wounded pride of the South has turned Sherman's memory into a curse.

Southerners thought of themselves as an oppressed people, the descendants of Scots-Irish immigrants driven out of their Celtic homelands by the English, flying the Confederate battle flag with its *X*-shaped cross of Scotland's patron saint and redolent of Scotland's "Lost Cause." The self-pity of the South pervades American popular culture, from Margaret Mitchell's *Gone with the Wind* to The Band's bathetic song "The Night They Drove Old Dixie Down." It is best known in the cover version by Joan Baez, an old civil-rights campaigner. Such is the pull of identity politics. With good reason, the descendants of Scots villagers expelled from the Highlands after the rebellion of 1746 may have thought themselves oppressed. Because they came from oppressed folk, their passion to better themselves burned all the more fiercely. When they set to build a slave empire, they could be stopped only by killing so many of them that insufficient numbers of them were left to form their ranks.

Sherman, who lived in the South and had many close Southern friends, understood that the ambitions of the South could be quelled only by a sea of blood. He is the decisive personality of the Civil War, yet there never has been a single cinematic treatment of the man. Twenty-one films, by contrast, portray Jesse James, the Confederate guerilla turned outlaw. He is the 50 Cent of the old South. I do not mean to draw a moral equivalency between would-be slave owners and the descendants of slaves, but the functional parallel is compelling.

CHAPTER 15

This Almost Chosen, Almost Pregnant Land

President Abraham Lincoln famously called Americans an "almost chosen people." That might qualify as America's national joke, for you can't be "almost chosen" any more than you can be almost pregnant. Lincoln's oxymoron frames the tension between the religious impulses that made America and the reality that ultimately it is one imperfect polity among many others. Idolatry attracts both wings of American politics: The right tends to confound the United States of America with the City of God, while the left makes an object of worship out of its utopian imagination.

The central role of religion continues to polarize Americans and confuse foreign observers. The working of faith in America's public square is more complex than Americans acknowledge or foreigners understand. One of the most insightful books about the subject is a study of the heavenly city versus the earthly city of our exile— *American Babylon: Notes of a Christian Exile*, by Father Richard John Neuhaus. Until his death on January 8, 2009, Neuhaus was the preeminent social conservative and Christian intellectual, founder of the monthly magazine *First Things*, and advisor to former president George W. Bush, but no less an even-handed critic for that.

"There is in America," he wrote, "a strong current of Christian patriotism in which 'God and country' falls trippingly from the tongue. Indeed, God and country are sometimes conflated in a single allegiance that permits no tension, never mind conflict, between the two." Neuhaus added that "this book is animated by a deeply and lively patriotism," adding, "I have considerable sympathy for Abraham Lincoln's observation that, among the political orders of the earthly city, America is 'the last, best hope of mankind.'"

On the left, utopian efforts to create a heaven on earth expressed American idolatry, for example, in the Social Gospel movement of Walter Rauschenberg: "Christianizing America and Americanizing Christianity." The liberal philosopher John Dewey embodied the drift of mainline Protestantism into a social-reform movement. The heir of this left-wing current is Rauschenberg's grandson, the late philosopher Richard Rorty, whose career was dedicated to proving the proposition that no proposition can be proven. It is even sillier than it sounds, in Neuhaus's amusing account. As Neuhaus says, Rorty writes that Dewey and his soulmate Walt Whitman "wanted [their] utopian America to replace God as the unconditional object of desire. They wanted the struggle for social justice to be the country's animating principle, the nation's soul." Rorty quotes favorably the lines of Whitman:

And I say to mankind, Be not curious about God,
For I who am curious about each am not curious about God.

"Whitman and Dewey," Rorty writes, "gave us all the romance, and all the spiritual uplift we Americans need to go about our public business." That is the left-wing version of American self-worship. American nationalism harbors a civic religion as well. There is a line of devotion that runs from the Puritans' "errand in the wilderness" to John F. Kennedy's inaugural. It is the American story, the American promise, that is invoked in Martin Luther King Jr.'s dream of the "beloved community" and in Ronald Reagan's vision of the "city on a hill." Some readers will be surprised and others scandalized by the suggestion that George W. Bush was in the tradition of Washington, Lincoln, Wilson, Kennedy, King, and Reagan in sounding the characteristic notes of the American story, but so it is. This is painfully clear, observed Neuhaus, in George W. Bush's second inaugural address. Bush said:

> We are led by events and common sense, to one conclusion: The survival of liberty in our land increasingly depends on the success of liberty in other lands. The best hope for peace in our world is the expansion of freedom in all the world. America's vital interest and our deepest beliefs are now one.... We go forward with complete confidence in the even triumph of freedom. Not because history runs on the wheels of inevitability; it is human choices that move events. Not because we consider ourselves a chosen nation; God moves and chooses as He wills.

Both the power and the danger of the story is in the sincerity with which it is told, Neuhaus commented. Good intentions go awry; we blind ourselves to our own capacity for self-deception when we cast ourselves in the role of God's agents in history's battle between "The Children of Light and the Children of Darkness," also the title of a book by Reinhold Niebuhr.

President Barack Obama famously called Niebuhr his "favorite philosopher," although his reading of Niebuhr has a distinctive slant. The Reuters reporter Tom Heneghan parsed the president's 2009 Nobel Prize acceptance speech against Niebuhr's writings and found parallels as well as divergences:

> Obama: "We must begin by acknowledging the hard truth that we will not eradicate violent conflict in our lifetimes."
>
> Niebuhr: "Nothing worth doing is completed in our lifetime."
>
> Obama: "I face the world as it is, and cannot stand idle in the face of threats to the American people."
>
> Niebuhr: "We take, and must continue to take, morally hazardous actions to preserve our civilization. We must exercise our power."
>
> Obama: "We do not have to think that human nature is perfect for us to still believe that the human condition can be perfected."
>
> Niebuhr: "The sad duty of politics is to establish justice in a sinful world."

There is a world of difference between Niebuhr's call for justice despite the fallenness of human nature and Obama's claim that "the human condition can be perfected." Niebuhr argued that, since those who exercise power in a fallen world are themselves sinners, power cannot be exercised without guilt. But whose guilt is in question? The answer to this question can be found in Obama's published writings and inferred from his relationship to his mother Ann Dunham, as I'll explain in the next chapter.

As Obama reads Niebuhr, the guilt pertains to the world's greatest power, the United States. In short, Obama appears to believe that America's influence in the world is malign.

Bush's second inaugural was an exercise in American self-worship, in its assumption that the free institutions of the United States were an earthly manifestation of the divine, such that the American government should become a Bureau of Missions for the cult of democracy. But it is manifestly false that America's security depends on the success of freedom elsewhere. China's political system is not free by Western standards, yet China poses no strategic threat to the United States. Dictatorships that support terrorism well may constitute a strategic threat to the United States, especially if they are able to employ nuclear weapons. But the United States could just as well wipe all of them off the face of the earth through preemptive nuclear bombardment, or let them fight each other to exhaustion, as try to foster democracy in their midst. America had no strategic imperative to promote democracy, only a narcissistic one.

As Neuhaus concluded in his book, however high our appreciation of America's achievement and promise, and whether that appreciation is expressed from the left, as in the case of Richard Rorty's work, or from the right, as in George W. Bush's speech, with its confidence in "a new order of the ages," the great danger is in forgetting that America, too, is Babylon. From a Christian vantage point every earthly city is an exile, like the Babylon whence the Jews of the sixth century were exiled after the fall of Jerusalem.

Christ's kingdom, Christians believe, is not of this world. Luther spoke of "two kingdoms"—namely, the political life of the corrupt world in contrast to the Kingdom of Heaven. To conflate them in the form of a "New Jerusalem" broke not only with Christian tradition but beggared Christian doctrine, for it presumed that man might redeem himself. If that is true, why did Jesus need to sacrifice himself? That, I believe, is what led to the extinction of Puritanism. Christians do not join the New Israel through their mere presence in a polity but by personal faith in God's Kingdom. The trouble is that Christianity cannot resolve the conundrum of free will and original sin. A handful of Christians, such as the Mennonites, will form small communities apart from the world and wait for divine grace to find them. That leads to irrelevance. Most Christians will go out into the world and reform it so that it is more amenable to grace, reverting, as it were, to the Hebrew roots of Christianity. As Neuhaus writes:

> In the 1860s the church of the *novus ordo seclorum* was shattered by the holy war to end slavery, and from that catastrophe emerged the most profound theologian of the civil religion. Lincoln's Second Inaugural Address, with its troubled reflection on the mysteries of providence, is in some ways worthy of St. Augustine, except, of course, that it is without Augustine's Church and therefore without the communal bearer of the story of the world by which all other stories, including the story of America, are truly told. American theology has suffered from an ecclesiological deficit, leading to an ecclesiological substitution of America for the Church through time.

There is no gainsaying Neuhaus's critique of the Puritans, who were playacting at being Jews with their vision of a new chosen people and a new promised land, as I explained in the previous chapter. Gentiles do not emulate the Jews, or "Judaize," with success, perhaps because Jewish continuity depends not only on faith but on blood ties. Still, the tiny band of English separatists who departed Europe in 1620, the second year of the Thirty Years' War, had better reasons to seek an "errand in the wilderness" than we easily can imagine today.

Whether the Puritans were right to conclude that Europe already had been lost for Christianity is a matter for historians to debate. But it is hard to imagine how Europe might have avoided the victory of communism or fascism were it not for the United States, now the only major nation in which Christianity remains at the center of public life. If the Puritans had not sailed to America in emulation of Israel leaving Egypt, the gates of hell well might have prevailed against St Peter.

According to Neuhaus, Lincoln appeared not only as the most profound theologian of the civil religion but arguably as the most profound American theologian of any religion. That is also the view of the evangelical historian Mark Noll in his book *America's God*. "Views of providence," Noll wrote, "provide the sharpest contrast between Lincoln and the professional theologians of his day." Noll muses that "the American God may have been working too well for the Protestant theologians who, even as they exploited Scripture and pious experience so successfully, yet found it easy to equate America's moral government of God with Christianity itself. Their tragedy—and the greater the theologian, the greater the tragedy—was to rest content with a God defined by the American conventions God's own loyal servants had exploited so well."

For America to draw inspiration from the Hebrew Bible is salutary, but for Americans to regard themselves as God's chosen is idolatrous. Because America is not a chosen nation, Neuhaus warned, "we should be uneasy even with Lincoln's sharply modified claim that we are an 'almost chosen' people." But "almost chosen" is like "almost pregnant," and the absurdity of Lincoln's joke suggests the possibility of a more benign reading. America brought into the world a new political form, the nonethnic democracy, a necessary but not sufficient condition for a Christian nation. America really is different from, say, Poland, the homeland of the greatest religious leader of our times. Pope John Paul II's last book, *Memory and Identity*, "is about Poland and being Polish, both of which John Paul explores and affirms in a way that many might think scandalously chauvinistic," Neuhaus observes. In some respects, Poland deserves the special admiration of her preeminent son. As a breakaway Soviet buffer state on the central front, Poland occupied center stage in the Cold War, and the Polish people led by the Catholic Church rose heroically to the occasion. The trouble is that Poland's story is coming to an end. The country's population (assuming constant fertility) will fall by almost 30 percent by midcentury, and by almost 60 percent by the end of the century, and the median age will rise from 36 to 56 years. Fertility might change, to be sure, but Poland (along with virtually all of Eastern Europe as well as Germany, Italy, and Japan) appears to have passed a demographic point of no return. Benedict XVI, for that matter, ranks by my reckoning as the best mind on the planet, but it is questionable whether today's Germany is capable of educating another Joseph Ratzinger. America's story will not end, at least not in the same way.

What we might call America's "Special Providence" is founded on its capacity to absorb the talented and energetic immigrants vomited out by the wars and persecutions of the Old World. America's fresh start made it congenitally receptive to Christianity. Only in its potential is America "almost chosen"; the extent to which it actually is Christian will depend not on its constitution but on its churches. Ultimately, the Puritan hope of forming a new chosen people in a new promised land only could fail, but it is hard to see how Christianity could have prevailed in the West without it. Sometimes, perhaps, Christians may have to emulate the Jews in order to remain Christians.

Of all the American sects who emulate the Jews, the Mormons must rank as the most enthusiastic. Their founder, Joseph Smith Jr., the forger, treasure hunter, magician, polygamist, and self-styled priest-king of the American continent, invented an American version of Europe's ethnically founded idolatry. Each European tribe that rebelled against Christianity styled itself the Chosen People. Smith concocted a tale in which Americans actually were the Chosen People, and America was the Promised Land of the ancient Hebrews where Jesus Christ himself walked after the resurrection. In short, Smith took to the extremes of fantasy and forgery an impulse toward national self-worship that always lurks somewhere in American Christianity. The Catholic Church does not consider them to be Christians at all. Despite the weirdness of Mormon theology (which asserts, among other things, that God once lived on another planet and was married), Mormons nonetheless imbibe American religion from the national ambience and have become a strangely American success story.

Part Four

Continental Drift

CHAPTER 16

When the Cat's Away,
the Mice Kill Each Other

History speaks of a Pax Romana, a Pax Britannica, and a Pax Americana but has no other nameable eras of sustained peace, for the simple reason cited by Henry Kissinger: Nothing maintains peace except hegemony and the balance of power. The balancing act always fails, though, as it did in Europe in 1914 and as it will in Central and South Asia precisely a century later. The result will be suppurating instability in the region during the next two years and a slow but deadly drift toward great-power animosity. Those who wanted an end to U.S. hegemony will get what they wished for. But they won't like it.

President George W. Bush thought that the United States could turn Kabul into Peoria, the archetypal American city in the state of Illinois. President Barack Obama thinks that Kabul is just as good as Peoria. America has shed idealist delusion—that imposing the outward form of democracy in Iraq or Afghanistan would implant its content—in favor of an even stranger delusion. It was mad to believe, with Bush, that America could remake the world in its own image. Given that more than half the world's languages will go extinct for lack of interest during the present century, it is even madder, with Obama, to turn foreign policy into an affirmative-action program for disadvantaged cultures. But those are the idiot twins of American idealism: Either one size fits all or size doesn't matter. I do not propose to draw a moral equivalence between Bush and Obama: Bush wanted to elevate American power and Obama wants to diminish it. Bush had better motives, but he was no less destructive of American influence.

Where are the realists? Self-styled realists, to be sure, idle at every corner on K Street. Professors John Mearsheimer and Stephen Walt, the enemies of the so-called Israel lobby, claim to be realists. Why, they ask, should America ally with Israel, a land of seven million people, and offend 1.3 billion Muslims, some of whom are sitting on a great deal of the world's oil? Why not force Israel to accept a peace on Arab terms—namely, a return to the 1967 borders and the division of Jerusalem? Why can't we be rational and sensible and sophisticated like our European allies? A widely shared fantasy, though, doesn't qualify as reality. Mearsheimer, Walt, and their kind are not realists at all, just majoritarian fantasists.

It is easy to confuse "realism" with a widely shared delusion. In the parlance of American foreign policy, "realism" means accepting a howling lie if it is accepted by a large enough number of people. The "realists" during the Reagan administration insisted that the Soviet Union was a successful, stable, and permanent fixture in the world-power equation. Reagan and his advisors saw in Soviet aggression a symptom of imminent internal breakdown. The head of plans at Reagan's National Security Council, Norman A. Bailey, told me in early 1981 that American rearmament would overstrain the Soviet economy and bring about the collapse of communism by 2007.

"No one nation can or should try to dominate another nation," President Barack Obama told the United Nations on September 23, 2009. "No world order that elevates one nation or group of people over another will succeed. No balance of power among nations will hold." Having renounced hegemony as well as the balance of power, Obama by year's end chose to prop up the power balance in the region with additional American and allied soldiers in Afghanistan. Obama chose the least popular as well as the least effective alternative. The U.S. president's apparent fecklessness reflects the gravity of the strategic problems in the region.

There is one great parallel, but also one great difference, between the Balkans on the eve of the First World War and the witch's cauldron comprising Pakistan, Afghanistan, Iran, and contiguous territory. The failure of the region's most populous state—in that case, the Ottoman Empire, and in this case, Pakistan—makes shambles out of the power balance, leaving the initiative in the hands of irredentist radicals who threaten to tug their sponsors among the great powers along behind them. But in 1914, both France and Germany thought it more advantageous to fight sooner rather than later. No matter how great the provocation, both India and China want to postpone any major conflict. The problem is that they may promote minor ones.

Without America to mediate, scold, and restrain, each of the small powers in the region has no choice but to test its strength against the others. That is why the major players in the region resemble a troupe of manic Morris dancers in a minefield.

What is most astonishing is that official Washington seems entirely oblivious to the crackup of American influence occurring in front of its eyes. None of the wonkish foreign-policy blogs, let alone the mainstream press, seem able to focus. That is not surprising, for official Washington and unofficial Washington have a wheel-and-spoke relationship. As the staff at the U.S. State Department and National Security Council work up policy papers, they send out feelers to the think-tank community and get feedback. This is what feeds the Washington rumor mill. The difference between this administration and every other administration I have observed is that there appears to be no staff work, no departmental effort, no National Security Council—nothing but President Barack Obama. Obama's penchant for "policy czars" has become the source of continuing controversy, with his opponents at Fox News and elsewhere complaining he has bypassed cabinet departments (whose senior staff require Senate confirmation) in favor of twenty-nine policy czars who report directly to him. Like Poo-bah in the *Mikado*, the president seems to be Lord High Everything Else, Secretary of Everything, and a nonstop presence before the television cameras. He has a cabinet, but it has met infrequently in full session since he took office. Some of his supporters are chagrined. The former publisher of the *New Republic*, Marty Peretz, who evinces buyer's remorse over Obama's Middle East policy, diagnosed the president with narcissistic personality disorder in his blog on October 4, 2009. The reason for Obama's peculiar mode of governance, though, may have less to do with his apparent narcissism than with his objectives. It is a credible hypothesis that this president holds views that he cannot easily share, even with his own staff. As he told the United Nations General Assembly on September 23, he truly wants a world without superpowers: "In an era when our destiny is shared, power is no longer a zero-sum game. No one nation can or should try to dominate another nation. No world order that elevates one nation or group of people over another will succeed."

What does Obama mean by this? How strongly does he feel that America should not be elevated above any other nation? There is some basis for the conjecture that his innermost sentiment is hardcore, left-wing, Third World antipathy to the United States. It now seems well established that his autobiography *Dreams of My Father* was ghostwritten by the former Weatherman Bill Ayers, now a professor of education in Chicago. Long rumored, this allegation is confirmed by the celebrity journalist Christopher Anderson in his new book, *Barack and Michelle: Portrait of an American Marriage.* Jack Cashill at *American Thinker* has been on this trail for a year, comparing Ayers's attributed writing to *Dreams*, and in my view made a strong case even before Anderson's book appeared. Ayers never repudiated the bombs he planted in public buildings during the 1960s. Obama's upbringing was leftist (which in itself proves nothing—so was mine). He was abandoned by three parents—his biological father Barack Obama Sr., his Indonesian stepfather Lolo Soetero, and his mother Ann Dunham, who left him with her parents to pursue doctoral research in anthropology in Indonesia. Dunham's communist sympathies from adolescence onward are widely reported; the African American poet Frank Marshall Davis, a Communist Party member, was a friend of his maternal grandfather Stanley Dunham and, according to *Dreams*, something of a mentor to young Obama. "Peasant Blacksmithing in Indonesia: Surviving against All Odds" was the title of Dunham's doctoral dissertation. Dunham's sympathy for the traditional life of Indonesians fighting against the encroachment of the global economy evidently left a huge impression on young Obama, for he thought their lives better than those of poor people in the United States. As he (or Bill Ayers) wrote in *Dreams of My Father*:

And yet for all that poverty [in the Indonesian marketplace], there remained in their lives a discernible order, a tapestry of trading routes and middlemen, bribes to pay and customs to observe, the habits of a generation played out every day beneath the bargaining and the noise and the swirling dust. It was the absence of such coherence that made a place like [the Chicago housing projects] so desperate.

That paragraph is a précis of his mother's doctoral dissertation and may be the most important point of self-revelation in Obama's collective utterances. The words may have come from Bill Ayers, but the sentiment is doubtless Obama's. In mature adulthood, Obama continued to identify with the leftist sentiments of his mother.

The failures of the Obama administration were made painfully obvious by WikiLeaks. From the first batch of headlines there is little in WikiLeaks' 250,000 classified diplomatic cables that a curious surfer would not have known from the Internet. We are shocked—shocked—to discover that the Arab Gulf states favor an invasion of Iran, that members of the Saudi royal family fund terrorism, that Pakistan might sell nuclear material to malefactors, that Saudi Arabia will try to acquire nuclear weapons if Iran does, that Israel has been itching for an air strike against Iran's nuclear facilities, that the Russian government makes use of the Russian mob, that the Turkish prime minister Recep Tayyip Erdogan tilts toward radical Islam, or that the Italian prime minister Silvio Berlusconi mixes politics and business. American career diplomats have been telling their masters in the Obama administration that every theater of American policy is in full-blown rout, forwarding to Washington the growing alarm of foreign leaders. In April 2008, for example, Adel al-Jubeir, Saudi Arabia's envoy to the United States, told General David Petraeus that King Abdullah wanted the United States "to cut off the head of the [Iranian] snake" and "recalled the king's frequent exhortations to the US to attack Iran and so put an end to its nuclear weapons program." Afghani president Hamid Karzai warned the United States that Pakistan was forcing Taliban militants to keep fighting rather than accept his peace offers. Pakistani government officials, other cables warn, might sell nuclear material to terrorists. The initial reports suggest that the U.S. State Department has massive evidence that Obama's approach—"engaging" Iran and coddling Pakistan—has failed catastrophically. The crisis in diplomatic relations heralded by the press headlines is not so much a diplomatic problem—America's friends and allies in Western and Central Asia have been shouting themselves hoarse for two years—but a crisis of American credibility. Not one Muslim government official so much as mentioned the issues that have occupied the bulk of Washington's attention during the past year—for example, Israeli settlements. The Saudis, to be sure, would prefer the elimination of all Israeli settlements; for that matter, they would prefer the eventual elimination of the state of Israel. In one conversation with a senior White House official, Saudi king Abdullah stated categorically that Iran, not Palestine, was his main concern; while a solution to the Arab–Israeli conflict would be a great achievement, Iran would find other ways to cause trouble. "Iran's goal is to cause problems," Abdullah added. "There is no doubt something unstable about them." There never has been a shred of evidence that an Israeli–Palestinian agreement would help America contain Iran's nuclear threat. The deafening silence over this issue in the diplomatic cables is the strongest refutation of this premise to date. How do we explain the gaping chasm between Obama's public stance and the facts reported by the diplomatic corps? The cables do not betray American secrets so much as

American obliviousness. The simplest and most probable explanation is that the president is a man obsessed by his own vision of a
multipolar world, in which America will shrink its standing to that
of one power among many and thus remove the provocation on
which Obama blames the misbehavior of the Iranians, Pakistanis,
the pro-terrorist wing of the Saudi royal family, and other enemies
of the United States.

Never underestimate the power of nostalgia. With a Muslim father and stepfather, and an anthropologist mother whose life's work
defended Muslim traditional society against globalization, Obama
harbors an overpowering sympathy for the Muslim world. He is not
a Muslim, although as a young child he was educated as a Muslim
in Indonesian schools. His vision of outreach to the Muslim world,
the most visible and impassioned feature of his foreign policy, draws
on deep wells of emotion.

Think of Obama as the anti-Truman. As David Brog recounts
in his book *Standing with Israel* (2006), President Harry S. Truman overruled the unanimous opposition of his cabinet and made
America the first country to recognize the new state of Israel in
1948. His secretary of state, wartime chief of staff George Marshall,
had threatened in vain to resign and campaign against Truman in
the next presidential election over the issue. Personal religious mo-
tivations, not strategy, guided Truman's decision. He was a Bible-
reading Christian Zionist who supported Israel as a matter of principle. Obama has the same sort of loyalty to the Muslim world that
Truman had toward the Jewish people. He cannot bring himself to
be the American president who ruins a Muslim land. It is wishful
thinking that the Iranian problem can be managed without bringing ruin to the Persian pocket empire. In many respects, Iran resembles the Soviet Union just before the collapse of communism.

It turned out that there were no communists in Russia outside the upper echelons of the party. There are very few Muslims in Iran outside of the predatory mullahcracy. According to Zohreh Soleimani of the BBC, Iran has the lowest mosque attendance of any Muslim country; only 2 percent of adults attend Friday services, a gauge of disaffection comparable to church attendance in Western Europe. Iran's fertility rate of about 1.6 children per woman, coincidentally, is about the same as Western Europe's. Iran has a huge contingent of young people, but they have ceased to have children. They have faith neither in the national religion nor in the future of their nation. The United Nations Office on Drugs and Crime, meanwhile, reports that fully 5 percent of Iran's adult nonelderly population of 35 million is addicted to opium. Alcoholism also is epidemic, despite the Islamic prohibition on alcoholic beverages, which must be smuggled into the country. The United States. won the Cold War by ruining Russia. Russia may never recover. In 1992, three years after the Berlin Wall came down, thousands of pensioners gathered daily near Red Square in the winter cold to barter old clothing or trinkets for food, and the tourist hotels swarmed with prostitutes. The collapse of communism did not usher in a golden age of Russian democracy, and the new government turned into the most rapacious plague of locusts ever to descend on a vulnerable economy. Break the Iranian mullahcracy, and Iran most likely will fall into demoralization and ruin. Punish Pakistan for its machinations with the Taliban, and the country likely will descend into civil war. Iran's nuclear ambitions and Pakistan's dalliance with terrorism both stem from the sad fact that they are failed states to begin with. Push them into a corner, and the failure will become manifest.

In fairness to Obama, benign neglect of Iran's nuclear ambitions has precedent in the administration of George W. Bush. Obama simply carried that neglect forward. Bush confirms in his memoirs what was evident at the time: He followed the advice of Defense Secretary Robert Gates and Secretary of State Condoleezza Rice to avoid open conflict with Iran. If provoked, Iran was capable of producing a large number of American casualties in Iraq in the advent of the 2008 elections. The difference between early 2008 and early 2010, to be sure, is that Iran has had two years to enrich uranium, consolidate its grip on Syria, insert itself into Afghanistan, stockpile missiles with Hezbollah in Lebanon and Hamas in Gaza, and build up its terror capabilities around the world. The window in which Iran may be contained is closing. Covert operations and cybersabotage might have bought some time, but benign neglect of Iran has reached its best-used-by date.

The cables, in sum, reveal an American administration that refuses to look at the facts on the ground, even when friendly governments rub the noses of American diplomats into them. Napoleon was a lunatic who thought he was Napoleon, and the joke applies to the forty-fourth U.S. president with a vengeance. Obama is beyond reality; he has become the lunatic who thinks that he is Barack Obama.

CHAPTER 17

In Praise of Premature War

Rarely in its long history has the West suffered by going to war too soon. On the contrary: Among the wars of Western history, the bloodiest were those that started too late. Why should that be the case? The answer, I believe, is that keeping the peace requires prospective combatants to maintain the balance of power—for example, between Athens and Sparta in the fifth century BC, between Catholic and Protestant states in the seventeenth century AD, and between the Central Powers and the Allies at the turn of the twentieth century. Once powers truly are balanced, however, neither side can win, except by a devastating war of attrition. Postponing war therefore creates equally matched opposing blocs who eventually will annihilate each other.

More than ever does this principle apply to the present race for nuclear weapons. It brings to mind the joke about the housewife in Hertfordshire who telephones her husband and says, "Dear, be careful driving home. The news report says that there is a maniac driving in the wrong direction on the motorway." He replies, "What do you mean, one maniac? Everyone is driving in the wrong direction!"

After the failure to find nuclear weapons in Iraq, much discussion has been spent on the legitimacy of the American-led invasion. Whether or not Saddam Hussein actually intended or had the capacity to build nuclear weapons is of trifling weight in the strategic balance. Everyone is planning to build nuclear weapons. They involve sixty-year-old technology no longer difficult to replicate. It hardly matters where one begins. "Kill the chicken, and let the monkey watch," as the Chinese say. The theocrats of Iran, the North Koreans, and soon many other incalculable reprobates have or will have such plans. It hardly matters which one you attack first, so long as you attack one of them. But isn't it cruel to cast the die for war before it is proven beyond doubt that war cannot be avoided? Given the frightful cost of war, should peace not be given every chance? Some wars, of course, should not be fought, such as the threatened hot war between the United States and the Soviet Union. In many cases, however, risk and reward are highly asymmetric; the cost of a short and nasty small war vanishes toward insignificance compared with the price of a grand war of attrition, particularly when nuclear weapons are concerned. Many writers, to be sure, have offered apologies for war. Under the title "Give War a Chance," Edward Luttwak wrote in *Foreign Affairs* (summer 1999):

> Since the establishment of the United Nations, great powers have rarely let small wars burn themselves out. Bosnia and Kosovo are the latest examples of this meddling. Conflicts are interrupted by a steady stream of ceasefires and armistices that only postpone war-induced exhaustion and let belligerents rearm and regroup. Even worse are UN refugee-relief operations and NGOs [non-

governmental organizations], which keep resentful populations festering in camps and sometimes supply both sides in armed conflicts. This well-intentioned interference only intensifies and prolongs struggles in the long run. The unpleasant truth is that war does have one useful function: it brings peace. Let it.

I have no quibble with Luttwak but propose to go further. He proposed to let small wars burn out; I propose to let some wars break out, the sooner the better. Historians allow that the Allies should have attacked Germany in 1936 rather than 1939, but they dismiss the First World War as "a tragic and unnecessary conflict," in the words of Sir John Keegan. Tragedy stems from necessity. From the Congress of Berlin in 1878, when Germany and Austria set limits to Russian expansion in the Balkans, pan-Slavism set Europe on a course toward inevitable war. France allied with Russia, seeking help against Germany after its humiliation in the Franco–Prussian War of 1871. Already in demographic decline, France knew that it could not wait one more generation to attack Germany. Germany knew that if Russia completed its railroad network its bulk might make it undefeatable a generation hence.

If Kaiser Wilhelm II had had the nerve to declare war on France during the 1905 Morocco crisis, Count Alfred von Schlieffen's invasion plan would have crushed the French within weeks. Russia's Romanov dynasty, humiliated by its defeat in the Russo–Japanese War and beset by popular revolt, likely would have fallen under circumstances more benign than what prevailed in 1917. England had not decided on an alliance with the Franco–Russian coalition in 1905. One major source of tension, the naval arms race between Germany and England, was yet to emerge. War in 1905 would have left Wilhelmine Germany the sole hegemon in Europe, with no prospective challenger for some time to come. Germany's indecision left the initiative in the hands of Russia, elements of whose secret service backed the Serbian terrorists who murdered the Austrian crown prince in 1914, forcing Germany into war under far less favorable circumstances. Both world wars of the twentieth century, in my view, started too late, with catastrophic consequences for Western Europe. America's Civil War, by contrast, was a war that began just in time, and I attribute the future flowering of the United States to Abraham Lincoln's ruthlessness in pushing the country into war.

Was it coincidence that France, England, and Spain determined to invade Mexico after Benito Juarez suspended debt-service payment to Mexico's European creditors in 1861, just as the American Civil War began? French, English, and Spanish forces landed in Mexico in December 1861, after the South's early victories in the Civil War convinced European governments that the slaveholders would prevail. By 1862, after Stonewall Jackson's success in the Shenandoah Valley, England came close to recognizing the Confederacy. In October of that year, William Gladstone, then chancellor of the exchequer, stated, "We may anticipate with certainty the success of the Southern States so far as regards their separation from the North." The Union half-victory at the Battle of Antietam in September came just in time to abort British recognition of the South. Had the war broken out two years later, the European powers already would have been entrenched in Mexico, providing the South with a natural ally against the Lincoln government and with a base from which to expand the slave system southward. America would have split in two (at least), and the history of the world would have been radically different, and radically worse.

If the South had bought time to ally with France under Napoleon III, who invaded Mexico in 1862, and with Britain under Lord

Palmerston, the Union never could have imposed a blockade on the Confederacy. The highly motivated Southern armies would have worn down the North with sufficient materiel. If the South had not seceded with a violent tantrum, firing on Fort Sumter in April 1861, the North might not have mustered the support for a civil war. The secession of the South was of no economic consequence to New England manufacturers who bought its cotton, and it was remote to the Midwestern farmers who eventually won the war under General W. T. Sherman. Northern outrage against the Southern initiation of hostilities gave a military mandate to Lincoln, who had won less than 40 percent of the popular vote in the 1860 presidential election.

John Brown, the insurrectionist hanged for treason after an abortive effort to spark a slave revolt, deserves a great deal of the credit for the missteps of the South. Through his raid on the Harpers Ferry arsenal with twenty-one men in 1859, he ostensibly sought to distribute the one hundred thousand firearms on hand to slaves. It had no chance of success, but it persuaded slaveholders that their worst-case scenario was to have their throats slit by mutinous slaves. Fear rather than rational calculation guided Southern policy, and the war came soon enough for the Union to triumph.

CHAPTER 18

Kierkegaard, Socrates,
and the Continental Op

"The Owl of Wisdom flies at night," by which G. W. F. Hegel meant that we understand what went wrong only after the sun has set on the empire we have the misfortune to inhabit. As America wakes up to the ruin of its world position, perhaps it will reflect on the false premises underlying its foreign policy. Worst among these is the notion that the United States can impose a rational constitution on whatever country it pleases. Under the George W. Bush administration, this drew credibility from the myth of Socratic statecraft as told by Leo Strauss and his students. If Greek rationalism, not Hebrew love, informs the American idea, then it must be America's mission to promulgate such rationalism among the less fortunate. War among civilizations erupts not because men are unreasonable but rather because existential fear drives them to it. The real Socrates, as opposed to the Straussian invention, has something disturbing to tell us about this.

Turning Socrates into an apostle of rationalism seems odd, for he drank the poison prescribed for him by an Athenian court in 399

BC rather than escape into exile (as Leo Strauss doubtless would have done in Athens, and in fact did in Germany). That was an existential rather than a rational choice. Although the Athenian mob condemned him, and Athens had fallen into ignominy after its surrender to Sparta five years earlier, Socrates preferred to die than to cease to be Athenian. Athenian philosophy presents a problem rather than a solution; try as one might, one cannot pry the Socratic cult of reason out of its context, which is Athenian piety. Socrates drank the hemlock not because he believed in metempsychosis but rather because he could not conceive of himself except as an Athenian. Lesser men than Socrates have displayed greater courage in the face of death, in the belief that their tribe would bear some part of their mortal existence into the future. Strauss thought Martin Heidegger the greatest philosopher of his time. Strip away all of Heidegger's word games, and his message reduces to this: "Authenicity"—being what you are—trumps abstract reason. If Socrates drank the hemlock to remain Athenian, what prevents me from supporting Hitler in order to remain German? Heidegger never apologized for his Nazism, not because he was a Nazi extremist but because his decision to become a Nazi was inextricable from his entire body of thought. To get around this problem Strauss had to invent an "exoteric" and an "esoteric" Plato.

The Danish theologian Søren Kierkegaard (1813–1855) remains a lone and cranky voice in the debate. U.S. policymakers would benefit from a few quiet hours with Kierkegaard, whose 1841 doctoral dissertation showed Socrates not as a system builder but as a destroyer who saw that Greek culture was a failure and who set out to tear down its premises. Socrates, in short, was an "ironist" for whom "the whole substantial life of Greek culture had lost its validity." The ironist, wrote Kierkegaard, is prophetic, but his position and situation are the reverse of the prophet's. The prophet walks arm in arm with his age, and from this position he glimpses what is coming.... The ironist, however, has stepped out of line with his age, has turned around and faced it. That which is coming is hidden from him, lies behind his back, but the actuality he so antagonistically confronts is what he must destroy; upon this he focuses his burning gaze.

Doubtless Kierkegaard had in mind Goethe's spirit that always negates—namely, Mephistopheles—who told Faust, "Alles was entsteht / Ist wert, dass es zu Grunde geht" (Everything that comes to be goes rightly to its ruin). Irony, said the Danish writer, "establishes nothing, because that which is to be established lies behind it. It is a divine madness that rages like a Tamerlane and does not leave one stone upon another."

Athens' hubris (or greed and corruption) led to the city's ruin in the Peloponnesian War of 431–404 BC, which America's critics cite as an analogous case of imperial overreach. Yet the Athenian tragedy reveals precisely the opposite, if we read Kierkegaard correctly. No culture founded on a restricted ethnicity and its particular gods can help but fail. Pericles boasted that Athens was great both in good and in evil, as was borne out by the massacre of the inhabitants of Melos in 416. The subtlest philosophy could not overcome Athens' particularism. It could expand only through empire—that is, collecting tribute by the threat of violence. In broader war, Athenian culture failed, and Socrates "used irony as he destroyed Greek culture" (Kierkegaard). In this respect Socrates' insistence (in *Phaedo*) that a wise man should welcome death, and that the only argument against suicide is obedience to the laws of the *polis*, echoes Sophocles' lament (in *Oedipus at Colonus*) that the dead are happier than the living and that those are happiest who never were born.

Three conflicting portraits of Socrates have come down to us. Besides Plato's hagiographic report we have not only the hostile depiction by the satirist but also a sympathetic account by the soldier Xenophon. The latter paints Socrates as an avuncular source of humdrum advice, however, whereas Plato's Socrates dwells in the realm of ideas, unperturbed by earthly concerns. Xenophon "has deflated his Socrates," and "Plato, like an artist, has created his Socrates in supernatural dimensions" (Kierkegaard). In *The Clouds*, meanwhile, Aristophanes shows yet another Socrates, a meddlesome troublemaker who leads a young man to beat his father after hearing Socrates' critique of traditional authority.

"But what was Socrates actually like?" asks Kierkegaard. "The answer is: Socrates' existence is irony.... Along with Xenophon, one can certainly assume that Socrates was fond of walking around and talking with all sorts of people because every external thing or event is an occasion for the ever quick-witted ironist; along with Plato, one can certainly let Socrates touch on the idea." Like Kierkegaard, Leo Strauss hoped to stitch together a single picture of Socrates from three divergent reports. Strauss, however, assumed that hidden among the contradictions was an esoteric science of statecraft discernible only to an elite of adepts. His students have spent the thirty years since Strauss's death bickering about what the great man really meant to say. That does not speak well for his argument. I suspect that, rather than there being an occult Straussian conspiracy, as some have suggested, Strauss worked himself into a maze of infinite regress. Those who wish to delve further into the Straussian labyrinth may consult his "Lectures on Socrates" in Thomas Pangles's collection, *The Rebirth of Classic Political Rationalism* (Chicago 1989).

The view of the Danish theologian illumines both the material and the historical context, which raises a question as to why Strauss remains so influential. The answer, I believe, is that Kierkegaard's understanding of Socrates leads to disturbing conclusions. If all the effervescence of Platonic reasoning does not lead to positive conclusions, what hope does reason give us? Philosophy (in Franz Rosenzweig's phrase) is a small child stuffing his fingers in his ears and shouting, "I can't hear you!" in face of the fear of death. Kierkegaard requires not a deduction but a leap of faith. Kierkegaard, that is, betrayed the philosophers and went over to the camp of the theologians, and the philosophers give him the cold shoulder. Rationalists as well as antirationalists fought over a straw man, Socrates, the supposed Apostle of Reason. Friedrich Nietzsche despised both faith and reason and chose Socrates as the whipping boy for reason. Rationalists such as Leo Strauss defend Socrates, without ever getting quite clear which Socrates they propose to save. Both rationalists and antirationalists get it wrong. The general disregard for Kierkegaard is understandable, for it is a most uncomfortable thing to conclude that philosophy has deposited us at the edge of the precipice of faith.

Strauss hung his political-philosophy hat on Thomas Hobbes, who threw out the traditional concept of God-given rights of man. He derived the social contract instead from man's brute instinct for self-preservation. In order to protect themselves against violence in the state of nature, men surrender part of their freedom to a ruler who in turn guarantees their security. By deriving natural rights from brute instinct rather than divine law, Strauss argued (in *Natural Right and History*, 1950), Hobbes invented modern political science—that is, a discipline distinct from faith. Thus he made it possible to create a practicable republic composed of selfish men, unlike the utopian vision of Plato, which depended on virtuous rulers. Kant summarized the modern viewpoint: "We could devise a constitution for a race of devils, if only they were intelligent."

If Strauss were correct, then building a democracy would not be much different from building a power plant. Once the components were assembled, it would run anywhere. If one country could learn how to do it, so could another; it might not run quite as smoothly in Iraq as in the United States but, then again, neither would a power plant.

History exposes Hobbes's "self-preservation instinct" as a chimera. If men have nothing more than physical self-preservation, self-disgust will stifle them. Strauss knew that Hobbes's approach leads inevitably to nihilism, and he proposed a return to Athenian political philosophy as an antidote, although what that might accomplish is unclear. His students still quibble fruitlessly over whether Strauss "stayed with the moderns" or "went back to Athens."

Strauss was a German Jewish theologian who lost his faith and came under the spell of the modernists' critique of tradition. On the one hand, he agreed with the critics of Christian civilization from Machiavelli through Heidegger. On the other, he perceived that the end of the old order of things led only to nihilism and destruction. Nietzsche and Heidegger refuted the absolutes of right and wrong as taught by revealed religion, insisting that men invented their own values as circumstances permitted. The Nazis idolized Nietzsche; Heidegger himself embraced National Socialism. That left Strauss in a profoundly uncomfortable position intellectually, given his fascination with Heidegger, as well as personally, as he had to flee Nazi Germany.

Caught between the collapse of tradition and the pyromania of the modernists, Strauss took the well-trodden path back to ancient Athens—that is, to the political philosophy of Socrates. Westerners who reject religion have been doing that since the Renaissance. Strauss, the theologian who began his career writing glosses on Jewish authorities, restyled himself as a classicist. As he wrote to Karl Lowith in 1946: "I really believe, although to you this apparently appears fantastic, that the perfect political order, as Plato and Aristotle have sketched it, is the perfect political order. I know very well that today it cannot be restored." What that means, we shall see below.

Once in America, Strauss's continental credentials and broad learning made him the guru of gullible Americans. Like the Gypsy Melchiades in Gabriel García Márquez's fantasy *A Hundred Years of Solitude*, the refugee scholar came from afar with irresistibly exotic wares. "Young Americans seemed, in comparison [to Europeans], to be natural savages when they came to the university. They had hardly heard the names of the writers who were the daily fare of their counterparts across the Atlantic, let alone took it into their heads that they could have a relationship to them," wrote the late Allan Bloom, Strauss's bestselling student. Americans want happy endings, and the enterprising Leo Strauss provided them with this one: Reason as taught by the Athenian political philosophers can provide solutions to modern problems of statecraft. His student Harry Jaffa spent a lifetime portraying the Founding Fathers of the United States as well as Abraham Lincoln as master logicians. To Jaffa, Lincoln was "the greatest of all exemplars of Socratic statesmanship.... Never since Socrates has philosophy so certainly descended from the heavens into the affairs of mortal men."

Yet there is the nagging problem of Heidegger, who rejected all tellers of absolute truth and Socrates most vehemently. As an impressionable young man, Strauss fell under Heidegger's influence and never quite shook it. Considering Heidegger's grandiose reputation, it is depressing to consider how cheap was the trick he played.

What is Being? he demanded of a generation that after the First World War felt the ground shaky under their feet. It is a shame that Eddie Murphy never studied philosophy, for then we might have had the following *Saturday Night Live* sketch about Heidegger's definition of Being with respect to Non-Being, or death. Hegel is said to be easier to understand in Italian translation, and Heidegger is clearer in Ebonics:

> What be "Be"? You cain't say that "Be" be, cause you saying "be" to talk about "Be," and it don't mean nothing to say that "Be" be dis or "Be" be dat. "Be" be "Be" to begin wit! So don't you be saying "Be" be "Be." You wanna talk about "Be," you gotta talk about what ain't be nothin' at all. You gotta say "Be" be what ain't "ain't-Be." Now when you ain't be nothing at all? Dat be when you be daid. When you daid you ain't be nothing, you just be daid. So "Be" be somewhere between where you be and where you ain't be, dat is, when you be daid. Any time you say "Be" you is also saying "ain't-Be," and dat make you think about being daid.

That is all there is to Heidegger's existential idea of Being-toward-death. Metaphysical pettifogging of this sort appeals to people whom the disintegration of social order has made uncertain about their sense of being. But in an important sense Heidegger's idea is correct. (It was also correct when it was Kierkegaard's idea earlier.) The enunciation of the concept *Being* dredges up the problem of mortality, Heidegger continued. What we are is defined by our response to mortality. But if we reject revealed religion as a response to mortality, we are creatures of circumstances. Men thus confront their mortality under particular circumstances, in what came to be called "radical historicism"—in, that is, the complete absence of absolute truths. What remains is arbitrary existential choice, guided by the contingent circumstances in which we happen to find ourselves. Heidegger's was to join the Nazis.

That left Strauss in the odd position of preaching the absolute truth of Socratic philosophy while giving credence to Nietzsche and Heidegger, who rejected all absolutes and Socrates more than anyone. The Straussians come out on every side of this question, leading to the charge that Strauss secretly taught a cynical, value-free theory of power to his inner sanctum of acolytes. No such thing is the case. Strauss is neither a Heideggerian historicist nor a Greek rationalist, but exactly the opposite. He was confused, but confused in a very special way. He was a Jew who lost his faith. Kierkegaard's ironic reading of Socrates is as good a place as any to reconstruct political philosophy. Disturbing as Kierkegaard's conclusion may be, his case is most convincing that Socrates was an ironist, a "revolutionary," the destroyer of the invalid old. Only in that sense is the United States Socratic: it is the embodiment of creative destruction, reinventing itself to the ruin of the remnants of history. Kierkegaard's Socrates—the ironist, not the system builder—yet may serve as an inspiration to U.S. policy.

To say that, if Americans read Rosenzweig rather than Strauss, they would make better policy is like saying, "If we had some ham, we could have ham and eggs, if we had some eggs." The American students of Leo Strauss did not understand him, or they would not take him quite so seriously. If they attempted to read Rosenzweig, their heads would spin. America has in fact brought forth its own existential philosopher, whose most important aphorism is this: "Plans are all right sometimes.... And sometimes just stirring things up is all right—if you're tough enough to survive, and keep your eyes open so you'll see what you want when it comes to the top."

I quote the Continental Op, that black sheep of American literature, the nameless detective of Dashiell Hammett's novel *Red Harvest* (1927). No man is a prophet in his own country, and the Continental Op is no exception. Hollywood embraced all of Hammett's heroes except the Op, whose casual destructiveness horrifies American sensibilities. We encounter the Op in a 1920s Western town, where the mine owner imported gangsters to break a strike, and the gangsters stayed to run the rackets. A brittle truce prevails among the various gangs, the corrupt police, and the mine owner. The Op willfully incites a gang war, deceiving colleagues and superiors. He dislikes authority, not least the one that pays him. Damsels in distress and downtrodden workers matter to him not at all. He is a loner without friends—short, fat, and alcoholic. His transient love interest is a demimondaine whose murder he neglects to prevent. He incites the war simply because he can, at great risk to his own life, which in any case he holds cheap. He manipulates rather than confronts. The story ends when everyone else is dead.

Numerous films borrowed *Red Harvest*'s plot outline, including Akira Kurosawa's *Yojimbo*, Sergio Leone's *A Fistful of Dollars*, Walter Hill's *Last Man Standing*, and the Coen brothers' *Miller's Crossing*, without, however, portraying Hammett's protagonist. In all of these loose adaptations the protagonist nearly dies to save a woman's honor. In *Red Harvest*, the corresponding woman is a prostitute, and the Op (who authentically likes her) is indirectly responsible for her murder. Nothing stands in the way of the avenger of blood. In the Coen brothers' reading (a conflation of two Hammett novels, *Red Harvest* and *The Glass Key*) the hero soft-heartedly spares the life of a petty criminal, to his near undoing.

The inability of American cinema to depict the most interesting character in all of American fiction reveals something about

American culture. The detectives and cowboys who infest American cinema descend from the silly chivalric literature that Miguel de Cervantes lampooned in Don Quixote. Americans (and even Japanese and Italians) want their tough guys to have a heart of gold. In the Kurosawa–Leone–Hill adaptations, the Toshiro Mifune–Clint Eastwood–Bruce Willis characters take great risk to aid a lady in distress. Hammett's Op cares about neither lady nor risk. His object is the mutual destruction of the contending parties, which he arranges with humor and enjoyment. At one point the Op arranges "a peace conference out of which at least a dozen killings ought to grow...pretending I was trying to clear away everybody's misunderstandings...and played them like you'd play trout, and got just as much fun out of it.... I looked at Noonan [the police chief] and knew he hadn't a chance in a thousand of living another day because of what I had done to him, and I laughed, and felt warm and happy inside." After another multiple murder, he opines, "I haven't had so much fun since the hogs ate my kid brother."

There is no "there" there in American culture, as Gertrude Stein said of Oakland. That is true because America is not a destination but a journey. Franz Rosenzweig described Christianity as a perpetual journey, an infinite midpoint between the promise of redemption at the crucifixion and its fulfillment at the end of days. By the same token, Americans remain in perpetual transition between the Old World culture they abandoned on arrival and the promise of redemption that always lies past the sunset. The most compelling image of American narrative art is the journey toward redemption: Huck and Jim rafting down the Mississippi, or John Wayne and Claire Trevor escaping toward the West in John Ford's *Stagecoach* (1939). Because it presumes a return to innocence, the journey is set most powerfully in a fairy-tale setting, such as Ford's Painted Desert location.

But the Continental Op already has made the journey and has no hope of redemption. In an uncanny dream sequence

> I walked...half the streets in the United States, Gay Street and Mount Royal Avenue in Baltimore, Colfax Avenue in Baltimore, Aetna Road and St. Clair Avenue in Cleveland, McKinney Avenue in Dallas, Lemartine and Cornell and Amory Streets in Boston, Berry Boulevard in Louisville, Lexington Avenue in New York, until I came to Victoria Street in Jacksonville.... Tired and discouraged, I went into the lobby of the hotel that faces the railroad station in Rocky Mount, North Carolina.

It is an image worthy of Gertrude Stein's witticism: Hammett's America has no "there," only a Kafkaesque series of transitions—streets, hotels, railway stations. Better than any other passage in American literature, perhaps, it evokes an America that is always journey but never destination. That is why America is the most Christian of nations, for Christian life—to use Franz Rosenzweig's expression—is an eternal journey. American Christianity has always revived itself from the transient path of people on the move, from the burnt-out district of upstate New York in the first years of the nineteenth century to the megachurches of today's exurbs. It is odd that it took an avowed atheist to construct the American dream sequence, but such is art.

America produces irredeemable outsiders like Hammett himself: a philandering alcoholic who burned himself out after half a dozen books and a handful of screenplays. Americans enjoy the comic outsider, invariably portrayed as an immigrant or regional character. They cheer on the loner who rides into town and rights all the wrongs, an Amadis of Gaul with six-guns. But a misfit who already has walked down every street and expects no redemption frightens Americans. That is why we never have seen American literature's most characteristic creation on the screen, which abounds with cynical tough guys but cannot abide an intelligent one. In any event, he upsets the French. "The last word in atrocity, cynicism, and horror," said Andre Gide of *Red Harvest*. Instability is his natural element. He acts unpredictably, even quirkily, to keep the other side off balance and to discover openings. The point is not so much that he despises authority but rather that it is meaningless to give him orders. In a destructive milieu, he is the agency of destruction. For wide swaths of the world, the Continental Op is a better guide than Leo Strauss.

CHAPTER 19

Christianity's New Heartlands

Christianity may flounder in Europe but find a new fulcrum in the global South, particularly Africa, and in China. The new Christians of the Southern Hemisphere confound enlightened Western prejudice and may bring Christianity back closer to its original purpose.

Ten thousand Chinese become Christians each day, according to the National Catholic Reporter's veteran correspondent John Allen, and 200 million Chinese may constitute the world's largest concentration of Christians by midcentury, and the largest missionary force in history. I suspect that even the most enthusiastic accounts err on the downside and that Christianity will have become a Sinocentric religion two generations from now. China may be for the twenty-first century what Europe was during the eighth through eleventh centuries and what America has been during the past two hundred years: the natural ground for mass evangelization. If this occurs, the world will change beyond our capacity to recognize it. Islam might defeat the Western Europeans, simply by replacing their diminishing numbers with immigrants, but it will crumble beneath the challenge from the East. China, devoured by hunger so many times in its history, now feels a spiritual hunger beneath the neon exterior of its suddenly great cities. Four hundred million Chinese on the prosperous coast have moved from poverty to affluence in a single generation, and 10 million to 15 million new migrants come from the countryside each year, the greatest movement of people in history. Despite a government stance that hovers somewhere between discouragement and persecution, more than 100 million of them have embraced a faith that regards this life as mere preparation for the next world. Given the immense effort the Chinese have devoted to achieving a tolerable life in the present world, this may seem anomalous. On the contrary: It is the great migration of peoples that prepares the ground for Christianity, just as it did during the barbarian invasions of Europe during the Middle Ages. The murder of the Reverend Bae Hyung-kyu three years ago, the leader of the missionaries still held hostage by Taliban kidnappers in Afghanistan, drew world attention to the work of South Korean Christians, who make up nearly 30 percent of that nation's population and send more evangelists out into the world than does any country except the United States. This is only a first tremor of the earthquake to come, as Chinese Christians turn their attention outward. Years ago I speculated that, if Mecca ever is razed, it will be by an African army marching north; now the greatest danger to Islam is the prospect of a Chinese army marching west. People do not live in a spiritual vacuum; where a spiritual vacuum exists, as in Western Europe and the former Soviet Empire, people simply die, or fail to breed. In the traditional world, people see themselves as part of nature, unchangeable and constant, and worship their surroundings, their ancestors, and themselves. When war or economics tear people away from their roots in traditional life, what once appeared constant now is shown to be ephemeral. Christianity is the great liquidator of traditional society, calling individuals out of their tribes and nations to join the *ekklesia*, which transcends race and nation. In China, communism leveled traditional society and erased the great Confucian idea of society as an extension of the loyalties and responsibility of families. Children informing on their parents during the Cultural Revolution put paid to that.

Now the great migrations throw into the urban melting pot a half-dozen language groups who once lived isolated from one another. Not for more than a thousand years have so many people in the same place had such good reason to view as ephemeral all that they long considered to be fixed, and to ask themselves, "What is the purpose of my life?" The World Christian Database offers by far the largest estimate of the number of Chinese Christians, at 111 million, of whom 90 percent are Protestant, mostly Pentecostals. Other estimates are considerably lower, but no matter; what counts is the growth rate. This uniquely American movement, which claims the inspiration to speak in tongues, like Jesus' own disciples, and to prophesy, is the world's fastest-growing religious movement. In contrast to Catholicism, which has a very long historic presence in China but whose growth has been slow, charismatic Protestantism has found its natural element in an atmosphere of official suppression. Barred from churches, Chinese began worshipping in homes, and five major "house church" movements and countless smaller ones now minister to as many as 100 million Christians. This quasi-underground movement may now exceed in its number of adherents the 75 million who are members of the Chinese Communist Party; in a generation it will be the most powerful force in the country. While the Catholic Church has worked patiently for independence from the

Chinese government, which sponsors a "Chinese Catholic Patriotic Association" with government-appointed bishops, the evangelicals have no infrastructure to suppress and no hierarchy to protect. In contrast to Catholic caution, John Allen observed, "most Pentecostals would obviously welcome being arrested less frequently, but in general they are not waiting for legal or political reform before carrying out aggressive evangelization programs." Allen added:

> The most audacious even dream of carrying the gospel beyond the borders of China, along the old Silk Road into the Muslim world, in a campaign known as "Back to Jerusalem." As [*Time* correspondent David] Aikman explains in *Jesus in Beijing*, some Chinese evangelicals and Pentecostals believe that the basic movement of the gospel for the last 2,000 years has been westward: from Jerusalem to Antioch, from Antioch to Europe, from Europe to America, and from America to China. Now, they believe, it's their turn to complete the loop by carrying the gospel to Muslim lands, eventually arriving in Jerusalem. Once that happens, they believe, the gospel will have been preached to the entire world. Aikman reports that two Protestant seminaries secretly are training missionaries for deployment in Muslim countries.

Where traditional society remains entrenched in China's most backward regions, Islam also is expanding. At the edge of the Gobi Desert and on China's western border with Central Asia, Islam claims perhaps 30 million adherents. If Christianity is the liquidator of traditional society, I have argued in the past, Islam is its defender against the encroachments of leveling imperial expansion. But Islam in China remains the religion of the economic losers, whose geographic remoteness isolates them from the economic transformation on the coasts. Christianity, by contrast, has burgeoned among the new middle class in China's cities, where the greatest wealth and productivity are concentrated. Islam has a thousand-year presence in China and has grown by natural increase rather than conversion; evangelical Protestantism had almost no adherents in China a generation ago. China's Protestants evangelized at the risk of liberty, and sometimes life, and possess a sort of fervor not seen in Christian ranks for centuries. Their pastors have been beaten and jailed, and they have had to create their own institutions through the house-church movement.

The growth of Christianity opens up possibilities for democratization. I do not propose that the Chinese must become Congregationalists before they can practice democracy. But political faith presumes a deeper sort of faith in the inherent worth of the humblest of one's fellow citizens. For a people to govern itself, it first must want to govern itself and want to do so with a passion. It also must know how to do so. Democracy requires an act of faith, or rather a whole set of acts of faith. The individual citizen must believe that representatives sitting far away in the capital will listen to his views, and he must know how to band together with other citizens to make their views known. That is why so-called civil society, the capillary network of associations that manage the ordinary affairs of life, is so essential to democracy. Americans elect their local school boards, create volunteer fire brigades, and raise and spend tax dollars at the local level to provide parks or sewers. China's network of house churches may turn out to be the leaven of democracy, like the radical Puritans of England who became the Congregationalists of New England. Freedom of worship is the first precondition for democracy, for it makes possible freedom of conscience. The fearless evangelists at the grassroots of China will, in the fullness of time, do more to bring U.S.-style democracy to the world than either all the nation-building bluster of President George W. Bush and his advisers or the passivity of Barack H. Obama

China and Korea are not alone as new centers of evangelical zeal. American Pentecostalism is also spreading rapidly through sub-Saharan Africa.

Philip Jenkins of Pennsylvania State University predicts a "historical turning point" in Christianity, "one that is as epochal for the Christian world as the original Reformation." In the October 2002 issue of the *Atlantic Monthly*, he wrote:

> In the global South (the areas that we often think of primarily as the Third World) huge and growing Christian populations—currently 480 million in Latin America, 360 million in Africa, and 313 million in Asia, compared with 260 million in North America—now make up what the Catholic scholar Walbert Bühlmann has called the Third Church, a form of Christianity as distinct as Protestantism or Orthodoxy, and one that is likely to become dominant in the faith.

This may look like a "Third Church" to Catholic eyes, but what I perceive is the proliferation of Anglo-Saxon—that is, American—Christianity, albeit in the patchwork raiment of local peoples. Growth of church membership in the Southern Hemisphere concentrates in denominations of American or British origin. Observes Jenkins:

> It is Pentecostals who stand in the vanguard of the Southern Counter-Reformation. Though Pentecostalism emerged as a movement only at the start of the twentieth century, chiefly

in North America, Pentecostals today are at least 400 million strong, and heavily concentrated in the global South. By 2040 or so there could be as many as a billion, at which point Pentecostal Christians alone will far outnumber the world's Buddhists and will enjoy rough numerical parity with the world's Hindus.

In an important book published in 2006, *The New Faces of Christianity: Believing the Bible in the Global South*, Jenkins seeks to further analyze and explain this phenomenon. The Bible, and above all the Hebrew Bible, speaks immediately to the new Christians of the Global South because their lives are fragile and fraught with danger, unlike the complacent and secure Euro-American Christians who find disturbing the actual Bible of blood and redemption. Southern Christians will dominate the religion within a generation or two, and this may bring it closer to its original purpose and character. This observation makes Jenkins's volume indispensable for his understanding not only of global change but also of what Christianity implies.

Southern Christians hold to biblical authority not because they are backward but because they have embraced the Bible for what it really is. Euro-American Christians who interpret scripture to suit their evolved cultural tastes are soon-to-be-ex-Christians. Another common misunderstanding is the idea that the uncertainty of African life makes the Bible more credible. But it cannot be the fragility of *individual* life that leads Africans to the Bible—for their lives always have been fragile—but rather the death of tribal existence. The intrusion of the global marketplace into traditional cultures makes individual life less uncertain, most obviously through the introduction of antibiotics. The child-mortality rate in sub-Saharan Africa has fallen by a third in the past generation, for example, despite the

AIDS epidemic. But the same global forces that make individual existence more secure destroy the basis of tribal existence.

The collapse of Africa's tribal existence explains the improbable fact that Africans of such disparate ethnicities embrace the *Hebrew Bible*—that is, Israel itself. Western Christians tend "to associate the Old Testament with those aspects of Christianity that they find uncongenial, including the stories of Creation and the Fall, the vision of God as angry judge rather than loving parent, the justification of war and ethnic cleansing, and the pervasive legalism," as Jenkins describes the "popular stereotypes" of the Hebrew Bible. Western liberals, Jenkins notes shrewdly, make concessions to Jewish sensibilities in deference to the continuing presence of Jews but intensely dislike the Jewish Bible. African Christians have no reason at all to placate the Jewish community, for there is none in most African countries, but love the Hebrew Bible. "Cultural affinities with the biblical world," Jenkins writes, "lead African and Asian Christians to a deep affection for the Old Testament as their story, their book.... While the vast majority of modern Africans have no direct experience of nomadism or polygamy, at least they can relate to the kind of society in which such practices were commonplace." This is invidious condescension, presuming that backward and ignorant Africans like the Bible because of merely contingent similarities with their own lives—exactly what the liberal critics of African "fundamentalism" maintain. A more convincing explanation of African identification with the Old Testament is that African Christians identify with ancient Israel because they desire to become part of the People of God, as tribal society disintegrates. This is all the more remarkable given the prevailing anticolonialist sentiment in Africa, which sympathizes with the Palestinian cause against the present state of Israel. The Book of Joshua, recounting ancient Israel's violent conquest of Canaan, is the most problematic book of the Bible for some African Christians.

The disintegration of tribal society provides part of the explanation. Another, and more profound, reason for African affinity with the Old Testament may be the influence of North American evangelical currents on African conversion. The missionaries sent by colonial powers—Catholic, Anglican, and to a lesser extent Lutheran—have been overtaken by denominations of North American origin, notably the Pentecostals, who now number 350 million worldwide. U.S. evangelical Christianity (as well as Pentecostalism and Mormonism), as I have tried to show in chapter 13, are unique in their identification with Israel, for Americans selected themselves out from among the nations and crossed the oceans to come to a New Land, in emulation of the tribes of Israel crossing the Jordan into Canaan. Evangelical Christianity centers on the rebirth of the individual out of his sinful, Gentile origin into Israel, into the People of God, by the miracle of Christ's blood. The prestige of American Christianity more than the mere primitivism of African life may explain why Africans have so little trouble with the Old Testament. Africans' appreciation of the concept of blood sacrifice is a source of wonder for Jenkins. He observes:

> Only readers in a culture familiar with sacrificial tradition are in a position to appreciate fully the numerous allusions to this practice throughout the New Testament. A quick search of the New Testament produces over ninety uses of the word "blood," not counting cognates or related concepts such as *altar* and *lamb*, so it is scarcely an exaggeration to describe the text as soaked with blood.... Appropriately, evangelical religion, with its central notion of being saved in the blood, has exercised immense appeal

in modern Africa. Recall the impact of hymns like the "Tukuten-dereza Yesu," the song of the blood of the lamb.

This is precisely correct as far as it goes, but again, it is frustrating that Jenkins does not take the issue one step further. The reason that blood is so important to Christianity (and not just evangelical Christianity) is that the Christian undergoes a change of ethnicity. As Africa emerges from tribalism—if it is to emerge at all—this is decisive. It is the Gentile flesh that is sinful by its nature, and, to overcome sin and gain the Kingdom of God, the Christian believes that he must be reborn into a new flesh, the flesh of Israel, through the blood sacrifice of Jesus Christ.

Because Jenkins's account is impressionistic rather than precise, he has difficulty addressing the issue of syncretism—that is, the Christian problem of having one's cake and eating it too. Christians too often wish to keep one foot in their Gentile past and another in the Kingdom of God. This dichotomy, I have argued earlier in this book, ultimately doomed European Christianity. The reader is left wondering whether, as reported by Jenkins, the hatred of some African theologians for the Book of Joshua reflects a syncretic bias on the part of some African Christians who see their ethnicities under pressure from colonialism.

Between 2000 and 2005, violence between Muslims and Christians in just one Nigerian province killed or expelled more than fifty thousand people, mainly Christian. Across Africa, repression by secular states often includes an incidental religious element because of the strong Muslim tradition in the armed forces; this predominance recalls the preference of colonial powers for Muslim "warrior races." Soldiers serving dictatorships tend disproportionately to be Muslim, and their critics and opponents are often Christian clergy.

One dies a vicarious death in order to secure eternal life. Unlike Christians or Jews, whose religions are based on vicarious sacrifice, Islam demands the self-sacrifice of its adherents, in keeping with its essentially militant character. Revealed religion puts blood at a distance; Abraham sacrifices a ram and spares his son Isaac, and God sacrifices his own son in order to spare humankind. That is why blood in Judaism became taboo, to be handled only by the priest or his surrogate, the ritual butcher. Usually a Catholic priest administers the Eucharist. Unlike Christianity or Judaism, Islam has no ritual of vicarious sacrifice. The Eid al-Ahda "commemorates" the post-Koranic tradition in the Hadith of Abraham and Ishmael but has no ritual function. According to a fatwa issued by the mainstream website *Islam Online*, and frequently cited by other Muslim sites, "Sacrifice is not a pillar of Islam.... Not only did the pagan Arabs sacrifice to a variety of gods in hopes of attaining protection or some favor or material gain, but so, too, did the Jews of that day seek to appease the One True God by blood sacrifice and burnt offerings. Even the Christian community felt Jesus to be the last sacrifice, the final lamb, so to speak, in an otherwise valid tradition of animal sacrifice (where one's sins are absolved by the blood of another). Islam, however, broke away from this longstanding tradition of appeasing an 'angry God' and instead demanded personal sacrifice and submission as the only way to die before death and reach fana or 'extinction in Allah.'" To sacrifice one's self for one's kind is the sine qua non of pagan cultures; revealed religion (Judaism and Christianity), unlike Islam, exempts the individual from this terrible requirement. Islam, with its demand for the self-sacrifice of every adherent, represents the last defense of traditional society, uniting the tribes into the ummah, whose definitive sacrament is jihad. Christianity lifts the mortal decree for those who repudiate traditional society and abandon their own ethnicity for a new and universal ethnicity, that of Israel. The people of the Southern Hemisphere increasingly are willing to substitute a universal Christian identity for their ethnic or tribal identity, choosing Christianity over Islam. If that is correct, we are witness to one of the most remarkable things to happen in world history. One cannot quite make sense of today's world without it. The new Christians of the South will surprise us for ill as well as good.

Part Five

Islam in Jeopardy

CHAPTER 20

Christian, Muslim, Jew

Why is it that civilizations quarrel? Mainstream Western thinking rejects the question. In the mind of the twentieth century, cultures, like lifestyles, simply exist and do not bear comparison. Religious relativists, such as Karen Armstrong, attempt to reduce all religions to an indistinguishable and insipid spiritual gruel. Critics of Islam such as Robert Spencer, on the other hand, never tire of pointing to the violent passages in the Qur'an. For years American conservatives sought to shoehorn the problems of the Islamic world into the box of the Western enlightenment: "freedom" versus "tyranny." All this has led to a useless exchange of Qur'anic quotations that show that Islam is loving or hateful, tolerant or bigoted, peaceful or warlike, or whatever one cares to show. Whether justified or not, Islam bashing is a waste of time. Anyone can quote the Qur'an, or for that matter the Bible, to show whatever one wants. A religion is not a text but a life. To understand Islam and its role in the present civilizational struggle, we must peer through the eyes of Muslims.

Judaism and Christianity have a violent past; one can point to the Deuteronomic injunction to exterminate the Canaanite tribes, or the crusades against Saxons or Cathars, just as easily as to Islam's bloody conquests. Some Muslim countries were more enlightened and tolerant of other religions than were some Christian countries at some points in history. Rehearsing the nasty bits of Muslim history tells us nothing about what distinguishes Islam from Judaism or Christianity. One glaring point of contention—the matter of wife beating—offers a thread that unravels the problem. Few if any Muslim religious authorities explicitly denounce wife beating, for which Surah 4:32 of the Qur'an offers explicit justification. The proponent par excellence of Islam with a Western face, the Swiss academic Tariq Ramadan, refused to condemn wife beating in a now notorious television debate with Nicolas Sarkozy in 2003. Challenged on Muslim support for wife beating as well as for the stoning of adulteresses, Ramadan only called for a "moratorium" on such practices, not outright repudiation. Wife beating is instructive not only because the enlightened West considers it repugnant but because the legal grounds on which the Qur'an sanctions it reveals an impassable gulf between Islamic and Western law. To every individual in Western society, of which protection from violence is foremost, the sovereign grants inalienable rights. Every individual stands in direct relation to the state, which wields a monopoly on violence. Islam's legal system is radically different: The father is a "governor" or "administrator" of the family—that is, a little sovereign within his domestic realm, with the right to employ violence to control his wife and children. That is the self-understanding of modern Islam spelled out by Muslim American scholars—and it is incompatible with the Western concept of human rights.

By extension, the power of the little sovereign of the family can include the killing of wayward wives and female relations. Execution for domestic crimes, often called "honor killing," is not mentioned in the Qur'an, but the practice is so widespread in Muslim countries—the United Nations Population Fund estimates an annual toll of five thousand—that it is recognized in what we might term Islamic common law. Muslim courts either do not prosecute so-called honor killings or prosecute them more leniently than other crimes. Article 340 of Jordan's penal code states, "He who discovers his wife or one of his female relatives committing adultery and kills, wounds, or injures one of them, is exempted from any penalty." Syria imposes only a two-year prison sentence for such killings. Pakistan forbids them but rarely punishes them.

Westernized Muslim scholars strive to justify the practice on Islamic legal grounds. Muslim traditional society is a nested hierarchy in which the clan is an extended family, the tribe an extended clan, and the state an extended tribe. The family patriarch thus enjoys powers in his realm comparable to those of the state in the broader realm. That is the deeper juridical content of the Qur'anic provision for wife beating in Surah 4:34:

[Husbands] are the protectors and maintainers of their [wives] because Allah has given the one more [strength] than the other, and because they support them from their means. Therefore the righteous women are devoutly obedient and guard in [the husband's] absence what Allah would have them guard. As to the women on whose part you fear disloyalty and ill conduct, admonish them first, refuse to share their beds, spank them, but if they return to obedience, seek not against them means of [annoyance]: for Allah is Most High, Great.

An essay by two law students at Michigan State University, Bassam A. Abed and Syed E. Ahmad, is cited often on Islamic websites as a credibly modern interpretation of Surah 4:34. Abed and Ahmad begin with the legal principle that sanctions wife beating—namely, that the husband is the "governor" or "administrator" of the family:

> The translator's use of the term "protectors" in the first line of the quote above is in reference to the Arabic term *qawaamoon* (singular: *qawaam*). *Qawaamoon* has been defined in various manners by different scholars and translators. Abul Ala Maududi has defined *qawaamoon* as "governors" and as "managers." *Qawaam* "stands for a person who is responsible for the right conduct and safeguard and maintenance of the affairs of an individual or an institution or an organisation [*sic*]."

The authors explain:

> The majority of jurists hold that the language of the "Discipline Passage" itself reveals a sequential approach to the discipline authorized. For them, the conjunction *wa* ("and") used between the various types of discipline signifies its chronological order. This approach guides a husband in disciplining his wife who is disobedient, regardless of how disobedience is defined. In following the disciplinary process, he must first admonish his wife, then desert her in bed, and finally physically discipline her as a last resort to marital reconciliation.

Beating is permitted, Abed and Ahmad explain, but only if it is done in a spirit of reconciliation:

The greatest controversy and misunderstanding of the "Discipline Passage" is in the final stage of the disciplinary process— "spanking" the disobedient wife. The reconciliatory purpose behind the passage's "spanking" provision helps debunk the misconceptions surrounding this disciplinary stage. A husband is not to "spank" his wife if his motivation in doing so is other than such reconciliation. "Spanking" out of anger, for punishment, or for retaliation is prohibited, running contrary to the reconciliatory rationale. Similarly, a husband cannot "spank" his wife to humiliate her, cause in her fear, or to compel her against her will. Islam permits "spanking" to remind the wife of her disobedience and to bring her back to obedience so as to facilitate marital reconciliation.

That is why traditional society is incompatible organically with the first principle of law in modern liberal democracy: The state wields the monopoly of violence. Sharia in principle cannot be adapted to the laws of modern democratic states, for it is founded on the deeply ingrained notion that the family is the state in miniature and that the head of the family may employ violent compulsion just as the state does. From the vantage point of Western family law, wife beating is an atrocity, even in the case that a devout Muslim wife were to accept being beaten. Family courts in the West would intervene to separate a wife beater from his family, in the interests of the children. The president of the North American Council for Muslim Women, Sharifa Alkhateeb, estimated in a 1998 study that physical violence occurred in about 10 percent of Muslim marriages in the United States. "The rates of verbal and emotional abuse may be as high as 50% based upon international studies and preliminary research in the U.S.," Alkhateeb's website states.

A misleading, indeed offensive, comparison often is made between sharia and Jewish religious law, or halacha. When the arch-
bishop of Canterbury in February 2008 proposed to admit sharia
into British courts, he cited the supposed precedent of halacha.
Observant Jewish communities in the Diaspora have submitted
civil matters to rabbinical courts for two thousand years without,
of course, having any authority other than the religious persuasion
of the litigants to pronounce judgment. Nowhere in the Hebrew
Bible, though, is wife beating sanctioned, and it is strictly prohibited
in the most ancient extant sources of postbiblical Jewish law. There
is a surface resemblance between sharia and halacha, to be sure,
but that is by construction. Islam, wrote the great German Jewish
theologian Franz Rosenzweig, is a parody of Judaism and Christianity, more of the former than of the latter, for on the surface the two
religions appear quite close. Both affirm the absolute unity of God.
Jews pray thrice daily facing Jerusalem, while Muslims pray five
times daily facing Mecca. Muslims may eat kosher food. And both
are regulated by religious law dispensed by clerical courts. Sharia
resembles halacha for the same reason the Qur'an resembles the
Torah: It is derived from it, with self-serving adjustments. (Ishmael,
rather than Isaac, becomes the heir of Abraham.) But the principles
of the two legal systems are radically different. That is why Jewish
observance of halacha never has clashed with the legal systems of
modern democracy, while sharia inevitably must conflict, and in the
most intractable and intimate way—in matters of family law.

Underlying this difference on the matter of wife beating is a
fundamentally different philosophy of law, deriving from a fundamentally different theology. As Harvard's Eric Nelson most recently
showed in *The Hebrew Republic* (2010), and as Michael Novak explained in his book *On Two Wings* (2002), American law rests on

Jewish roots. Jewish law proceeds from God's covenant with each member of the Jewish people. The notion of an intermediate sovereign, such as Islam's "governor" of the family, is inconceivable in Jewish law, for there is only one sovereign, the King of kings. The powers of the earthly sovereign derive from God and are limited by God's laws. The American founding notion of "inalienable rights" stems from the Hebrew concept of covenant: A grant of rights implies a Grantor, and an irreversible grant implies a God who limits his own sovereignty in covenant with mankind. From the vantage point of Islam, the idea that God might limit his own powers by making an eternal covenant with human beings is unthinkable, for Allah is absolutely transcendent and unconditionally omnipotent. From a Hebrew and, later, Christian standpoint, the powers of the earthly sovereign are limited by God's law, which irreversibly grants rights to every human being. Islam can make no sense of such self-limitation of the divine sovereign and therefore never has produced a temporal political system subject to constitutional limitations.

In Islam, the family father has the ability to be a petty tyrant in his own home. That may explain the great mystery of modern Islam, why nearly a billion and a half human beings have failed over eight centuries to produce scientific or cultural figures whose names the world recognize. Even in Joseph Stalin's Russia, individuals could find refuge in their families and in creative pursuits not discouraged by the state—for example, pure science and classical music. Islam can make the family itself an oppressive institution. The issue of wifebeating thus uncovers radically opposed principles of social organization, founded on radically different religious anthropologies. Decisive in the above analysis of Surah 4:32 is the analogy between the husband and the head of a political subdivision or organization. The state in traditional society devolves its authority to the cells from which it is composed, starting with the family, which is a state in miniature, whose patriarch is a "governor" or "administrator." Traditional society is organized like a nested set of Russian dolls: The clan is the family writ large, the tribe is an extension of the clan, the state is an alliance of the tribes, and the relationship of citizen and sovereign is reproduced at each level.

When Rosenzweig argues that Islam is to be understood as a throwback to paganism, that is precisely what he means. He saw, rather than three Abrahamic religions, only two religions arising from the self-revelation of divine love, with Islam as a cryptopagan pretender: a parody of Christianity and Judaism. He was no Islamophobe, observing that Islam during certain eras evinced greater tolerance and humaneness than Christian Europe. But he was emphatic that truly foundational differences distinguish Judeo-Christian religion from Islam. Rosenzweig predicted a prolonged conflict of civilizations between Islam and the West. "The coming millennium will go down in world history as a struggle between Orient and Occident, between the church and Islam, between the Germanic peoples and the Arabs," he forecast in 1920—in part because Islam is "a parody of revealed religion," while Allah is an apotheosized despot, "the colorfully contending gods of the pagan pantheon rolled up into one." Contemporary academic thinkers almost universally eschew Rosenzweig's view of Islam. But it makes no sense to affirm his depiction of the unique bond between Jews and Christians— their response to God's self-revelation through love—while ignoring what makes this bond so different from other human responses to the transcendent. In Rosenzweig's theology, the soul's awareness of God begins with his love, and from this arise both faith and authentic human individuality. The existential condition of being loved is what uniquely characterizes the Christian and Jew, as opposed to the pagan, for whom God must remain hidden.

Rosenzweig's characterization of Islam as pagan appears strange at first glance, for we habitually classify religions according to their outward forms and identify paganism with manifestations of polytheism or nature worship. Insisting on the uniqueness of Allah and suppressing outward expressions of idolatry, Islam appears the opposite of a pagan religion. Rosenzweig, however, requires us to see faith from the existential standpoint of the believer, who in revealed religion knows God through God's love. For Rosenzweig, paganism constitutes a form of alienation from the revealed God of Love; Allah, the absolutely transcendent God who offers mercy but not unconditional love, is therefore a pagan deity.

All humankind acknowledges the divine, Rosenzweig insists in *The Star of Redemption*, because humans are mortal. From the fear of death arises the perception of the transcendent, and, in the pursuit of eternal life, one proceeds to life, as he avers in the book's final words. The path to human life, however, requires a life outside time—that is, in the Kingdom of Heaven. Man cannot abide his mortal existence and the terror of death without the prospect of eternal life. Rosenzweig's existential theology looks through the patina of received doctrine to the spiritual life of the congregation and its attempt to create for itself a life beyond the grave. How different faiths—different modes of living—address the fear of death creates a unique vantage point from which to understand how profoundly Christianity, Judaism, and Islam differ from one another. Rosenzweig's existential theology is embedded in what he calls a sociology of religion. He considers not only the individual's response to the fear of death but also, and more important, the response of entire peoples to the threat of extinction. It is not only our own death that we fear—under some circumstances we may not fear it at all—but rather the death of our race, our culture, our language, and with them the death of the possibility that some trace of our presence on earth will persist through our successors.

Perhaps Rosenzweig's most influential claim holds that Judaism and Christianity complement each other. The Jew "converts the inner pagan" inside the Christian, such that the living presence of the Jewish people creates a counterweight to the Gnostic impulses in Christianity. "Before God stand both of us," he wrote, "Jew and Christians, laborers at the same task":

> It is only the Old Testament that enables Christianity to defend itself against Gnosticism, its inherent danger. And it is the Old Testament alone, because it is more than just a book. The arts of allegorical interpretation would have made short work of a mere book. If, like Christ, the Jews had disappeared from the world, they would denote only the Idea of a People, and Zion the Idea of the midpoint of the world, just as Christ denotes only the Idea of Man. But the sturdy and undeniable vitality of the Jewish people—to which anti-Semitism itself attests—opposes itself to such "idealization." That Christ is more than idea—no Christian can know this. But that Israel is more than an idea, the Christian knows, because he sees it.... Our presence stands surety for their truth.

In the post-Holocaust world, after neopaganism nearly conquered Europe, the contention that Christianity requires the presence of the Jews found great resonance. Yet his formulation stems from a theological sociology with broader application. Pagans have only the fragile and ultimately futile effort to preserve their physical continuity through blood and soil. Their hope for immortality takes the form of a perpetual fight for physical existence, which one day they must lose. Therefore, a pagan people, ever sentient to the fragility of their existence, are prepared to fight to the death.

It is hard to dismiss Rosenzweig's view of Islam as an expression of Jewish prejudice, for he also rejected Zionism and celebrated the virtues of a Judaism removed from the temporal constraints of nationhood. He formed his view of Islam during the First World War, as a German soldier (and an ally of Muslim Turkey), long before Arab–Jewish conflict was a concern to most Jews. Indeed, Jews of Rosenzweig's generation tended to view Islam as more hospitable to Judaism than was Christianity. Although most of Rosenzweig's comments about Islam are found in book 2 of *The Star of Redemption*, it is book 3, his portrayal of the encounter of the peoples with mortality, that establishes the context—for it is there that he explains the "pagan world of fate and chance," which applies to paganism's manifestation in Islam.

Rosenzweig argues that pagan society cannot foster authentic human individuality but dissolves the individual into an extension of race or state. "For the isolated individual, his society is the society," he writes.

> In the thoroughly organized state, the state and the individual do not stand in the relation of a whole to a part. Instead, the state is the All, from which the power flows through the limbs of the individual. Everyone has his determined place, and, to the extent that he fulfills it, belongs to the All of the State.... The individual of antiquity does not lose himself in society in order to find himself, but rather in order to construct it; he himself disappears. The well-known difference between the ancient and all modern concepts of democracy rightly arise from this. It is clear from this why antiquity never developed the concept of representative democracy. Only a body can have organs; a building has only parts.

Written before the consolidation of communist power in Russia or the creation of the European fascist state, this passage was prescient, for it characterizes the modern neopagan state as well as the heathen societies of antiquity. In his book *The Crisis of Islamic Civilization* (2009), the former Iraqi minister Ali A. Alawi argues that the notion of a human individual as an autonomous entity endowed with free will is simply absent from Islamic thinking and impossible to describe in the Arabic language. Only God has individuality and uniqueness; the individual is merely an instrument. The Arabic word for "individual"—*al-fard*—does not have the implication of a purposeful being, imbued with the power of rational choice, but carries the connotation of singularity, aloofness, or solitariness. *Al-fard* is usually applied as one of the attributes of supreme being, in the sense of an inimitable uniqueness. It is usually grouped with others of God's attributes to establish the absolute transcendence of the divine. Man is simply unable to acquire any of these essential attributes. "Therefore," concludes Allawi, "to claim the right and the possibility of autonomous action without reference to the source of these in God is an affront." This is a remarkably clear formulation of a central premise of Islam, for it makes clear why individuality in the Western sense is inconceivable within Islam: An absolutely transcendent God leaves no room at all for the individual. The individual acquires from God whatever appearance of individuality he might have, but he has no autonomy, in sharp contrast to the Western notion.

It is a commonplace to compare Islamic theocracy to the totalitarian regimes of the twentieth century. That has been the approach of such critics as Daniel Pipes, Paul Berman, and the Dutch parliamentarian Geert Wilders, among others. But Islam is much older than modern totalitarian forms, and Allawi, like Tariq Ramadan and other modern Islamic philosophers, offers a persuasive case that the "totalitarian" character of Islamic society requires no emulation of European models but stems directly from Islam itself. Following Rosenzweig, perhaps for a comparison we should look backward, to the integralism of ancient pagan society to make sense of Islam's need to embrace every aspect of public and private life, rather than forward, to the totalitarian political movements of the twentieth century. Islamic civilization is not a caricature of modern totalitarian political movements; on the contrary, totalitarian movements are neopagan, and like all pagan political forms dissolve the individual into a mere extension of the polity. Allawi's explanation of why the individual disappears into the Islamic whole bears comparison to Rosenzweig's account; they differ only in whether they think this is a good thing or a bad thing.

His understanding of the individual is also the starting point for Rosenzweig's characterization of Islam as pagan and Allah as an apotheosized despot. He begins, in other words, with a general characterization of pagan society as a "thoroughly organized" society in the absence of God's self-revelation through love. Then, he considers Islam as a specific case of a paganism that parodies the outward form of revealed religion. "In an authentic confession of faith," he argues, "there always is this testimony, namely, that one's personal experience of love must be more than the experience of just one individual; that He whom the soul experiences in its love cannot be simply an illusion or a self-deception of the beloved soul, but that He actually lives." And so God "achieves through the witness of the believing soul a tangible and visible reality beyond Hiddenness, beyond his Hiddenness, which he possessed in a different way in heathendom."

By the same logic, Islam's confession of faith cannot be a confession of faith at all: "Islam's confession, 'God is God,' is no confession of faith, but a confession of nonfaith [ein Unglaubensbekenntnis].

It confesses in this tautology not a revealed God, but a hidden one. Nicholas of Cusa says rightly that a heathen, indeed an atheist, could profess the same." Revelation, according to Rosenzweig, occurs through the soul's awareness of God's love, and human individuality arises from the soul's response to being loved. In pagan society, where God remains unrevealed, the individual exists only as an organ of the collective of state or race. The pagan's sense of immortality therefore depends solely on the perpetuation of his race, and his most sacred act is to sacrifice himself in war to postpone the inevitable day when his race will go down in defeat.

Rosenzweig's spiritual characterization of pagan society is the starting point for his sociology of religion: an understanding of the response of whole peoples to mortality and transcendence. Uniquely among the peoples of the world, the Jews believe that a covenant with the Creator of heaven and earth makes them an eternal people.

> Because it trusts only in its self-created eternity and on nothing else in the world, [the Jewish people] really believes in its eternity, while the peoples of the world in the final analysis reckon with their own death, just as does the individual, at some point, be it ever so remote.

And further:

> War as it was known to the peoples of antiquity was in general only one of the natural expressions of life, and presented no fundamental complications. War meant that a people staked its life, for the sake of its life. A people that marched to war took on itself the danger of its own death. That mattered little as long as the peoples regarded themselves as mortal.

Islam, Rosenzweig continues, transforms the defense of the homeland into an offensive against the prospective enemies of the homeland, such that Europe had to defend itself against the "encroaching heathenism of the half-moon." Military incursions, to be sure, are not the likeliest form of attack on traditional society in the twenty-first century; the infiltration of popular culture and the encroachment of the global marketplace pose an existential threat to some traditional societies as dire as conquering hordes. It is against such new threats to pagan culture that Islam spills the blood of its sons on the soil of their homelands today. Holy war is the sine qua non of Islam, precisely because war is the most sacred act of pagan society in general. Rosenzweig:

> The concept of the Path of Allah is entirely different from God's path. The paths of God are the disposition of divine decrees high above human events. But following the path of Allah means in the narrowest sense propagating Islam through holy war. In the obedient journey on this path, taking on one's self the associated dangers, the observance of the laws prescribed for it, Muslim piety finds its way in the world. The path of Allah is not elevated above the path of humankind, as far as the heaven stretches above earth, but rather the path of Allah means immediately the path of his believers.

For this reason, God's special love for the weak and defenseless— the quality that characterizes the God of Jews and Christians—is inconceivable in Islam:

> Unlike the God of faith, Allah cannot go before his own [people] and say to their face that he has chosen them above all others in

all their sinfulness, and in order to make them accountable for their sins. That the failings of human beings arouse divine love more powerfully than their merits is an impossible, indeed an absurd thought to Islam—but it is the thought that stands at the heart of [Jewish and Christian] faith.

Franz Rosenzweig was quite prepared to believe that Islam was more humane and tolerant than Christianity during some of its history. But that historical fact remains beside Rosenzweig's point, for he sees Islam as the path of obedience: "The path of Allah requires the obedience of the will to a commandment that has been given once and for all time. By contrast, in [Judeo-Christian] brotherly love, the spore of human character erupts ever anew, incited by the ever surprising outbreak of the act of love."

Traditional peoples fight to the death, even in the knowledge that one day they must lose their existential fight for existence. The pagan's personality is an extension of race and state, in Rosenzweig's view; therefore, it dies with the death of his society. He risks nothing by sacrificing his life to preserve his society. Rosenzweig's sociology helps us to make sense of contemporary conflicts. Rarely if ever in recorded history has suicide played the central role in military conflict that it does today in the Islamic world. The explanation for self-destructive behavior on a grand scale is that the spiritual death ensuing from the dissolution of traditional society provokes greater fear than does the fear of physical death.

This leads to Rosenzweig's definitive characterization of Islamic life. The Christian and Jewish liturgical years recapitulate a journey to redemption. His chapter on Jewish life begins with the blessing recited multiple times during the reading of the Torah at the Sabbath service: "Blessed be He who planted eternal life among us."

That introduces Rosenzweig's elaboration of the Jewish idea of eternity in the physical continuity of an eternal people. The Sabbath is the foundation of Jewish life, the day on which the Jew eschews earthly endeavor and enjoys, as it were, a foretaste of the Kingdom of Heaven: "In the circle of weekly sections, which annually run through the entire Torah, the spiritual year is traversed, and the steps of this course are the Sabbaths."

Judaism for Rosenzweig is a self-sustaining eternal fire, nourished by the physical continuity of the Jewish people. Christianity is a perpetual journey toward salvation, directing these rays outward. The lives of Christian and Jewish communities, as experienced through the liturgical calendar, express the world's own journey toward redemption. Yet Islam lives in the perpetual present of prehistory:

> The path of Allah leads his believers into the real peoples of real epochs in time. But how does it think of these peoples and epochs? In the [Judeo-Christian] Kingdom they come forward in a continuous, if incalculable, augmentation of life.... In Islam, by contrast, all worldly individuality stands under the sign of prehistory, that is, negation. It is always new, and never something that develops gradually. Here every epoch in time stands in immediate relation to God, and not merely every epoch, but all individuality in general.... Historical epochs therefore are placed in no relation whatever to each other; there is no growth from one to the other, no "Spirit" that goes through all of them and unifies them.

In the case of Islam, Rosenzweig concludes, "the concept of the future is poisoned at its root." Only through the action of God in history, through the growth of the kingdom in contrasting epochs, he argues, is it possible to recognize the "gift of eternity" in the present moment. Sacred time, the content of the Jewish and Christian liturgical calendars, does not exist in Islam.

Rosenzweig's treatment of the response of peoples to the prospect of national mortality informs his understanding of paganism in general and Islam in particular.

> The God of Muhammad is a creator who well might not have bothered to create. He displays his power like an Oriental potentate who rules by violence, not by acting according to necessity, not by authorizing the enactment of the law, but rather in his freedom to act arbitrarily. By contrast, it is most characteristic of rabbinic theology that it formulates our concept of the divine power to create in the question as to whether God created the world out of love or out of righteousness.

Allah's creation is, therefore, a mere act of "magic." Muslim theology "presumes that Allah creates every isolated thing at every moment. Providence therefore is shattered into infinitely many individual acts of creation, with no connection to each other, each of which has the importance of the entire creation. That has been the doctrine of the ruling orthodox philosophy in Islam. Every individual thing is created from scratch at every moment. Islam cannot be salvaged from this frightful providence of Allah."

With his mention of "orthodox philosophy in Islam," Rosenzweig is referring to the eleventh-century normative theology of al-Ghazali, still recognized as the preeminent Muslim theologian. Al-Ghazali rejected Greek-derived philosophy, and asserted that Allah personally and immediately directs the motion of every molecule by his

ineffable and incomprehensible will, directly and without the media-
tion of natural law. Al-Ghazali abolished intermediate causes—that
is, laws of nature—leaving great and small events to the caprice of
the absolute tyrant of the universe. In place of Hellenistic reasoning, Islam turned to a literal reading of the Qur'an, and developed
a theology of divine caprice. Rosenzweig's objections to al-Ghazali
are rooted in the critiques made by Maimonides and St. Thomas
Aquinas. In fact, there is a striking parallel between Rosenzweig's
restatement of the medieval critique and Pope Benedict XVI's discussion of Muslim theology at Regensburg on September 12, 2006.

As all the world now knows—after riots and protests broke out
across the world—Benedict quoted the Byzantine emperor Manuel
II Paleologus: "Show me just what Muhammad brought that was
new, and there you will find things only evil and inhuman, such as his
command to spread by the sword the faith he preached." The pope
continued: "The emperor, after having expressed himself so force-
fully, goes on to explain in detail the reasons why spreading the faith
through violence is something unreasonable. Violence is incompatible with the nature of God and the nature of the soul. 'God,' he says,
'is not pleased by blood—and not acting reasonably is contrary to
God's nature.'" The decisive statement in this argument against violent conversion is this: Not to act in accordance with reason is contrary to God's nature. For the emperor, a Byzantine shaped by Greek
philosophy, this statement is self-evident. But for Muslim teaching,
God is absolutely transcendent. His will is not bound up with any
of our categories, even that of rationality. As the French Islamist R.
Arnaldez has pointed out, the eleventh-century Muslim theologian
Ahmad Ibn Said Ibn Hazm taught that Allah was not bound even
by his own word, that nothing would oblige him to reveal the truth
to us, and, should Allah will it, we should have to become idolaters.

What are we to make of this? Benedict went on to insist that "God does not become more divine when we push him away from us in a sheer, impenetrable voluntarism; rather, the truly divine God is the God who has revealed himself as logos and, as logos, has acted and continues to act lovingly on our behalf." And this, indeed, suggests that Rosenzweig's existential theology, which proceeds from the soul's experience of love in God's self-revelation, can find its way back to agreement with the medieval Christian and Jewish refutation of al-Ghazali.

In his recent book *The Closing of the Muslim Mind: How Intellectual Suicide Created the Modern Islamist Crisis* (2010), Robert R. Reilly also takes up the theme of al-Ghazali's abandonment of Hellenistic reason and blames it for the subsequent decline of Muslim civilization and the rise of radical Islam. Reilly argues that Western civilization is founded on reason, whereas normative Islam embraces irrationality. The absence of scientific accomplishment in the Muslim world after the twelfth century should indeed make clear that something is amiss in Islamic thinking. But there is something missing in Reilly's account.

"What Thomas Aquinas did for Christianity, someone needs to do for Islam," Reilly concludes. Sound theology, he appears to believe, would fix the problems in the Muslim world. But the influence of doctrine on the daily life of faith communities is subtler. We have to consider not only what people think but also how they think. To make sense of what a religion teaches and what the faithful actually believe, we must understand theology not only objectively (as a statement about God and the world) but also existentially—that is, we must understand in light of how the faith community lives its religion in ordinary life. The doctrines taught by religious authorities may or may not penetrate into the life of that religion's adherents. The Catholic Church teaches that all Christians are reborn into the People of God and that this new spiritual allegiance takes precedence over their Gentile origin. Nonetheless, the Christians of Europe slaughtered each other during the twentieth century while the Church watched helplessly. Muslims well might retort that, whatever their deficiencies, they never created a comparable disaster. Christian civilization survived the world wars and the expansion of communism only because America defeated first Nazism and then communism. Yet American Christianity does not quite fit the Hellenistic model. Catholicism has become the largest American Christian denomination, in part due to Hispanic immigration; America's religious character remains Protestant, scriptural, and enthusiastic rather than Catholic and philosophical. Whether this is a good thing or a bad thing is beside the point. The point is that a charismatic biblical literalist in rural America has a great deal in common with American Catholics but neither has much in common with Muslims.

A rationalist approach to theology is not what distinguishes Massachusetts from Mecca. The Massachusetts Bay Colony was founded by radical Protestants who poured contempt on "Popish Authors (Jesuites especially)" who "strain their wits to defend their Pagan Master Aristotle," in the words of the Puritan leader Increase Mather (1639–1723). American evangelicals, the most devout segment of the Christian population, tend to be fideist rather than philosophical. What is it that unites Catholic Thomists and evangelical fideists (as well as observant Jews) but divides all of them from Muslims? It is the biblical belief that God loves his creatures. A loving God, in the biblical view, places man in a world that he can comprehend, which is to say that, out of love for humankind, God establishes order in the universe. Al-Ghazali abhors the idea of divine love: "When there is love, there must be in the lover a sense of incompleteness; a recognition that the beloved is needed for complete realization of the self," he wrote. But since Allah is perfect and complete, this notion of love is nonsensical. "There is no reaching out on the part of God...there can be no change in him; no development in him; no supplying of a lack in Himself." The trouble is that, in this case, al-Ghazali simply reproduces Aristotle's definition of God as the unmoved mover. In this case it is Christians who must fall back on scripture, and it is al-Ghazali who defends the rational view of Greek philosophy.

Objectively speaking, the answer to the question "Are Muslims less rational than Christians?" is a flat "no." The Jewish idea that the maker of heaven and earth cares with his creatures and suffers along with them seemed idiotic to the Greeks and still seems idiotic to the vast majority of philosophers today. The trouble is that we cannot speak objectively about human reason. Reason is not an abstraction floating in some intellectual ether but rather *our* reason, the reason of our lives. Whether it is demonstrable or not, the Judeo-Christian notion of divine love is what makes possible the rational ordering of human existence. Whether al-Ghazali was a bad philosopher compared to Aquinas is beside the point: Muslim life is irrational because of the concept of divine love as expressed in the covenant between God and man. Existential rationality, the rationality of ordinary life, proceeds from the biblical concept of covenant.

Rosenzweig's analysis of foundational differences between Judeo-Christian religion and Islam holds more than historical interest for us today. The challenges of theological dialogue with Islam that have been noted by Benedict XVI, among others, should alert us that an existential divide separates Islam and the Judeo-Christian

West. Rosenzweig is provocative, perhaps even disturbing, in his treatment of Islam. But it seems unlikely that we will make sense of the civilizational debate without grappling with the issues that he raised almost a century ago.

CHAPTER 21

Crisis of Faith in the Muslim World
—and the Islamist Response

Islam is a pagan parody of Judeo-Christian religion, says Franz Rosenzweig. But how does Islam respond to the encroachment of the modern world?

In Europe, a decline in religious faith underlies its demographic decline, as I have argued in chapter 1. In the footsteps of Western Europe, Islam also faces a crisis of faith that will bring about a demographic catastrophe in the middle of the present century. Given the prominence of what Westerners call "Islamic fundamentalism," it seems odd to speak of a crisis of faith in the Islamic world. Striking statistical evidence supports this conclusion, however, as I'll explain below.

Although the Muslim birthrate today is the world's second highest (after sub-Saharan Africa), it is falling faster than the birthrate of any other culture. In the case of Iran, Algeria, and many other Muslim countries, the fertility rate in 2050 is expected to fall below two children per woman. Iran's fertility rate has already fallen to just over 1.7 children per female, according to the latest figures from the United Nations Populations Division. A generation ago, it stood at 6.5—the fastest decline in fertility ever recorded. Along with most of the Muslim world, Iran therefore faces a population bust that will raise the proportion of dependent elderly in the population to 28 percent in 2050, from just 7 percent today. America's fertility rate—the average number of children per woman—has stabilized at just around the replacement level. That is why America's ratio of elderly dependence will stabilize around 2030. Even Saudi Arabia, the bastion of Islamic conservatism, will show a fertility rate below replacement level within two decades, according to UNDP projections published in 2009.

Total Fertility, Selected Arab Countries

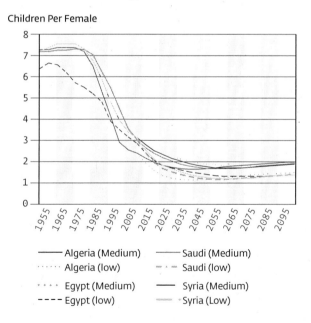

Children Per Female

——— Algeria (Medium) ———— Saudi (Medium)
· · · · · Algeria (low) ～ · ～ Saudi (low)

· · · · Egypt (Medium) ——— Syria (Medium)
– – – – Egypt (low) ～～～～ · Syria (Low)

Source: United Nations Population Division

I think the UN estimates err on the high side, as they have world-wide for the past twenty years. Modernization is likely to push fertility down further than the demographers now calculate. No single measure of modernization captures this transformation, but most of the variation in fertility can be explained by a single factor, literacy: As Muslims (and especially Muslim women) learn to read, they drift away from traditional faith. The birthrate drops in consequence. The joke in New York goes, "How do you stop a Jewish girl from having sex? Marry her." The data suggest that the way to stop a Muslim girl from having babies is to educate her. A wide range of fertility rates characterizes the Islamic world. This wide spectrum expresses different degrees of modernization. Where traditional conditions prevail, characterized by high rates of illiteracy (and especially female illiteracy), the fertility rate remains at the top of the world's rankings. But where the modern world encroaches, fertility rates are plummeting to levels comparable to those in the industrial world. In the non-Muslim world, literacy alone explains 46 percent of variation in population growth. In the Muslim world, however, the link between rising literacy and falling population growth is much more pronounced: Among the thirty-four largest Arab countries, just one factor, the difference in literacy rates, explains 60 percent of the difference in the rate of population growth in 2005. Not a surprising result considering that the Muslim world begins with extremely high population growth and extremely low literacy rates.

The population of Somalia, where only a quarter of adults can read, is growing at an enormous 4 percent per year, with a fertility of more than 6.2 children per woman. At that rate, the number of Somalis will double in just 18 years. But in Algeria, where 62 percent of adults can read, the population growth rate is only 1.4 percent per year. At that rate it would take fifty years for the population to double. Qatar, with a literacy rate close to 80 percent, has a population growth rate of just 1.2 percent.

Why does population growth fade in response to rising literacy in the Muslim world? Traditional society is everywhere fragile, not only in the Islamic world; by definition it is bounded by values and expectations handed down from the past, to which individuals must submit. Most members of religious groups adhere to their beliefs because they were born into a faith and learned no other way to live. Traditional society admits of no heresy or atheism because religion governs the socialization of individuals. Once the bonds of tradition are broken and each individual may choose for herself what sort of family to raise, religious faith becomes the decisive motivation for bringing children into the world. Urbanization, literacy, and openness to the modern world will suppress the Muslim womb.

Nowhere is this more obvious than in Iran. The restoration of an all-embracing Islamic society is an idea whose time already has come and gone in the Shi'ite Islamic Republic of Iran. Ayatollah Khomeini's revolution attempted to retard the disintegration of Persian society, but it appears to have accelerated the process. Efforts to isolate Iran from the cultural degradation of the American "great Satan" have produced a corrupt kleptocracy, endemic materialism, and social pathologies worse than those in any Western country. Its demoralization is shown by the proliferation of prostitution: according to some claims, 300,000 women are whoring in Tehran alone, many of them university educated. What persuades women to employ their bodies as an instrument of commerce, rather than as a way of achieving motherhood, is not just poverty, for poor women bear children everywhere, but deracination and cultural despair. Prostitution is a form of psychic suicide; writ large, it is a manifestation of a national death wish. The clerical regime vacillates between repressing prostitution and sanctioning it through "temporary marriages," an arrangement permitted under Shi'ite jurisprudence. In the latter case the Muslim clergy in effect become pimps, taking a fee for sanctioning several "temporary marriages" per woman per day. The same networks that move female flesh across borders to Europe and the Middle East also provide illegal passage for jihadis, and the proceeds of human trafficking often support Islamist terrorists. From Jakarta to Kuala Lumpur to Sarajevo to Tirana, the criminals who trade in women overlap with jihadist networks. Prostitutes serve the terror network in a number of capacities, including suicide bombing. The Persian prostitute is the camp follower of the jihadi, joined to him in a pact of national suicide. President Mahmud Ahmadinejad, understanding that life as Iranians know it is coming to an end, has proposed drastic measures commensurate with the need.

The demographic position of the Islamic world has set a catastrophe in motion. It is hard enough for rich nations to care for a growing elderly population, but it is impossible for poor nations to do so. If America faces discomfort, and Europe faces crisis, Muslim countries face breakdown. Iran depends on oil exports for the state subsidies that keep its population fed and clothed—and Iran will no longer be able to export oil after 2020, according to some estimates. Apart from oil, Iran exports mainly fruits and nuts. Its most talented people have emigrated, leaving behind only the leeches of the bazaar who hope to grow fat on state oil money. Between 2005 and 2050, the shift from workers to pensioners will mean that pensioners make up 21 percent of Iranians, 19 percent of Turks and Indonesians, and 20 percent of Algerians. That is almost as bad as the German predicament, where each employed worker will have to support a pensioner in 2050. A simple way to express the problem is that German productivity must rise by 0.8 percent per year between now and 2050 simply to maintain the same standard of living, for that is the rate of productivity growth that would allow a smaller number of German workers to produce the same amount of goods and services. That is not inconceivable; during the 1990s, German productivity grew at such levels. Productivity growth in the Arab world and Iran on the other hand has been low or negative, and it is not likely to improve. Only 1 percent of the Arab population owns a personal computer. It is delusional to believe that the Arab world, which now exports (net of oil) as much as Finland, might come to compete with China, India, and the rest of Asia in the global market for goods and services. Of China's 1.3 billion people, 400 million are integrated into the world division of labor, and millions more are becoming urbanized, literate, and productive each year. India remains behind China but has good prospects for success. It is not a good thing to come late to the table of globalization: In a world that has little need of subsistence farmers and even less need of university graduates with degrees in Islamic philosophy, most of the Muslim world can expect small mercy from the market. Just as the Muslim population peaks, the one bounty that nature has bestowed on the Arabs, oil, will begin to diminish. According to the U.S. Department of Energy, at the present rate of production growth, 2 percent, conventional oil production will peak just before 2050. In short, the Muslim world half a century from now can expect the short end of the stick from the modern world. It has generated only two great surpluses, people and oil. By the middle of the century both of these will have begun to dwindle.

America, on the other hand, can ameliorate the impact of an aging population by raising productivity (so that fewer workers produce more GDP), attracting more skilled immigrants (and increasing its tax base), and, in the worst case, tightening its belt. American life will not come to an end if more people drive compact cars instead of SUVs, or if for vacation they go camping instead of to Disney World. But the Islamic world is so poor that any reduction in living standards from present levels will cause social breakdown. Negotiating the demographic decline of the twenty-first century will be treacherous for countries that have proven their capacity to innovate and grow. For the Islamic world, it will be impossible. That is the root cause of Islamic radicalism, and there is nothing that the West can do to change it.

A generation hence, Iran will not have the resources to provide infrastructure for the more than fifty thousand rural villages inhabited mainly by elderly and infirm peasants. America's fertility rate—the average number of children per woman—has stabilized near the replacement level. That is why America's ratio of the workforce to the elderly dependent will stabilize around 2030. Before the First World War, army general staffs began war planning with demographic tables, calculating how many men of military age they might feed to the machine guns. Demographics still provide vital strategic information, albeit in quite a different fashion. Today's Islamists think like the French general staff in 1914. The pool of unemployed Arabs has reached 25 million in 2010—enough young men to fight a war during the next thirty years. Because of the decline in Muslim birthrates, Islam has one generation in which to establish a global theocracy before it hits a demographic barrier.

Most of the world's cultures will go into oblivion without a fight, either because they cannot or do not wish to fight for survival. Some scholars hold that declining birthrates and population growth will make violence less likely. In my view, the population dynamics described above will lead not to less violence but to more. Similarly, a school of thought presented by Daniel Pipes holds that terrorism obstructs the quiet work of political Islamism, whereby Islamists advance their cause with Westerners who respond as slowly boiled frogs are supposed to, not noticing a thing, in Pipes's telling. I think this is wrong; the Islamists have to strike quickly and decisively, not only to advance their cause in the West but also to consolidate their power in home countries where conditions will become unstable before long. Of the world's endangered cultures, only one can and will fight to perpetuate itself, and that is Islam. Militancy is not unique to Islam. Twice during the twentieth century the nations of Europe fought each other for preeminence, with the result of their common ruin. Yet Islam's decline was not an accident, nor is the fearsome response to that decline offered by the Islamist radicals. Born in militancy, Islam among the world's religions offers a unique justification for conquest. If the owl of wisdom flies at night, as Hegel said of philosophy, so does the buzzard of militant Islamism. The war that Islam will offer the West in its final throes will be a tragic, terrible, and prolonged one that cannot be avoided, but only fought to exhaustion. Islam has one generation in which to turn its foothold in Western Europe into a governing power, before the effects of slowing population growth set in.

Islam has enough young men to make its stand during the next thirty years. Because of mass migration to Western Europe, where twenty million Muslims already live, the worst of the war might be fought on European soil.

Part Six

Demographics and Depression

CHAPTER 22

The End of Leverage

There is nothing complicated about finance. It is based on old people lending to young people. Young people invest in homes and businesses; aging people save to acquire assets on which to retire. The new generation supports the old one, and retirement systems simply apportion rights to income between the generations. Never before in human history, though, has a new generation simply failed to appear. The world kept shipping capital to the United States over the past ten years, however, because no other market could absorb the savings of the senescent populations of Europe and Asia. The financial markets, in turn, found ways to persuade Americans to borrow more and more money. If there weren't enough young Americans to borrow money on a sound basis, the banks arranged for a smaller number of Americans to borrow more money on an unsound basis. That is why subprime, interest-only, no-money-down, and other mortgages waxed great in bank portfolios. In a nutshell, that's the explanation for the financial crisis that erupted in 2008.

The spiritual malaise underlying the great extinction of the nations that I have described in the first part of this book has also caused the financial crisis.

An enormous hoax has been perpetrated on global financial markets during the past ten years. An American economy based on opening containers from China and selling the contents at Wal-Mart, or trading houses back and forth, provides scant profitability. Where the underlying profitability of the American economy was poor, financial engineering managed to transform thin profits into apparently fat ones through the magic of leverage. The income of American consumers might have stagnated, but the price of their houses doubled during 1998 through 2007, thanks to the application of leverage to mortgage finance. The profitability of American corporations might have slowed, but the application of leverage in the form of mergers and acquisitions financed with junk bonds multiplied the thin band of profitability. Wall Street and the City of London rode an unprecedented wave of profitability by providing overpriced leverage to consumer and corporate markets. Led by the financial engineers at Lehman, the securities industry grew an enormous infrastructure of staff, systems, and financial exposure. They were so successful that, when the music stopped, there was no way to liquidate this mechanism gracefully. It could only be allowed to collapse.

In effect, Americans borrowed a trillion dollars a year against the expectation that the 10 percent annual rate of increase in home prices would continue, producing a bubble that now has collapsed. Except in size and global impact, it is no different from the real-estate bubble that contributed to the devaluation of the Thai baht devaluation in 1997.

Lehman Brothers survived the American Civil War, two world

wars, and the Great Depression, but the firm that set the standard in fixed-income markets was liquidated in September 2008, marking a definite turning point in the financial and economic crisis. Potential losses were so toxic that none of the major financial institutions were willing to acquire it. It is tempting to see in the failure of Lehman Brothers and the forced merger of Merrill Lynch with Bank of America a failure of "corporate culture." In the case of a great financial firm that has weathered many storms, the failure of a business culture contains more information. Credit markets connect what we do today with what we plan for the future. Because the future is uncertain, we must have faith in the outcome, which is why the word *credit* derives from the same Latin root that denotes belief in the religious sense. We require a certain degree of trust in our counterparties. It is the job of the great financial firms to create trust between borrowers and lenders and establish a link between the present and the future.

It is of small account in the great scheme of things, but in the sad, strange little world of business studies, Lehman's culture was held up as an exemplar, a beacon to the ambitious and avaricious. Lehman's demise is a minor event next to the travails of America's mortgage guarantee agencies, which required a government bailout, to be sure, but it is a landmark in the unraveling of American corporate governance.

By a charming coincidence, the two great failures in the securities industries to date occurred at the extreme antipodes of the corporate-cultural spectrum. Lehman was the second great American securities firm to have failed in 2008, following the March demise of Bear Stearns, the shards of which were swept up by JPMorgan Chase. Bear was a group of scrappy outsiders, led by Jews of no social pedigree. Jimmy Cayne, the firm's president, never finished college and began his career literally trading scrap metal. Bear's managers played bridge, and prided themselves on having no corporate culture except a piranha's instinct for the next trade. A book of memos by Bear's former CEO Alan Greenberg circulated some years ago, including a lampoon in which the Bear chief, considering his competitors who had bitten the dust over the years, categorized them according to the management philosophy each had embraced—"total quality management" and other such shibboleths. As a matter of scruffy pride, Bear rejected corporate culture and management philosophy. At Bear, partners ran their own businesses and hid their best methods from their colleagues to prevent anyone from cutting in on their action. The favorite method of management communication was the one-minute phone call. Lehman held meetings to plan the meeting that would set the agenda for the meeting that would make the decision, and of course every department and interest had to be represented. That was called "teamwork." As a result, all of Lehman's resources were mustered for the projects to which the firm set its priorities.

Tongues clicked across Wall Street when Bear went down for the last time. "Nobody liked [Bear's] Jimmy Cayne," a senior fellow at Lehman Brothers offered, "but everybody likes [Lehman Brothers CEO] Dick Fuld." Everyone may like Dick Fuld, who presides over a socially connected, politically involved army of networking specialists who have one of Wall Street's best stock of favors done and collectible in return. But no one liked Fuld well enough to buy his firm, which apparently has been rejected at any price by a Korean bank, by Barclay's Bank of the UK, and finally by Bank of America.

The failure of Lehman and Bear Stearns did not reflect the breakdown of a particular kind of corporate culture. What took both firms down, rather, is a sudden break in the chain of expectations between the present and the future. Today's savers no longer can have any confidence that they will earn enough to fund their retirements by putting money at risk. They have discovered that, in one form or another, their investments have fed a securities-market bubble rather than the creation of value.

One wants to ask the Wall Street wizards who currently constitute the talent pool for the incoming administration, "If you so smart, how come you ain't rich no more?" Manhattan's toniest private schools, harder to get into than Harvard, quietly are looking for full-tuition pupils now that the children of sacked Wall Street bankers are departing for public schools in cheaper suburbs. In 2008, Harvard University's president, Drew Faust, warned of budget cuts to come due to "unprecedented losses" to its $39 billion endowment.

The cleverest people in the United States, the Ivy-pedigreed investment bankers, have fouled their own nests as well as their own net worth, and persuaded the taxpayers to bail them out. If these are the best and the brightest of today, America is in very deep trouble. The one-trick wizards of Wall Street had one idea, which was to ride the trend and pile on as much leverage as credulous investors and crony regulators would allow. It has gone pear-shaped, and those who didn't cash out early along with the cynics are poor. Fortunately for them, Obama will let them play with the budget of the U.S. federal government for the next four years. Failed financiers run the Obama transition team. It used to be that the heads of great industrial companies got the top cabinet posts. Now it is the one-trick wizards. After George W. Bush fired former treasury secretary Paul O'Neill, who had run Alcoa, the last survivor of the species was Vice President Dick Cheney, the former CEO of Halliburton. Obama's bevy of talent comes from finance. American industrialists have become figures of ridicule, like the pathetic chief executive of General Motors, Rick Wagoner, begging for a government loan. Stocks rallied on November 22 ,2008, on reports that Obama would give the Treasury post to Geithner, the New York Federal Reserve Bank president and the architect of the biggest bailout in history. He doubled the size of the Federal Reserve's balance sheet to more than $2 trillion, through the purchase of such risky assets as the commercial paper of near-bankrupt American auto companies. That is in addition to the Treasury's $700 billion bailout plan. Investors like the idea of trillion-dollar transfers from public funds to private companies.

A case in point is the reported implosion of the Harvard and Yale endowments. For years, these giant funds were held up as proof that superior intelligence was the ticket to excess returns. During the ten years through 2007, Harvard and Yale produced compound annual returns of 15 percent and 17.8 percent, respectively, far better than the market, the average endowment, or the average hedge funds—only to blow up in 2008 by frightful proportions not yet released. The "super endowments" sailed past their peers by loading up real estate, commodities, and "private equity," precisely the sectors that underwent necrosis in 2008. Private equity is the subprime version of corporate finance, acquiring nonpublic companies with a minimum down payment and the maximum of debt. David Swenson, the legendary manager of the Yale Endowment, learned one trick: Buy on dips in the equity market, with all the borrowed money he could get. The alumni network on Wall Street made sure that the university endowments were first in line for the hottest deals. That worked until 2008.

For a quarter of a century, the inbred products of the Ivy League puppy mills have known nothing but a rising trend in asset prices. About the origin of this trend, they were incurious. The Reagan administration in 1981 had encountered a stock market trading 50 percent below its the long-term trend. Reagan restored the equity market to trend by cutting taxes, suppressing inflation, and easing some regulations. The private-equity sharps were fleas traveling on Reagan's dog. They simply rode the trend with the maximum of leverage. Now that the stock market has collapsed, the private-equity strategies cannot repay their debt, and their returns have evaporated. Note that equity investors spent a decade in the cold, from 1973 to 1983; it may be even worse this time. The maturities on debt issued to finance private equity deals will come due long before the recovery. We know that, over the long term, the average investment cannot grow faster than the economy, for investments ultimately are valued according to cash flows, and cash flows stem from economic growth. Real American gross domestic product grew by 2 percent a year on average between 1929 and 2007. Whence came the enormous returns to the Ivy League? Some of them surely came from betting on the right horses, but most came from privileged access to leverage.

One recalls Ferdinand I of Austria (1793–1875), deposed for incompetence after the 1848 Revolution, who apocryphally shot an eagle and said, "It's got to be an eagle, but it's only got one head!" Ferdinand thought the two-headed bird of his family crest was the norm, just as the pink-shirted, suspender-wearing Ivy Leaguers thought that two-digit returns were the norm for their investments. The same privileged access to leverage allowed the investment banks to produce return on equity in excess of 20 percent year in, year out, by selling structured products. For the ten years through 2007, American homeowners joined the party, with returns in excess of 20 percent of their home equity (10 percent home-price appreciation more than doubles with leverage). Investment banks were levered long the leverage, so to speak. The more leverage the world demanded, the more Wall Street could charge for ever more arcane methods of packaging leverage, and the higher the returns to leverage providers. That explains how a Washington political operative like Rahm Emanuel, Obama's former chief of staff, who studied ballet rather than balance sheets, could earn a reported $16.2 million in two and a half years at Wasserstein Perella, the mergers-and-acquisitions boutique. At the height of the bubble, Bruce Wasserstein's firm sold out to Germany's Dresdner Bank for the fairy-tale sum of $1.6 billion. Even the crumbs from Wasserstein's loaf could make a Chicago politician rich.

Without leverage, the clever folk around Barack Obama are fleas without a dog. None of them invented anything, introduced an important new product, opened a new market, or did anything that reached into the lives of ordinary people. They wore expensive cufflinks, read balance sheets, exercised regularly, sat on philanthropic boards, and assumed that their flea's ride on the Reagan dog would last forever. All they knew was leverage. Now that the world is de-levering, they are trying to put leverage back into the system. One almost can hear Mortimer Duke, Don Ameche's charcter in *Trading Places*, shouting, "Now, you listen to me! I want trading reopened right now. Get those brokers back in here! Turn those machines back on!"

It won't work. The United States lived in Lever-Lever Land too long. Like Peter Pan, the country has refused to grow up. The object of the stimulus plans offered by the last two administrations is to return to Lever-Lever Land—that is, to debt-financed consumption. It won't work. Leverage is for the young, who borrow to build homes and start businesses. The financial crisis forces Americans to act their age, to save rather than borrow and spend. For a world economy geared to servicing the once-insatiable maw of American consumption, that is very bad news. Recovery cannot begin until

Americans have restored their decimated wealth by saving—an effort that will take years—or until the youthful emerging markets start importing from the United States rather than exporting to it. America's leaders haven't yet had the required moment of clarity. Its financial leaders still think the problem is a matter of mere confidence. These were the same people who swallowed their own sales pitch. The crisis began in June 2007 with the failure of a Bear Stearns hedge fund backed by partners' money, and peaked in September 2008 with the failure of Lehman Brothers, a shop where managers famously had to drink the Kool-Aid. Wall Street fell on its own sharp elbows and died. Firms that survived the Great Depression have failed or merged into a mockery of their former piratical selves. Why did the kidders succeed in kidding themselves? Don't blame them: Think of a middle-aged Peter Pan unwilling to admit that he shouldn't be flying. Like Sauron in *The Lord of the Rings*, who was not evil at the beginning, the instruments of monetary destruction that caused the present crisis began as the agents of upward mobility and entrepreneurial change. Mortgage-backed securities (MBS), leveraged buyouts (LBOs), collateralized debt obligations (CDOs), asset-backed securities (ABS), and even subprime mortgages unleashed American energy during the 1980s and made the U.S. economy the wonder of the world. At the outset, the alphabet soup of finance helped entrepreneurs and households to leap over barriers to market entry and make markets more efficient. Because financial innovation had done so much good, its practitioners refused to believe that it could do so much harm. America was younger then. The baby boomers were in their twenties and thirties when Ronald Reagan took office in 1981, and they needed all the capital they could borrow. All the instruments of monetary destruction that rained ruin on American markets in 2008 came into the world as good things. They arrived at a moment when America needed more debt. Can America return to Lever-Lever Land? Not a chance. America is much an older country than it was during the tech boom of the 1990s. J. M. Keynes's "animal spirits" are made mainly of testosterone. America had loads of that.

Young (25–50) Versus Older (50–64) American Workers

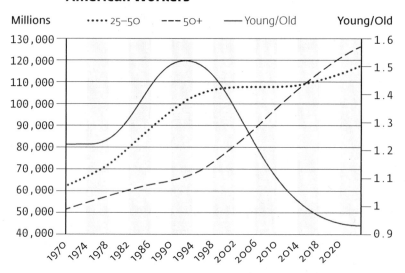

Source: United Nations Population Prospects

In the mid-1980s, America was young and was getting younger. Its ratio of younger (25 to 50) to older (50 to 65) workers peaked in the mid-1990s, when it had 1.5 citizens aged 25 to 50 for every one citizen aged 50 to 64. Those were heady times. The children of the baby boomers were happy to work for stock options, live on pizza, and spend twenty hours a day in a loft launching an Internet startup. Joining a startup was a rite of passage for bright young college graduates, and the exuberant young people of America momentarily persuaded the world that they had discovered a fountain of youth.

Ten years later, the number of aging workers and young workers is about even. The young programmer who worked for stock options during the 1990s still owns them, and all of them are worthless. He or she is pushing forty, with teenaged children who need money for college. Youth needs leverage. The Reagan Revolution of the 1980s, which launched the quarter-century expansion of 1983 through 2007, rested on three kinds of leverage: home mortgages, junk bonds, and leveraged buyouts. Turning mortgages into mortgage-backed securities made it easy for young families to buy homes and easy for entrepreneurs to draw working capital from the value of their homes. Junk bonds allowed emerging companies without the balance-sheet strength of their big competitors to enter the market and take on entrenched interests. And leveraged buyouts allowed clever upstarts to evict stodgy managers and make capital more efficient. The financiers who created these markets were giants. The mortgage-backed securities market allowed savers in the aging Rust Belt states of America to lend money to young families in the Sun Belt. Later, it allowed investors around the world to invest in American homes. Federal agencies that standardized and guaranteed U.S. mortgages made securitization possible, by creating a generic form of mortgage that could be bundled into securities.

The world's appetite for American mortgage-backed securities, though, grew out of bounds as an entire generation neared retirement in Europe and Japan, and the newly prosperous savers of Asia sought secure investments. America could not produce enough of the standardized, government-backed home mortgages to satisfy demand. Mortgages with risky credit constituted a tiny portion of total issuance during the 1990s but grew to $800 billion a year of issuance by 2006 before the market crashed to zero during 2008. Wall Street appropriated Milken's old idea of pooling credit risk and selling different grades of risk to different investors and applied it with a vengeance to risky mortgages, creating the subprime disaster of 2008.

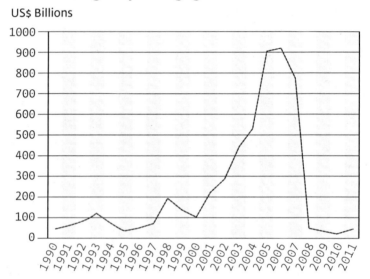

Non-Agency Mortgage-Backed Securities

Source: SIFMA (Securities Industry and Financial Markets Association)

Michael Milken, the creator of the modern high-yield bond market, might have been history's best judge of credit. By the time Milken went to jail on largely technical securities infractions in 1989, an army of imitators had turned the high-yield market into a manufacturing machine for soon-to-default credits, which helped trigger the recession of 1990. Milken invented the collateralized bond obligation—a pool of securities whose credit risk could be assigned to different investors willing to assume different degrees of risk in return for more or less income. During the 1980s, junk bonds gave entrepreneurs access to clubby capital markets that had favored the stodgy Fortune 500. Sadly, this market financed a wave of telecom startups during the technology bubble of the late 1990s. At the peak of the bubble in 1999, telecom made up a third of high-yield issuance, and the vast majority of the sector defaulted with little recovery for investors. The technology debacle discredited the market's original mission—namely, to promote entrepreneurship; it had done far too good a job with the wrong sort of risks. By the mid-2000s, Wall Street had stood the junk-bond market on its head: If investors were once burned and twice shy of new market entrants with low credit ratings, they would buy junk bonds from long-established companies that used to have investment-grade ratings. Wall Street proceeded to issue vast amounts of low-quality debt to fund leveraged buyouts of industry-leading giants—for example, $33 billion for Health Care Associates in 2006, $36 billion for Equity Office Properties Trust, nearly $40 billion for the utility TXU—for a total of $350 billion of leveraged buyouts in 2006, compared with just $50 billion in 2003. Wall Street sold junk bonds to finance the LBOs, and the junk bonds in turn were sold into alphabet-soup trusts such as collateralized debt obligations. Michael Milken's old vehicle for dealing out risks to different classes of investors became an assembly line for levering up corporate balance sheets. To accommodate the leverage boom in American and overseas corporate finance, issuance of collateralized debt obligations rose almost tenfold between 2002 and 2006, before falling to zero in 2008.

Nearly $1 trillion of these structured instruments have been written off in the past year. The U.S. Federal Reserve has added more than $1 trillion to its balance sheet, buying hundreds of billions of dollars' worth of structured instruments from banks, not to mention roughly $300 billion of commercial paper issued by U.S. corporations that otherwise could not raise money. The Treasury has injected more than $300 billion of capital into the banking system and insurance companies, with full-dress bailouts for two of the largest players in the structured finance market, American International Group and Citigroup. Some analysts worry that inflation is lurking behind the Fed's exploding balance sheet. I am less concerned. Aging people buy future goods (securities) for their retirement rather than current goods. Demographic decline is deflationary, as Japan should have taught the world by now.

Global Issuance of CDO's
(Collateralized Dept Obligations)

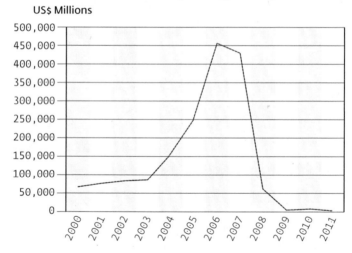

Source: SIFMA (Securities Industry and Financial Markets Association)

Aging workers, who soon will predominate in the American workforce, missed their chance to accumulate savings for retirement and education during the boom years of 2002 through 2008. Instead, they borrowed cheap money from foreigners and gambled on real estate. Many analysts have drawn attention to the link between America's zero percent personal savings rate and the current account deficit (see figure below). Americans' home equity probably is worth half of what it was three years ago, and may fall a great deal further. If they had a retirement savings plan, it is probably down by 40 percent or so. If they still have a job, they need to save as much as they can and make up for lost time. All the stimulus in the world won't persuade them to spend now that they know that they can't retire on the price of their houses.

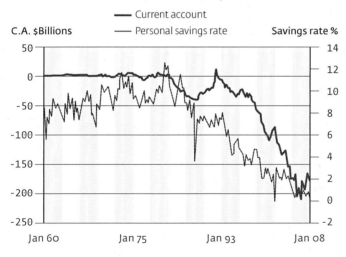

America Substituted Capital Imports for Savings: the Savings Rate Fell in Line with the Current Account Deficit

Source: St. Louis Federal Reserve

America's aging Peter Pans have discovered that happy thoughts and fairy dust no longer entitle them to fly. The young people of America led the world economy during the 1980s and 1990s, but now they are older, struggling to pay down mortgages that might be worth more than their homes, and to put something aside for a retirement that they never may be able to afford.

CHAPTER 23

The Keynes Conundrum

Written jointly with Prof. Reuven Brenner

What happens when government applies an old economic theory to a new recession? Nothing good. The most practical man of business is usually the slave of a defunct economist, John Maynard Keynes observed seventy-five years ago, in reference to the theories he proposed to overthrow, and this judgment applies with force to his continuing grip on the minds of the world's policymakers. Public debate about responses to the economic crisis remains circumscribed by Keynes's vocabulary. The Group of Twenty remains locked into Keynesian orthodoxy: debating whether governments should pursue "austerity," diminishing spending while cutting deficits and debts, or "stimulus," offering a "stimulative" monetary policy while increasing spending. None of the leaders of the world's top economies has uttered a pip about creating incentives to rebuild equity and revive the entrepreneurial spirits of their people, which is the only way to stop debts from compounding on public and private balance sheets. In the years following the publication, in 1936, of his *General Employ-*

ment, Interest, and Money, Keynes admitted that his new language was obscure and often misleading and that his analysis stood in dire need of rethinking. He even called his followers "fools." His early death, in 1946, allowed obscurity to ossify into academic orthodoxy and come to distort public discourse to this day.

Why has his rule lasted so long? How did so many clever people become the slaves of this defunct economist? His language and analyses were entirely wrong, but, during the Great Depression of the 1930s, his call for governments to step in quickly as financial intermediaries when private intermediaries were shutting down was the correct one. And he correctly fought a conventional wisdom that then favored balanced budgets as a response to the crisis. The crash of the equity market and the banking system had wiped out most of America's wealth. Institutions and households lacked the means to invest and restart the economy, until the government provided it in the form of war spending after 1939. When individuals and corporations lack the ability to issue debt, government becomes, by default, the financial intermediary. An increase in government debt in such exceptional cases constitutes an increase in wealth and can pave the way back to healthy capital markets. In 1790, Alexander Hamilton did just that when he persuaded the nascent United States to fund the Revolutionary War debt at par; he restored credibility in the country's currency and fiscal and monetary discipline. Later, future Nobelist Robert Mundell showed that an increase in government debt may *sometimes* represent wealth. It happens when a well-funded public debt (to borrow Hamilton's term) is supported by future prosperity, which implies both more creation of assets and more tax revenues. Tax cuts stimulate growth and produce an increase in wealth when the rise in tax revenues exceeds the interest that the government pays on the bonds it issued to cover the initial loss in revenue. This insight underlay the "supply-side economics" of the Reagan administration, unfortunately reduced even by some of its backers into simplistic caricature. Yet, as Mundell observed, curing the stagflation of the 1970s required fighting inflation with tight monetary policy while promoting the creation of assets through tax incentives. That is just what Paul Volcker's Federal Reserve and the Reagan administration did during the early 1980s, launching a quarter century of noninflationary prosperity. Keynes taught that all forms of aggregate demand were equivalent, such that fiscal policy and monetary policy merely increased or reduced short-term spending power but had nothing to say about restoring the conditions for rebuilding a country's assets. Politicians, however, liked the Keynesians' claim that governments could solve all the problems of the economy by taxing, spending, and manipulating interest rates— without raising difficult subjects such as the accountability of government bureaucracies or fluctuating exchange rates. Whether the politicians believed in the nonsense is irrelevant: It was convenient for them to behave as if they did. And economists were pleased to have a theory that elevated their status to the modern equivalent of court astrologers. After the 2008 crash, a generation of academics learned in the minutiae of the 1930s Depression, including the Federal Reserve chairman Ben Bernanke and White House adviser Lawrence Summers, were entrusted with the execution of Keynes's old prescriptions. The great economic crisis that began in 2007 and has not yet abated was supposed to have been Keynes's decisive triumph—the crisis in which governments actually did what he urged them to do during the Great Depression, and the proof that an elite of puppeteers could make the innumerable actors in economic life dance into recovery. After several years of the largest peacetime deficits the modern world has ever known, and the lowest global level of interest rates in history, Keynes's remedy has clearly failed. The world economy has not recovered. Instead, the locus of crisis has shifted to the balance sheets of the governments whose spending powers were supposed to have been the solution to the crisis.

Keynes' idea is simple. In fact, it is simple by construction, for it focuses on the very short term within a closed economy. If consumers won't spend, the government will spend for them; if businesses won't invest, the government will invest for them; and if investors won't take risks, the central bank will reduce the yield on low-risk investments to almost nothing. The risk taking of entrepreneurs, the cleverness of inventors, the skills and motivation of the workforce, the competitiveness of industries—all the granular reality of a dynamic society, chugging along through trial and error—vanish into Keynesian aggregates like gross domestic product, price indices, productivity, and so forth. Behind all the technical language stands the assumption that bureaucracies, with no business experience whatsoever, can somehow make wise decisions about allocating capital—and do so quickly. These gross simplifications take on the aura of academic theurgy when packaged into seemingly complex mathematical models that occult their ridiculous assumptions. No economic recovery will ever occur until governments bury, once and for all, the Keynesian concept of aggregate-demand management and instead take measures to revive incentives to rebuild risk-capital financing by mobilizing the country's entrepreneurial talent.

The policy debate is a blame game, but one played by blind men with an elephant. Some say that if the Federal Reserve had not kept interest rates so low for so long, there would have been less credit expansion and fewer defaults. Others say that if the Fed had paid more attention to the external value of the dollar than to price indices or GDP, it would have suppressed the developing bubble in home prices. Still others argue that without official support for sub-prime securitization, the vast subsidies provided by government-sponsored mortgage funders, and the monopoly position of the heavily conflicted rating agencies, the securitized debt bubble might have been contained. Yet others argue that the proprietary trading focus of deposit-taking institutions made the payments system vulnerable to panic. All these observations are true, and all of them are misleading, for the crisis arose not from any of these errors as such but rather from the Keynesian mindset of policy makers and regulators that prevented them from identifying these problems before they combined to threaten the financial system and the long-term health of the economy.

A decisive issue was the role of "shadow banking"—that is, the expansion of unregulated derivatives such as credit default swaps and collateralized debt obligations (CDOs). Two trillion dollars of CDOs, which hold assets in trust and pay income to investors with varying degrees of seniority, were issued between 2004 and 2008. These instruments allowed rating agencies to classify the majority of CDOs as virtually default proof, which in turn allowed banks to drastically reduce the amount of capital required to hold them. In short, derivatives vastly increased the leverage in the banking system. "Shadow banking" made short work of the old Keynesian definition of monetary "aggregates." It was no longer possible to speak of "aggregate" demand generated by a homogeneous sort of money controlled by the central bank through traditional open-market operations. Unregulated derivatives decoupled the real world of banking from the imagined one of aggregate monetary policy. Policymakers kept talking about the "aggregate," homogeneous kind of money, devising policies in its terms, when they should have concentrated their attention either on the institutions needed to manage *the different kinds* of domestic moneys coming into existence or prohibit the existence of "shadow banking." Shadow banking would never have gained the significant role it did unless people believed that the Federal Reserve would be there to supply the needed liquidity in the event of a run on the shadow banking system, too, and believed that "every money was created equal." The panic of 2008 (in distinction from the still-ongoing crisis) occurred when people realized that this was not the case. The run on the shadow banking system contaminated the *payment* system, and, without a functioning payment system, no economy can survive. Economies can survive without capital markets financing long-term investments, although not very well—as communism did for most of the last century. Economies also can survive for a few months if capital markets that just replenish inventories suddenly freeze. But once the payment system collapses, panic ensues, and the economy shuts down. Hyperinflation is the usual result, although, as the events of 2008 showed, a collapse of the payment system also can result in a run against money-market funds and other deposit-taking institutions, and the effects can be just as fearful. The panic happened, in part, because central bankers relied for decades on the Keynesian view that "money" is a homogeneous *aggregate* that central bankers controlled. While they were acting as if this were the case, the financial industry in effect printed its own money. The problem was neither obscure nor insoluble. If the Federal Reserve had only paid attention to entrepreneurial changes in the financial system rather than operating under the illusion of "aggregates," it could have imposed constraints on the shadow banking system with the same effect that constraints have on ordinary deposit banking.

The derivatives disaster offers one example of how poorly the Keynesian framework and its dependence on aggregates has served economic policy. Another example is the misleading measurement of the so-called inflation rate, which continues to lull the central bank into complacency about the long-term impact of zero interest rates. The cost of housing constitutes nearly a third of the consumer price index (CPI). Measuring that cost has always been problematic. But the errors compounded during the last decade in particular, as houses ceased to be mere domiciles and instead became a new, putatively liquid-asset class. This happened because laws, regulations, and government-backed entities such as the federal mortgage insurers subsidized the housing market directly or indirectly. These subsidies drastically altered the nature of this asset class as well as the meaning of "inflation rates." Initially, scholars and politicians rationalized the subsidies, claiming that home ownership stabilizes communities, gives people a stake in the system, and provides bootstrap capital for business start-ups. These observations were accurate as long as the terms *ownership* and *equity* kept their meaning. In fact, the subsidies encouraged homeowners to reduce their equity by taking on as much leverage as possible. By 2007, homeowners enjoyed ownership only on paper, holding a small margin of equity against a great deal of debt. These distortions in the housing market played hob with the inflation indices, as Americans bought homes in the expectation of flipping them. Rents meanwhile remained stable, and rent is what the Bureau of Labor Statistics measures to determine the cost of housing. As a result, the housing component in price indices—30 percent of the index—barely changed. To many observers, including at the Federal Reserve, the stability of this price index suggested that there was no excessive credit creation *in spite of* the rapid increase in home prices. The resulting false readings led to wild misjudgments on the part of the Greenspan and later the Bernanke Federal Reserve Board, who did not believe that their lax monetary policy caused excess credit creation. The 35 percent fall in the trade-weighted dollar index and the quadrupling of the gold price between 2002 and mid-2009 should have made clear that something was woefully amiss, although the CPI failed to flash an alarm signal. Whatever one thinks about the gold price, that the market was willing to pay four times as much for a traditional inflation and devaluation hedge should not have gone unnoticed by the somnolent wizards of Constitution Avenue.

The collapse of the credit expansion raises the prospect of deflation, and the Keynesian elite now proposes to ward off this danger by returning to the inflationary policy that brought about the crisis in the first place. The International Monetary Fund's chief economist, Olivier Blanchard, offered what he called a "bold innovation" in February 2010, proposing that central banks pursue 4 percent inflation. Evidently Blanchard thinks that people will happily accept a 22 percent reduction in their wages over five years and a 48 percent reduction over ten years. Professional deformation on this scale attests to the triumph of Keynes over common sense. The reasoning of proponents of such policies—Paul Krugman advocates even higher inflation rates—is that the fear of inflation would lead people to spend money before its purchasing power declined. The Keynesians did not stop to ask how Americans could begin a spending spree after the colossal wealth destruction of the past several years, just before the largest retirement wave in American history. Perhaps the wildest distortion of all occurs in the measurement of the central aggregate in the Keynesian model, the gross domestic product. Earlier in 2010, the world was shocked, shocked to find that a series of Greek governments had lied outright about the size of the country's GDP, national debt, and other aggregate measures. As early as 2006, however, Europe's statistical bureau, Eurostat, had threatened Greece with lawsuits over its statistical fabrications. Hungary now is facing a similar problem, the newly elected government acknowledging that the official numbers were little more than statistical illusions. What does this imply about aggregate figures published with such solemnity by national statistics bureaus? This is nothing new. Back in 1987, Italy announced the year of *il sorpasso,* "the year we leapfrogged you." The Italian National Institute of Statistics (ISTAT), the government's statistics office, arbitrarily added an extra 18 percent to its estimate of Italy's "real national income." The adjustment was needed to show that Italy conformed to the evolving European Community requirements for debt and deficit ratios to national income. ISTAT simply asserted that Italy had a black market constituting between 20 percent and 30 percent of its economy and offered the 18 percent boost as a "conservative" adjustment. Greek politicians made similar statements when Eurostat confronted them, putting the size of the country's black market above 25 percent.

No outrage greeted these assertions. On the contrary, the statisticians went back to work churning out aggregate indices, and Keynesian economists plugged them into ever more recondite models. It might have seemed appropriate to ask if it were true that certain countries have black markets encompassing a quarter or a third of economic activity, and, if it were true, why. But no one did because the claim provided the data necessary to continue the Keynesian assumptions. The economics profession was content with government fabrications until early in 2010, when it seemed clear that Greece, as well as some other southern European countries, might not be able to service the debt that it had assumed on the strength of its aggregate economic measures. In politics, as in business, only the threat of bankruptcy forces lies into the open. As an advocate of emergency measures during the 1930s, Keynes, as we have said, deserves some credit. His legacy in economic theory, though, has been malignant. It is easy to explain why he drew support during the 1930s. It is harder to explain why the Keynesian model, with its inherent tendency to drive off the road, has survived so long. Part of the answer is that countries devoted to "Keynesian" policies had a run of good luck that covered up the systematic errors of economic policy. And the memory of this run of good luck still beguiles politicians and their advisers, who yet hope that the easy times will come back.

A major source of that good luck was the migration of capital and talent spurred by troubles elsewhere. Until 1989, most of the world suffered under communist or other dictatorial regimes prone to violent political upheaval. Whatever talent and capital was able to escape from the dictatorships arrived on the shores of a handful of Western countries, foremost among them the United States. The export of human and financial capital to the United States and a few other countries helped cover up accumulating mistakes. In politics as in business, competitors survive not because they are clever but because the competition is stupider. The massive flow of talent and capital to Western shores until 1989 had consequences that economists have not acknowledged, let alone measured. Consider the present debate about taxation. Paul Krugman intoned in a recent *New Yorker* interview: "I don't advocate a marginal tax rate of 70 percent, but it's worth noting that we had rates in that range all through the 1960s and much of the 1970s, without much evidence that effort at top levels was being crippled. So that's feasible."

Well, it is *not* feasible—unless the rest of the world were to move to even higher marginal tax rates, which is not going to happen. The United States was able to sustain that marginal tax rate during the 1970s because it seemed like tax paradise compared to the rest of the world. When the United Kingdom imposed a 90 percent marginal tax rate, its best talent fled to the United States and Canada—the Beatles included. The flow of talent and capital covered for many domestic mistakes within the United States. When America enjoyed a monopoly as a destination for talent and capital, governments were able to impose high tax rates, for capital had few other viable destinations.

Observers such as Paul Krugman believe that the past can be replicated because they do not understand that past, particularly the sources of the Western nations' good luck. His is the Keynesian mindset: a short-run view of a closed economy. But the American monopoly did not last. Communism collapsed in 1989, and the previously unstable and chaotic countries of Asia turned into economic tigers within a decade. Other parts of what we then called the "Third World"—a term that rings quaint today—developed political stability and economic success. Western countries, whose workers are used to living far better than people with similar skills in the rest of the world, are in trouble. They find themselves with a generation of employees in the public and private sectors who have been pampered by the extraordinary and nonrepeatable circumstances of the past fifty years. Greece is the industrial world's first casualty, with Portugal, Italy, Spain, and perhaps even France not far behind. Some American political jurisdictions, notably California, are suffering similar crises. These casualty countries are all democracies. But political parties are slow to correct the accumulated mistakes of decades. Capital markets are forced to correct mistakes much faster; the markets are signaling that, unless governments move swiftly, they risk default. Rather than learn their lesson and abandon Keynes, European governments have responded by throwing him into reverse, through fiscal austerity that suppresses growth and increases the real burden of public debt. What their countries need is to let their people leverage their entrepreneurial talents and build up assets. Unless this is done, the world economy will remain locked into a stagnation punctuated by periodic crises.

Lasting prosperity stems from innovation and entrepreneurship. It is easy to talk about this, but hard to bring it to life. To match talent and capital, and to sort out winning ideas from the failures, societies must build their risk capital and sustain the entire maze of institutions that maintain accountability among investors, entrepreneurs, and intermediaries. Accountability requires the continuous reevaluation of entrepreneurial experiments and the ability to intervene to shut them down through bankruptcy, to prevent costly errors from compounding. Government bureaucracies are the worst conceivable arbiters of failure and success because bureaucrats are rewarded not by the success of enterprise but by political constituencies that often have reason to avoid the consequences of failures. So-called speculators play an indispensable role, for they provide the liquidity needed during the long years that elapse between the floating of an idea and its successful execution. Matching talent and capital and sorting winning ideas from failures do not look difficult on paper. But a political culture that fosters the entrepreneurial spirit, tolerating trial and error and allowing the innovative newcomer a shot against entrenched interests, has been a relative rarity even in Western history.

Only through a long and fitful process of trial and error did Western societies develop the institutions that support entrepreneurship. Stock and commodity exchanges, investment banks, mutual funds, deposit banking, securitization, and other markets have their roots in the Dutch innovations of the seventeenth century but reached maturity, in many cases, only during the past quarter of a century. Among the Western nations, the United States has been the venue most friendly to entrepreneurship, although the direction of the present administration—which has expanded the government lock on financial markets to an extent never before seen in peacetime—has taken the country in a different, and troubling, direction.

Washington has turned the financial industry into the equivalent of a quasi-governmental public utility. The federal government provides emergency capital and cheap money to the banks, and the banking system in turn finances the federal deficit. The present administration has turned American capital markets into a state-influenced oligopoly, antithetical to entrepreneurial innovation. It is not surprising that venture capital, business start-ups, and other indicators of entrepreneurial activity remain depressed, and the economy shows little sign of recovery. In this situation it is not a good sign that the same cast of characters who led the financial system over the cliff—including Federal Reserve chairman Bernanke and former New York Federal Reserve Bank president (now treasury secretary) Timothy Geithner, both with bureaucratic and academic experience only—continue to direct policy. The public officials and leaders of financial institutions who managed their way into the crisis have little incentive to ask tough questions about what went wrong, much less to change the way that things are done. It is time to drive out the Keynesians and adopt a different benchmark altogether. The goal of economic policy should be to help individuals and firms sustain entrepreneurial risk taking over an extended period of time. It is not difficult to identify what should be done, and in what sequence. Maintaining confidence in the currency and the payments system is the first order of business: If systemic risk overwhelms portfolio decisions, investors will not take risks on innovation. The Federal

Reserve's reliance on the CPI led to errors in monetary policy, which some Keynesians now propose to repeat. There is a better way to guide monetary policy toward a stable currency. As I will explain in chapter 25, global currency stabilization, starting with a fixed-parity arrangement between the U.S. dollar and a convertible Chinese yuan, would provide a new yardstick for monetary stability.

The governments of the G20 misuse tax policy as an instrument to manage aggregate demand, oscillating between "stimulus" and "austerity." We have already seen, in the sad case of Western Europe, that reshuffling debt from private to public balance sheets only infects public credit with systemic risk and ultimately leads to the collapse of both public and private credit. The choice is not between austerity and stimulus through government spending but between stagnation and innovation. Government policy must foster independent sources of risk capital. In the 1790s, or the 1930s, or the 1980s, increasing government debt helped to do this, but it is very hard to argue that this was the case in 2010. The policy lever that can best influence risk taking today is fiscal. Governments should reduce taxes on capital income and eliminate taxes on capital gains entirely. Spending cuts must be second in the sequence, after tax reductions have generated more risk capital and employment. Cutting spending first will cause a sharp drop in employment, with no collateral benefits through additional deployment of risk capital. The worst course of action would be for the federal government to arrogate to itself the role of the private institutions slowly established by the efforts of tens of thousands of talented individuals. Restoring conditions for long-lasting prosperity requires risk investments that create assets, which in turn help create seed capital for new entrepreneurs, in a virtuous cycle. Government job creation produces at best temporary incomes, diverting capital from creation of assets.

The United States is now at a critical juncture. The economy has failed to respond to the administration's Keynesian patent medicine. Washington has the option to either start this "virtuous cycle" and adjust capital markets, taxes, and regulations accordingly or be doomed to decades of mediocre performance.

CHAPTER 24

Demographics and Depression

Three generations of economists immersed themselves in study of the Great Depression, determined to prevent a recurrence of the awful events of the 1930s. And as our current financial crisis began to unfold in 2008, policymakers did everything that those economists prescribed. Following John Maynard Keynes, President Bush and President Obama each offered a fiscal stimulus. The Federal Reserve maintained confidence in the financial system, increased the money supply, and lowered interest rates. The major industrial nations worked together, rather than at cross-purposes as in the early 1930s. In other words, the government tried to do everything right, but everything continues to go wrong. We labored hard and traveled long to avoid a new depression, but one seems to have found us nonetheless.

So is this something outside the lesson book of the Great Depression? Most officials and economists argue that, until home prices stabilize, necrosis will continue to spread through the assets of the financial system, and consumers will continue to restrict spending. The sources of the present crisis reach into the capillary system of the economy: the most basic decisions and requirements of American households. All the apparatus of financial engineering is helpless beside the simple issue of household decisions about shelter. We are in the most democratic of economic crises, and it stems directly from the character of our people. Part of the problem in seeing this may be that we are transfixed by the dense technicalities of credit flow, the new varieties of toxic assets, and the endless iterations of financial restructuring. Sometimes it helps to look at the world with a kind of simplicity. Think of it this way: Credit markets derive from the cycle of human life. Young people need to borrow capital to start families and businesses; old people need to earn income on the capital they have saved. We invest our retirement savings in the formation of new households. All the armamentarium of modern capital markets boils down to investing in a new generation so that they will provide for us when we are old. To understand the bleeding in the housing market, then, we need to examine the population of prospective homebuyers whose millions of individual decisions determine whether the economy will recover. Families with children are the fulcrum of the housing market. Because single-parent families tend to be poor, the buying power is concentrated in two-parent families with children.

Now, consider this fact: America's population has risen from 200 million to 300 million since 1970, while the total number of two-parent families with children is the same today as it was when Richard Nixon was president, at 25 million. In 1973, the United States had 36 million housing units with three or more bedrooms, not many more than the number of two-parent families with children—which means that the supply of family homes was roughly in line with the number of families. By 2005, the number of housing units with three or more bedrooms had doubled to 72 million, though America had the same number of two-parent families with children. The number of two-parent families with children, the kind of household that requires and can afford a large home, has remained essentially stagnant since 1963, according to the Census Bureau. Between 1963 and 2005, to be sure, the total number of what the Census Bureau categorizes as families grew from 47 million to 77 million. But most of the increase is due to families without children, including what are sometimes rather strangely called "one-person families." In place of traditional two-parent families with children, America has seen enormous growth in one-parent families and childless families. The number of one-parent families with children has tripled. Dependent children formed half the U.S. population in 1960. Today, they add up to only 30 percent. The dependent elderly doubled as a proportion of the population, from 15 percent in 1960 to 30 percent today.

If capital markets derive from the cycle of human life, what happens if the cycle goes wrong? Investors may be *unreasonably* panicked about the future, and governments can allay this panic by guaranteeing bank deposits, increasing incentives to invest, and so forth. But something different is in play when investors are *reasonably* panicked. What if there really is something wrong with our future—if the next generation fails to appear in sufficient numbers? The answer is that we get poorer. The declining demographics of the traditional American family raise a dismal possibility: Perhaps the world is poorer now because the present generation did not bother to rear a new one. All else is bookkeeping and ultimately trivial. This unwelcome and unprecedented change underlies the present global economic crisis. We are grayer, and less fecund, and as a result we are poorer, and will get poorer still—no matter what economic poli-

cies we put in place. We could put this another way: America's housing market collapsed because conservatives lost the culture wars
even back while they were prevailing in electoral politics. During
the past half century, America has changed from a nation in which
most households had two parents with young children. We are now
a mélange of alternative arrangements in which the nuclear family is merely a niche phenomenon. By 2025, single-person households may outnumber families with children. The collapse of home
prices and the knock-on effects on the banking system stem from
the shrinking count of families that require houses. It is no accident that the housing market—the economic sector most sensitive
to population—was the epicenter of the economic crisis. In fact,
demographers have been predicting a housing crash for years, in
light of the demographics of diminishing demand. Wall Street and
Washington merely succeeded in prolonging the housing bubble for
a few additional years. The adverse demographics arising from cultural decay, though, portend far graver consequences for the fund-
ing of health and retirement systems. Conservatives have indulged
in self-congratulation over the quarter-century run of growth that
began in 1984 with the Reagan administration's tax reforms. A prosperity that fails to rear a new generation in sufficient numbers is
hollow, as we have learned to our detriment during the past year.
Compared to Japan and most European countries, which face demographic catastrophe, America's position seems relatively strong,
but that strength has only postponed the reckoning, by keeping the
world's capital flowing into the U.S. mortgage market right up until
the crash at the end of 2007. As long as conservative leaders de-
livered economic growth, family issues were relegated to Sunday
rhetoric. Of course, conservative thinkers never actually proposed
to measure the movement's success solely in units of gross domestic

product, or square feet per home, or cubic displacement of the average automobile engine. But delivering consumer goods was what conservatives seemed to do well, and they rode the momentum of the Reagan boom.

Until now. Our children are our wealth. Too few of them are seated around America's common table, and it is their absence that makes us poor. Our prospects are diminished not only by the absolute count of children, to be sure, but also by the shrinking proportion of children raised with the moral and material advantages of two-parent families. The capital markets have reduced the value of homeowners' equity by $8 trillion and of stocks by $7 trillion. Households with a provider aged 45 to 54 have lost half their net worth between 2004 and 2009, according to Dean Baker of the Center for Economic and Policy Research. There are ways to ameliorate the financial crisis, but none of them will replace the lives that should have been part of America and now are missed.

This suggests that nothing economic policy can do will entirely reverse the great wave of wealth destruction. President Obama made *hope* the watchword of his campaign, but there is less for which to hope, largely because of the economic impact of the lifestyle choices favored by the same young people who were so enthusiastic for Obama. The Reagan reforms created new markets and financing techniques and put enormous amounts of leverage at the disposal of businesses and households. The 1980s saw the creation of a mortgage-backed securities market that turned the American home into a ready source of capital, the emergence of a high-yield bond market that allowed new companies to issue debt, and the expansion of private equity. These financing techniques contributed mightily to the great expansion of 1984 through 2008, and they were the same instruments that would wreak ruin on the financial system. During the 1980s the baby boomers were in their twenties and thirties, when families are supposed to take on debt; twenty years later, the baby boomers were in their fifties and sixties, when families are supposed to save for retirement. The elixir of youth turned toxic for the aging. Unless we restore the traditional family to a central position in American life, we cannot expect to return to the kind of wealth accumulation that characterized the 1980s and 1990s. Theoretically, we might recruit immigrants to replace the children we did not rear, or we might invest capital overseas with the children of other countries. From the standpoint of economic policy, neither of those possibilities can be dismissed. But the contributions of immigration or capital export will be marginal at best compared to the central issue of whether the demographics of America revert to health.

Life is sacred for its own sake. It is not an instrument to provide us with fatter IRAs or better real-estate values. But it is fair to point out that wealth depends ultimately on the natural order of human life. Failing to rear a new generation in sufficient numbers to replace the present one violates that order, and it has consequences for wealth, among many other things. Americans who rejected the mild yoke of family responsibility in pursuit of atavistic enjoyment will find at last that this is not to be theirs, either. It will be painful for conservatives to admit that things were not well with America under the Republican watch, at least not at the family level. From 1954 to 1970, for example, half or more of households contained two parents and one or more children under the age of 18. In fact as well as in popular culture, the two-parent nuclear family formed the normative American household. By 1981, when Ronald Reagan took office, two-parent households had fallen to just over two-fifths of the total. Today, less than a third of American households constitute a two-parent nuclear family with children. Housing prices are collapsing in part because single-person households are replacing families with children. The Virginia Tech economist Arthur C. Nelson has noted that households with children would fall from half to a quarter of all households by 2025. The demand of Americans will then be urban apartments for empty nesters. Demand for large-lot single-family homes, Nelson calculated, will slump from 56 million today to 34 million in 2025—a reduction of 40 percent. There never will be a housing-price recovery in many parts of the country. Huge tracts will become uninhabited except by vandals and rodents.

All of these trends were evident for years, and duly noted by housing economists. Why did it take until 2007 for home prices to collapse? If America were a closed economy, the housing market would have crashed years ago. The paradox is that the rest of the industrial world and much of the developing world are aging faster than the United States. In the industrial world, there are more than 400 million people in their peak savings years, 40 to 64 years of age, and the number is growing. There are fewer than 350 million young earners in the 19-to-40-year bracket, and their number is shrinking. If savers in Japan can't find enough young people to lend to, they will lend to the young people of other countries. Japan's median age will rise above 60 by midcentury, and Europe's will rise to the mid-50s.

America is slightly better off. Countries with aging and shrinking populations must export and invest the proceeds. Japan's households have hoarded $14 trillion in savings, which they will spend on geriatric care provided by Indonesian and Filipino nurses, as the country's population falls to just 90 million in 2050, from 127 million today. The graying of the industrial world creates an inexhaustible supply of savings and demand for assets in which to invest them—which is to say, for young people able to borrow and pay loans with interest. The tragedy is that most of the world's young people live in countries without capital markets, enforcement of property rights, or reliable governments. Japanese investors will not buy mortgages from Africa or Latin America, or even China. A rich Chinese won't lend money to a poor Chinese unless, of course, the poor Chinese first moves to the United States. Until recently, that left the United States the main destination for the aging savers of the industrial world. America became the magnet for savings accumulated by aging Europeans and Japanese. To this must be added the rainy-day savings of the Chinese government, whose desire to accumulate large amounts of foreign-exchange reserves is more than justified in retrospect by the present crisis. America has roughly 120 million adults in the 19-to-44 age bracket, the prime borrowing years. That is not a large number against the 420 million prospective savers in the aging developed world as a whole. There simply aren't enough young Americans to absorb the savings of the rest of the world. In demographic terms, America is only the leper with the most fingers. The rest of the world lent the United States vast sums, rising to almost $1 trillion in 2007. As the rest of the world thrust its savings on the United States, interest rates fell and home prices rose. To feed the inexhaustible demand for American assets, Wall Street connived with the ratings agencies to turn the sow's ear of subprime mortgages into silk purses, in the form of supposedly default-proof securities with high credit ratings. Americans thought themselves charmed and came to expect indefinitely continuing rates of 10 percent annual appreciation of home prices (and correspondingly higher returns to homeowners with a great deal of leverage).

The baby boomers evidently concluded that one day they all

would sell their houses to each other at exorbitant prices and retire on the proceeds. The national household savings rate fell to zero by 2007, as Americans came to believe that capital gains on residential real estate would substitute for savings.

After a $15 trillion reduction in asset values, Americans are now saving as much as they can. Of course, if everyone saves and no one spends, the economy shuts down, which is precisely what is happening. The trouble is not that aging baby boomers need to save. The problem is that the families with children who need to spend never were formed in sufficient numbers to sustain growth. In emphasizing the demographics, I do not mean to give Wall Street a free pass for prolonging the bubble. Without financial engineering, the crisis would have come sooner and in a milder form. But we would have been just as poor in consequence. The origin of the crisis is demographic, and its solution can only be demographic. America needs to find productive young people to lend to.

The world abounds in young people, of course, but not young people who can productively use capital and are therefore good credit risks. The trouble is to locate young people who are reared to the skill sets, work ethic, and social values required for a modern economy. In theory, it is possible to match American capital to the requirements of young people in venues capable of great productivity growth. East Asia, for example, has almost 500 million people in the 19-to-40-year-old bracket, 50 percent more than that of the entire industrial world. The prospect of raising the productivity of Chinese, Indians, and other Asians opens up an entirely different horizon for the American economy. In theory, the opportunities for investment in Asia are limitless, but political trust, capital markets, regulatory institutions, and other preconditions for such investment have been inadequate. For aging Americans to trust their savings to young Asians, a generation's worth of institutional reforms would be required. It is also possible to improve America's demographic profile through immigration. Some years ago Cardinal Baffi of Bologna suggested that Europe seek Catholic immigrants from Latin America. In a small way, something like this is happening. Europe's alternative is to accept more immigrants from the Middle East and Africa, with the attendant risks of cultural hollowing out and eventual Islamicization. America's problem is more difficult, for what America requires are highly skilled immigrants. Even so, efforts to export capital and import workers will at best mitigate America's economic problems in a small way. We are going to be poorer for a generation and perhaps longer. We will drive smaller cars and live in smaller homes, vacation in cabins by the lake rather than at Disney World, and send our children to public universities rather than private liberal-arts colleges. The baby boomers on average will work five or ten years longer before retiring on less income than they had planned, and young people will work for less money at duller jobs than they had hoped.

In traditional societies, each extended family relied on its own children to care for its own elderly. The resources the community devoted to the destitute—gleaning the fields after harvest, for example—were quite limited. Modern society does not require every family to fund its retirement by rearing children; we may contribute to a pension fund and draw on the labor of the children of others. But if everyone were to retire on the same day, the pension fund would go bankrupt instantly, and we all would starve. The distribution of rewards and penalties is manifestly unfair. The current crisis is particularly unfair to those who brought up children and contributed monthly to their pension fund, only to watch the value of their savings evaporate in the crisis. Tax and social-insurance policy should reflect the effort and cost of rearing children and require those who avoid such effort and cost to pay their fair share. Numerous proposals for family-friendly tax policy are in circulation, including recent suggestions by Ramesh Ponnuru, Ross Douthat, and Reihan Salam. The core of a family-oriented economic program might include the following measures:

Cut taxes on families. The personal exemption introduced with the Second World War's Victory Tax was $624, reflecting the cost of "food and a little more." In today's dollars that would be about $7,600, while the current personal exemption stands at only $3,650. The personal exemption should be raised to $8,000 simply to restore the real value of the deduction, and the full personal exemption should apply to children.

Shift part of the burden of social insurance to the childless. For most taxpayers, social-insurance deductions are almost as great a burden as income tax. Families that bring up children contribute to the future tax base; families that do not get a free ride. The base rate for social-security and Medicare deductions should rise, with a significant exemption for families with children, so that a disproportionate share of the burden falls on the childless.

Make child-related expenses tax-deductible. Tuition and health care are the key expenses here with which parents need help.

Change the immigration laws. The United States needs highly skilled, productive individuals in their prime years for earning and family formation.

We delude ourselves when we imagine that a few hundred dollars of tax incentives will persuade individuals to form families or keep them together. A generation of Americans has grown up with the belief that the traditional family is merely one lifestyle choice among many. But it is among the young that such a conservative message could reverberate the loudest. The young know that the promise of sexual freedom has brought them nothing but emptiness and anomie, as I tried to explain in chapter 8. They suffer more than anyone from the breakup of families. They know that abortion has wrought psychic damage that never can be repaired. And they see that their own future was compromised by the poor choices of their parents. It was always morally wrong for conservatives to attempt to segregate the emotionally charged issues of public morals from the conservative growth agenda. We know now that it was also incompetent from a purely economic point of view. Without life, there is no wealth; without families, there is no economic future. The value of future income streams traded in capital markets will fall in accordance with our impoverished demography. We cannot pursue the acquisition of wealth and the provision of upward mobility except through the reconquest of the American polity on behalf of the American family. The conservative movement today seems weaker than at any time since Lyndon Johnson defeated Barry Goldwater. There are no free-marketeers in the foxholes, and it is hard to find an economist of any stripe who does not believe that the government must provide some kind of economic stimulus and rescue the financial system. But the present crisis also might present the conservative movement with the greatest opportunity it has had since Ronald Reagan took office. The Obama administration will certainly face backlash when its promise to fix the economy through the antiquated tools of Keynesian stimulus comes to nothing. And as a result, American voters may be more disposed than they have been for several generations to consider fundamental problems. The message that our children are our wealth, and that families are its custodian, might resonate all the more strongly for the manifest failure of the alternatives.

CHAPTER 25

The Needle's Eye

Written jointly with Prof. Reuven Brenner

Even if America does not raise sufficient numbers of children, it still has access to the largest and least exploited resource in the world: the underutilized human capital of the poor half of the world. The destinies of the aging but affluent people of the West and the young but impoverished people of the Global South are joined—and joined by a very simple economic fact: The old tend to have savings, while the young tend to have energy. To fund their retirements, old people must find young people to whom they can lend. And to start families and businesses, young people must find old people from whom they can borrow. The extreme poverty of so many in the Global South offends morality for many reasons, but one reason hardly anyone seems to mention is that this poverty persists despite the economic interests of the world's people being complementary. We ought to help the poor, and we need to improve our own economic situation—yet, somehow, we seem unable to do either. This isn't a failure of charity. It's a failure of intellect, a failure of law, and a failure of imagination. Capital *wants* to flow from the West to high-return outlets in the South, but Third World corruption and First World insularity combine to block these mutual needs and interests.

Despite its recent financial woes, the United States remains the only actor on the world stage that can break down the barriers impeding the natural flow of capital around the world. In that sense, our present economic crisis is both a prod and an opportunity for American leadership to act in the interest of both America and the world. With the continued rise in American unemployment, despite nearly a trillion dollars in fiscal stimulus and more than eight trillion dollars in federal subsidies and guarantees to the financial system, this mutual dependency should be glaringly obvious. Americans, at the cusp of the biggest retirement wave in their history, must save as they never have before, particularly after the wealth destruction of the recent past. As they reduce consumption in order to save, employment falls—so far that one in five American adults is unemployed, underemployed, or "discouraged from seeking employment." Americans could increase both their savings and their employment by exporting manufactured goods. The trouble is that America has neither the capacity to manufacture such exports nor the customers to buy them. Half the world thirsts for capital, while half the world is drowning in it. Two decisive actions would help open the floodgates that separate the capital-thirsty Global South from the capital-rich savers of the West. We need, first, monetary policy to stabilize currencies—currencies of developing nations, in particular—while creating conditions for the rapid development of their domestic capital markets. And we need fiscal and regulatory changes to encourage savings and investment in the United States, to rebuild its equity.

In many ways, America's present position resembles that of the final years of the Carter administration, when Keynesian fiscal stimulus and lax monetary policy gave the country the worst of both worlds: economic stagnation and a collapsing currency. The present administration's policy mix of "Keynesian deficit spending" and near-zero interest rates will not produce a recovery either. In fact, by going down this road, we can only make matters worse. Post-Carter, the Reagan administration trampled on economic convention by applying the economist Robert Mundell's idea of combining tight monetary policy (to save the dollar) and tax cuts (to encourage investment and risk taking). This prescription began the longest economic boom in American history—and the nation can look forward to another long economic boom, if policymakers have the courage and imagination to throw out Keynesian convention. But, as Mark Twain said, history does not repeat itself; it only rhymes. We cannot simply replay the tape of the Reagan years, and we have to do something else to save the dollar from a devaluation spiral and rebuild equity. In 1981, Ronald Reagan faced a situation very different from what we face. The personal savings rate stood at 10 percent, and America was lending to the rest of the world rather than borrowing from it. The top marginal tax rate was 70 percent, and the baby boomers were young and ready to take risks, rather than about to retire.

Today, America is coming out of a decade without savings, and for years it has been borrowing from the world instead of lending to it. Rather than exporting and saving, America is vacuuming capital out of the rest of the world and going further into debt. Once we exclude the option of admitting a few million skilled, entrepreneurial young immigrants—as Israel did from Russia two decades ago—the present crisis can be solved only by opening the world to American exports and restructuring the American economy to create the necessary export capacity. The risk is that America's credit will be exhausted, leading to the collapse of the dollar and its role as the world's main reserve currency. Paradoxically, preventing the dollar's collapse also represents a once-in-a-century opportunity for American leadership. Our present fiscal and monetary policies degrade the dollar's value and force part of the burden of financing a misguided fiscal stimulus onto America's trading partners. They have no alternative for the moment but to shoulder this burden, however reluctantly. But they will not do so forever.

The United States should establish a fixed parity for the dollar with the currencies of its largest trading partners, starting with China. By stabilizing the dollar against the yuan and, eventually, other currencies, the United States can create a shield behind which the capital markets of developing countries can flourish and capital can continue to flow to the United States. Developed nations can protect themselves against sudden shifts in the flow of capital, but poor nations with nascent capital markets cannot. Currency stability is the first precondition for the creation of capital markets in the developing world.

The irony of America's predicament is that, as the government struggles unsuccessfully to revive consumer demand, the global demand for American products appears almost bottomless. Most of the young people of the world live in countries with capital markets that are primitive, inefficient, corrupt, and risky. But their demand for capital—to build homes, water systems, energy plants, cell-phone towers, schools, highways, and railroads—is just as large as the demand, among the aging savers of the West, for safe capital instruments with a better return than zero. There are only two ways to bridge this gap: Bring the capital to the young people, or bring the young people to the capital. Tens of millions of illegal immigrants make their way from Latin America to the United States, or to Europe from Africa and Asia, in search of the financing that might give them employment.

Hungry and frightened people do not wait for their governments to address the central concern of the day. They vote with their feet. Among the facts that a moral view of economics ought to consider, this one has been badly neglected: The failures of economic policy generate the social problems associated with illegal migrants. If we want a more stable world, then we must give people more opportunities in their own countries. Our old mistakes, in the shape of debts, are compounding on corporate and governmental balance sheets. In Washington, however, the problem is taken to be not the compounding of debt. Rather, the Obama administration (influenced, apparently, by the Keynesian outlook of Larry Summers, director of the White House's National Economic Council) insists, our financial crisis endures because Americans save too much and spend too little. And so, to restart the economy, the government has to spend money, in the form of an $800 billion stimulus package.

There are two things terribly wrong with this notion. The first is related to the fact that the administration perceives the situation through the Keynesian notion of a diminished "marginal propensity to consume." But, as I have explained in the previous chapters, Keynes was constructing a short-run model of a closed economy, and the United States today confronts the accumulation of long-run problems. A huge jump in the retirement rate coincides with the collapse of an asset-price bubble that has left a dangerous level of debt on domestic balance sheets. The consumer-driven model cannot be restored, because the problem it faces has nothing to do with the random, temporary shifts in psychology ("animal spirits") that Keynes noted. The problem we face instead is that the accumulation of mistakes and loss of wealth happened just as the baby boomers were about to retire.

The second thing wrong with the administration's present course stems from an insular focus on spurring consumer spending within the United States, the lip service paid to global cooperation notwithstanding. The solution to the savings–investment disparity does not lie in tinkering with government spending but in helping savers and investors come together across national frontiers. We can correct the balance sheets of both the United States and its trading partners by financing the capital markets in places where young people actually live. Barriers of politics, law, regulation, and institutional practice—together with volatile reserve currency—stand between young people who need capital and old people who need investments. These barriers perpetuate the imbalances that the world will have to manage while restoring accountability to Western financial markets. These imbalances can be fixed. The tools to do so are well understood and have been thoroughly tested. But these solutions are at present invisible on the political horizons in Washington. Currency policy is the key to opening the world to American exports. What seem like minor errors in Western monetary policy have devastating effects on developing economies. The large industrial economies are like oceangoing vessels designed to withstand typhoons; ten-meter waves may roil them but will not sink them. Not so for the fragile craft in their wake. As former Federal Reserve chairman Paul Volcker once observed, the deep financial markets of industrial nations allow participants to hedge against large shifts in currency parities. Not so for the shallow, inefficient financial markets of developing nations, in which the vast majority of firms do not qualify as derivative counterparties and the yield curve is not liquid past the two-year mark. A case in point is the Asian financial crisis of 1997.

During the early 1990s, Thailand pegged its baht to the dollar. When the dollar rose sharply against the yen, Thai purchasing power rose sharply against that of Japan, then Thailand's largest trading partner. The rising baht prompted short-term capital flows into Thailand and fueled a real-estate bubble not unlike the United States' bubble of recent years. In Thailand, the bubble collapsed in 1997, and the Thai currency collapsed along with the country's real-estate market and banking system.

China, in particular, is the natural fulcrum for America's proper economic policy. China's requirements for infrastructure and capital equipment are enormous: Two-thirds of its 1.3 billion people still live in conditions of extreme backwardness. But rather than invest in its own interior, China has diverted its savings to securities in Western currencies as a rainy-day hedge against potential political and economic disruption. America should help China stabilize its currency by a solemn and formal agreement to link the renminbi (or yuan, as it is more commonly known) to the dollar; China in turn should make its currency convertible and open its capital market to American institutions. Other countries may wish to participate in this arrangement; with the world's two largest and most dynamic economies as an anchor, a Sino–American currency agreement would quickly become the point of orientation for the rest of Asia and eventually for other countries. China's demand for savings, to be sure, stems in part from its one-child policy, which requires Chinese to provide for their retirement with financial assets rather than offspring. But a good deal of Chinese savings is precautionary. With a nonconvertible currency and limited outlets for investment, Chinese are apt to exaggerate their rainy-day savings. In effect, China needs to reduce its saving rate drastically while America increases hers. Why wouldn't just letting China's currency be convertible on its own, without coordinating with the United States, be part of the solution, as some propose?

The simple answer is that China's capital markets—and, by extension, its political system—are still too fragile to withstand the tsunami-sized capital flows caused by the dollar's instability. Dollar devaluation sends capital rushing into China, distorting asset prices. By contrast, a repetition of the global liquidity crisis that followed the failure of Lehman Brothers could provoke massive capital flows out of China, in a repeat of the 1997 Asian crisis. As long as the United States subjects its currency to extreme volatility, China cannot take the risk of making its own currency convertible. Notwithstanding China's fast economic growth, Beijing is profoundly aware of the dangers to stability that arise from disparities between the country's prosperous coast and backward interior. The Chinese government claims that it is correcting the economic mistakes of fifty years of rigid communism, and it must bet on policies to create employment quickly for about 25 million people every year for the next few years to prevent discontent from boiling over into social unrest.

Yet China does not have the financial, legal, or administrative capacity to match people and capital. Its efforts to spend a fifth of its gross domestic product on infrastructure face enormous problems of governance. In the United States, voters approve public spending at the local level, and the federal system provides checks and balances against abuse of public funds. China, like all emerging countries, must rely on the probity of a small number of officials with enormous power, and the rule of men, instead of the rule of law, is never an effective check against corruption. After Beijing sends a cadre of officials to clean out corruption in a province or an agency, it must send a second group to clean out the corruptions of the first.

Corruption intensifies the risk of political instability because extreme wealth disparities are less tolerable if people perceive them as arbitrary and unrelated to merit and achievement. No developing country has ever overcome corruption by hiring more police. The only way out of the vicious circle is to make it possible to earn more money through honest markets than through corruption. Creating open and efficient capital markets in China will not eliminate corruption, but it will create parallel and ultimately more compelling opportunities. To collaborate with the United States and other Western countries in the development of an internal capital market is profoundly in China's interest. Stabilizing currency parities is not a panacea but a precondition. Establishing the rule of law, eliminating corruption, and deepening financial institutions are indispensable, but confidence in local currencies comes first.

At the same time, America should ease restrictions on Chinese and other foreign investment in American companies. For narrow political reasons, the United States has rebuffed Chinese efforts to acquire equity in major American brands. China wants to reduce its exposure to American debt in favor of equity in firms that produce what it requires: food, energy, minerals, and technology. A crucial part of stabilizing the dollar is to increase global demand for dollars by selling more American assets to reduce America's overhang of foreign debt.

A partnership on this scale would constitute a revolution in American policy. For all its rhetoric about global cooperation, the Obama administration has followed an egregious unilateralism in economic policy, running the federal deficit to 12 percent of gross domestic product in a vain effort to reanimate the atavistic model of a forever-young consumer-based economy. As of the third quarter of 2009, the Federal Reserve was buying Treasury securities at an annual rate of nearly $700 billion, and commercial banks (with cheap funding from the Federal Reserve) were buying Treasuries at an annual rate of $350 billion. Directly and indirectly, the United States is monetizing debt at a trillion-dollar annual rate. Little wonder, then, that the dollar's exchange rate is falling and its status as a reserve currency is in doubt. The trend cannot be sustained. The world eventually will cease accumulating dollar assets, placing America's capacity to finance its deficit in jeopardy.

Opening the world for American exports is half the task. The other half requires restoring the nation's export capacity. Despite the present crisis, America remains the world's strongest platform for innovation. America continues to lead in every field of technology: software, communications equipment, aircraft, biotechnology, and electricity production. China plans to install more than twenty nuclear-power plants per year and could benefit from double that number; America possesses the world's best nuclear-reactor technology but not the capacity to fill Chinese demand. The way to increase American export capacity is economically simple, but it requires visionary political leadership. We have been borrowing in order to consume; we need now to save in order to invest. We need to shift the tax burden, moving it away from savings and investment and toward consumption. We should replace individual and corporate income taxes with consumption-based taxes (value-added and sales taxes). Instead of attempting to revive the dead horse of consumer-driven growth that the present administration is beating, we should make our tax policy encourage savings and investment at the expense of consumption.

If America looks outward, toward the young people of the Global South, rather than inward, toward the exhausted consumers of the baby boom, the ensuing economic boom could outpace the great expansion begun by the Reagan administration. There are close to two billion people in China and the countries in its immediate periphery, and a further 1.1 billion people in India. Half the world's population lives in emerging Asia, and that region's productivity could triple in a generation. America has the capacity to generate innovations and commercialize them in the world's largest and fastest-growing markets. Tax and monetary policy can create a conveyor belt that takes American innovations and turns them into productivity gains among billions of people in the Global South. Out of the present crisis, the world might enjoy one of the longest and fastest economic booms in history. Or it might remain in an economic mire for the foreseeable future.

Part Seven

Endings

CHAPTER 26

Overcoming Ethnicity

Never have things been better for one half of humankind, and never have things been worse for the other. The decisive divide in today's world lies between nations that have a future and nations that don't. Contrary to the prevailing pragmatism, which demands that we take every society on its own terms, an objective criterion has emerged that does not easily fade in the wash—namely, the desire to live. Samuel Huntington did the world an enormous service by changing the subject from comparative social systems to civilizations based on religion. His book *The Clash of Civilizations and the Remaking of World Order* (1996) reintroduced into geopolitics a radically tragic dimension that statesmen have yet to embrace. "The Iraq war was the supreme expression of the belief that Islamic civilizations are not different from Western ones in any fundamental way. It was the expression not of a hard-headed doctrine but of a woolly-minded one and, as such, a repudiation of ideas Huntington held his whole life," Christopher Caldwell observed in the *Financial Times* on January 2, 2008. After boldly introducing the subject, Huntington unfortunately left the next set of questions to forage for themselves. That great incompatibilities exist between some civilizations and others is an important insight.

Why do some civilizations, for example "Confucian" (that is, Chinese) and Western, seem highly compatible, while others, such as Western and Islamic, appear condemned to clash? A three-stage answer is required to answer the great question that Huntington left open. First, why do civilizations exist? Second, by what criteria can we judge their success or failure? Third, why should their goals conflict with each other?

I submit that the basis for our great civilizations (Judeo-Christian, Chinese, Hindu, Islamic) is existential. Civilizations exist because men wish to overcome death and have learned that ties of blood and language are not sufficient to win immortality. They require a form of social organization that rises above mere ethnicity, that promises a higher form of continuity between the dead and the yet unborn. But supplanting the ties of blood and language is a daunting task at which most civilizations ultimately fail. Half of the world's population now lives in three supraethnic states—that is, states in which citizenship has no ethnic connotation. These are China, India, and the United States. The three great supraethnic states are internally stable and have little cause for conflict anywhere on their borders, let alone with each other. Empires have existed throughout recorded history but always with fragile borders and mortal conflict with their rivals. In addition to the three billion inhabitants of China, India, and the United States, we may add nearly another billion people on China's periphery whose prospects for peace and prosperity are robust thanks to the strength of the supraethnic states. This is a great turn for the better in the blood-soaked history of humankind. During the long darkness of prehistory, two-fifths of males could expect to die violently in every generation. War has overshadowed human society throughout all of history but less so today than ever before. Most of humanity lives in states where each man may sit under his own vine and fig tree, and there is none to make him afraid. In other parts of the world life is less secure than it ever has been. For the first time in recorded history, most of the world's peoples are failing of their desire to live. All right-thinking people believe in "the equal rights of nations large and small," in the words of the United Nations charter—in short, they believe that every nation and every culture has equal rights to recognition, security, and dignity. The UN charter responded to the predation of powerful empires on nations that very much wanted to live. Today the existential threat to most of the world's peoples comes not from without but from within. A majority of earth's cultures is at risk of demographic death.

As I have discussed throughout this book, half of the world's languages will disappear by the end of the twenty-first century and up to 90 percent by the end of the twenty-second. The majority of these are spoken by a few hundred people each in the New Guinea highlands, and the rest are scattered around the pockets of humanity left behind by the global economy. A small army of ethnologists is trying to record and analyze the thousands of languages that will fall silent forever during the next two or three generations. It is not only the languages of primitive peoples that are endangered. Countries in which communism extirpated religion face catastrophic rates of population decline. A century from now, a geriatric remnant may be the only speakers of Latvian, Estonian, Lithuanian, Ukrainian, Georgian, and other secondary but significant Western languages.

The prospective extinction of nations, cultures, and languages has become the leading source of instability for the twenty-first century. Never before in human history have so many people held their lives so cheap. Among other things, this explains why suicide has become a widespread technique of war fighting for the first time. The phenomenon has become so widespread that it begs for a neologism. For lack of a better word, we shall call it "ethnosuicide." Europe is at peace for the first time in its history, such that the bestselling book on current European history is James Sheehan's *Where Have All the Soldiers Gone? The Transformation of Modern Europe* (2008). A better question is, "Where have all the Europeans gone?" Europe is at peace but not secure, for most European nations have birthrates so low that they will lose economic viability within the next fifty to hundred years.

Wealthy Europe stands on the same side of a global divide with the endangered peoples of the New Guinea highlands and the disappearing languages of the Siberian taiga. Europe is ill at ease over the attenuation of its culture in the face of mass immigration from the Middle East and Africa, an immigration that the Old World needs in order to replace its own declining ranks but that threatens to destroy its identity. Radical Islam would be a minor footnote if not for the possibility that Europe may be ruled by a Muslim majority a century hence, and that the Islamicization of Europe may give new impulse to a religion that elsewhere is immured in economic backwardness. Why have so many branches of the human family lost the will to live? And what does the despair of Stone Age peoples in New Guinea have in common with the despair of modern peoples who choose not to reproduce? The answer, as I have argued in this book, is that mortality becomes unbearable in the face of modernity. Sentience of morality distinguishes us from lower animals. From the sentience of mortality arises culture—the capacity to order our behavior consciously rather than by instinct. Unlike animals, human beings require more than progeny: They require progeny who remember them. To overcome mortality we create culture, a dialogue among generations that links the dead with the yet unborn. Whether or not we pray to a personal god or confess a particular religion, the existential question remains the same. Without the hope of immortality we cannot bear mortality. Cultures that have lost the hope of immortality also lose the will to live. Culture is the stuff out of which we weave the perception of immortality. With sad frequency, ethnic groups will die rather than abandon their way of life. Historic tragedy occurs on the grand scale when economic or strategic circumstances undercut the material conditions of the life of a people, which nonetheless cannot accept assimilation into another culture. That is when entire peoples fight to the death.

We cannot make a future for ourselves without our past. All cultures worship at the shrine of their ancestors. They exist to ward off the presentiment of death. Breaking continuity with the past implies that our lives have no meaning past our own physical existence. If we do not continue the lives of those who preceded us, nor prepare the lives of those who will follow us, then we are defined by our physical existence and nothing more. In that case we will seek to maximize our pleasure. It is perfectly possible for entire peoples to live only for their own pleasure and feel nothing for their prospective obliteration. How else should we explain fertility rates in Europe and Japan at barely half of replacement? The world wars discredited their traditional cultures, and their populations do not appear concerned about their own survival. That cannot, of course, be typical of the human condition or there would be no human race to begin with. Ethnosuicide follows on the death of faith in the future. My research supports the conclusions of Philip Longman, George Weigel, and others who link the respective declines of belief and birthrates.

But what belief is in question? The families of humankind have learned to believe in only two things: a supernatural god, or themselves. (For most of history, we worshiped ourselves, or what amounts to the same thing, our image in nature). Our ancestors cheated death through the perpetuation of blood and culture. They could step outside their own culture as little as animals could shed their instincts. In peril of their lives, men marched to war and women gave birth to perpetuate their tribes, without second thoughts, indeed without the capacity for second thoughts. Not until late antiquity does universal empire encroach on the prerogative of tribe in culture, first with Alexander and then with Rome. With the advent of empire, the peoples for the first time considered their mortality from the vantage point of a social entity not restricted to race. And with it also comes, among the Hellenistic and Roman upper classes, the first attenuation of the will to live. How the encroachment of empire in late antiquity might have influenced the will to live of tribes whose names we barely know and whose customs and language are lost forever, we only can guess. But we know that mere ethnicity no longer is a credible vehicle for continuity in a world dominated by supraethnic states.

A great gulf is fixed between the successful supraethnic states and the ethnicities marking time until they die out of ennui and self-loathing. Ethnicity is fading as a credible basis for personal identity or national life, for the nations have learned that they are mortal, and their sentience of mortality is a sorrow too great to bear. The love of the peoples for their own nation was "sweet and pregnant with the presentiment of death" in 1919 when Franz Rosenzweig considered the consequences of the First World War, in which all the nations of Europe fought unashamedly for their own supremacy.

But the presentiment of death has turned into a bitter, earthen taste in the mouths of the nations, who have lost the illusions that sustained their national lives during the past two centuries. Europe's Second Thirty Years' War, of 1914–1945, destroyed the nations' pretensions to eternal life in their own ethnic skin. It is not only that nationalism is dead; nationalism itself carries the taste of death, for the nations—"a drop of the bucket" and "dust on the balances"— must perish.

Only one nation conceives of itself as eternal, and that is Israel, whose belief that God's love for its ancestor establishes its immortality beyond the death of the universe itself (Psalm 102). In the West, nations came by the hope of immortality through Christianity, which offered the eternal promise of Israel to the Gentiles, but only on the condition that they cease to be Gentiles, through adoption into an Israel of the Spirit. Israel is the exception that proves the rule, the single universal nation whose purpose is the eventual recognition of the one God by all of humankind. The history of the world is the story of man's search for eternity. That is what Rosenzweig meant when he said that the history of humanity is the history of Israel. It is not the tiny Jewish nation, but rather the promise of eternal life vouchsafed first to the Jews, that stands at the center of Western history. Christian Europe came into being by absorbing invader and indigenous alike into a supraethnic Christian empire whose universality was expressed by a single religious leader whose authority transcended kingdoms, a single church, and a single language for liturgy and learning. Europe arose from universal Christian empire and it fell when the nationalities mutinied against their foster mother the Church and fought until their mutual ruin.

Hilaire Belloc's famous quip—"Europe is the faith, the faith is Europe"—was precisely correct. Europe came into being before a single Frenchmen or German was born, at the crowning of Charlemagne as Holy Roman emperor in AD 800. Voltaire was only partly correct—the Holy Roman Empire was neither Roman nor an empire, but it was holy. European monarchs donned the robes of ancient Rome like small children playing dress-up, and the power of their emperors was more symbolic than real. But the unifying concept of Christendom is what made it possible to create nations out of the detritus of Rome and the rabble of invading barbarians.

Why do European nations exist in opposition to Europe? The fact that they do is, I believe, a measure not of Europe's political maturity but rather of its decadence. The German language in its modern form was born at the court of Emperor Charles IV at Prague, when Teutonic grammar was standardized on the Latin mold. Dante Latinized his local Tuscan dialect to create an "eloquent vulgate." The Catholic monarchs imposed the Castilian language on the fractious Iberian tribes, without complete success, as the survival of philological relics such as Catalan and Galician makes clear. Why is there a Germany and not merely a Brandenburg, Bavaria, Franconia, Swabia, and Hanseatic League? Why is there a Spain and not merely a Navarra, Andalusia, and Castile? It is because European languages and European literature made possible a common discourse within the great national divisions. Europe's common faith and the institutions that supported it created this common culture as an expedient for worship and administration. Europe *is* the faith, for the faith gave birth to Europe. Under church and empire, the nations owed fealty to a higher power by virtue of the authority of faith. Its common language was Latin, and its ultimate authority was pope rather than emperor. The empire was weak, but it was holy, as a series of German emperors discovered when they attempted to substitute their own secular power for the ultimate authority of faith. Henry IV stood bareheaded in the snow for three days waiting for Pope Gregory VII to reverse his excommunication in 1077; the Staufen dynasty came to a terrible end after its prolonged war with the papacy in the second half of the thirteenth century. Without the faith, Europe's civil society could not exist, and a challenger to the authority of faith, no matter how powerful, ultimately would have had to fail.

Nationalism as an antipode to empire did not effervesce from the rising bourgeoisie or develop out of Protestantism. It was the invention of Cardinal Richelieu during the reign of Louis XIII, as I have explained. Richelieu for the first time proposed that the welfare of Christendom could be represented in a single European nation, whose particular interests thus defined the interests of the Christian world. Europe's nationalism of the nineteenth century was a response to France, specifically to Richelieu's successor Napoleon Bonaparte. One can trace the roots of nationalism to Romantic interest in the songs and stories of the European peoples, to Johann Herder and Johann Fichte, and so forth—but it should be remembered that the "Romantics" took their name from Rome. Their object was to renew the medieval Church. When Napoleon invaded the rest of Europe with a mass popular army, the other nations of Europe responded by creating mass armies. German nationalism was born at the Battle of Leipzig in 1813, when all Germany stood on the same field for the first time since the Thirty Years' War—but this time on grounds of sovereignty, not of religion. Ethnically defined nationalism led Europe into the First and Second World Wars, from which it has not recovered, and from whose wounds it yet might die. Europe's secular nationalism stands in contrast to popular sovereignty on a Christian foundation in the United States—it was not just "the people," though, but what Abraham Lincoln called an "almost chosen people" that made this possible.

The mantle of Christian empire passed to the United States of America, which is Christian by construction if not by constitution. The notion of national sovereignty that replaced the Christian empire as Europe's defining principle after the Treaty of Westphalia in 1648 overthrew the foundation on which Europe was built. The founding of America as a nonethnic state restored it, in a sturdier form. America and China have nothing of importance to quarrel over, and an innate affinity for each other. China was never a nation but a cultural construct uniting many tongues and tribes through a unified administrative platform and philosophy.

Francesco Sisci, *La Stampa*'s Asia editor and a frequent contributor to *Asia Times Online*, argues persuasively that Christianity will play a crucial role in unifying China in the future. China's rate of Christian evangelization, moreover, may make China the fulcrum of Christian life within a generation or two. India is the hybrid of an ancient civilization embracing thirty modern languages, united by the Anglo-Saxon import of parliamentary democracy. The adaptation of Hindu civilization to modern democratic governance is one of the miracles of modern times, and India's prosperity and stability are not in question. Islamic civilization remains the great frustration of world polity.

Islam parodies Christianity. Christianity proposes to incorporate all of humanity into the new People of God, by effecting an inner transformation of every individual. By this transformation, Christians believe, all of humanity can become holy. Islam offers a universal religion not of inner transformation but of obedience. Precisely this form of surface universalism ensures that Muslims carry the baggage of traditional life into the new religion, for it offers no point of departure from traditional society. As a universal religion, Islam can only universalize the aspirations of the tribes

356

it assimilates, rather than transform them, and it cannot rid itself of its pagan heritage. Instead, it lashes out against the encroachment of more adaptive civilizations: Western, Chinese, and Hindu. The Great Divergence separates the supraethnic states—America, China, and India—from the vulnerable ethnicities of the world. All ethnic states are failed states or eventually failed states.

There is one exception, and that is Israel, for Israel does not understand itself as a nation like other nations but rather as a bridge, between man and the eternal, over which all of humanity ultimately shall pass. I do not think it is a coincidence that, of all the world's industrial nations, only Israel and the United States have a positive population growth rate. In some cases a sick culture may recover; in other cases it is possible only to make the patient comfortable. Statecraft cannot decide ex ante which cultures should persist and which should disappear; no human agency has the authority, much less the right, to condemn peoples, languages, and cultures to the dustbin of history. By the same token, if whole peoples lose the desire to continue and they insist on disappearing, no outside agency can stop them from doing so. Managed mortality is the correct response of statecraft to the self-destructive impulses of peoples who no longer wish to exist. A healthy polity has the responsibility to prevent terminally ill neighbors from dragging it down with them. The type of man we encounter in the dying nations, not only in the remote rivulets of the human current but on the Baltic, the Black Sea, and the Sea of Japan, is a stranger to modern social science. He is neither Sigmund Freud's man, driven by libido, nor economic man, pursuing utility. He is averse not to life's hardships and dangers but to life itself, for he rejects life precisely at a moment when hardship and danger have begun to fade. He suffers from the restless heart that St Augustine ascribes to those who are far from God.

The world's political future depends not on the character of sovereign states but on the character of supraethnic states, as much as it depended on the character of Christian empire a thousand years ago. The heritage of Western thought prepares us inadequately for these questions, but Augustine is not a bad place to start.

CHAPTER 27

The Happiest Country in the World

Envy surrounds no country on earth as it does the state of Israel, and with good reason: Nearing the sixty-fifth anniversary of its founding, this country is, by objective measures, the happiest nation on earth. It is one of the wealthiest, freest, and best educated, and it enjoys a higher life expectancy than Germany or the Netherlands. But most remarkable is that Israelis appear to love life and hate death more than any other nation. If history is made not by rational design but by the demands of the human heart, as I have argued, the light heart of the Israelis in the face of continuous danger is a singularity worthy of a closer look.

Can it be a coincidence that this most ancient of nations, and the only nation persuaded that it was summoned into history for God's service, consists of individuals who appear to love life more than any other people? As a simple index of life-preference, I plot the fertility rate versus the suicide rate of thirty-five industrial countries—that is, the proportion of people who choose to create new life against the proportion who choose to destroy their own. Israel stands alone, positioned in the upper left-hand quadrant, or life-loving, portion of the chart.

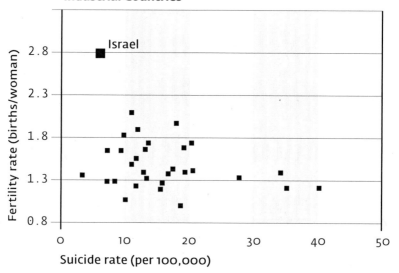

Loving Life versus Loving Death

Fertility Rate versus Suicide Rate in 35 Selected Industrial Countries

Source: United Nations

Those who believe in Israel's divine election might see a special grace reflected in its love of life. In a world given over to morbidity, the state of Israel still teaches the world love of life, not in the trivial sense of joie de vivre but rather as a solemn celebration of life. I argued, "It's easy for the Jews to talk about delighting in life. They are quite sure that they are eternal, while other peoples tremble at the prospect of impending extinction. It is not their individual lives

Suicide and Fertility Rate
of 35 Selected Industrial Countries

	Suicide Rate (per 100,000)	Fertility Rate
Israel	6.2	2.77
United States	11	2.1
France	18	1.98
Iceland	12	1.91
Ireland	9.7	1.85
Denmark	13.6	1.74
Finland	20.3	1.73
Serbia	19.3	1.69
Sweden	13.2	1.67
Netherlands	9.3	1.66
United Kingdom	7	1.66
Canada	11.6	1.57
Portugal	11	1.49
Switzerland	17.4	1.44
Estonia	20.3	1.42
Croatia	19.6	1.41
Germany	13	1.41
Bulgaria	13	1.4
Russia	34.3	1.4
Austria	16.9	1.38
Greece	3.2	1.36
Hungary	27.7	1.34
Slovakia	13.3	1.34
Italy	7.1	1.3
Spain	8.2	1.3
Poland	15.9	1.27
Slovenia	25.6	1.27
Ukraine	23.8	1.25
Bosnia	11.8	1.24
Belarus	35.1	1.23
Czech Republic	15.5	1.23
Japan	24	1.22
Lithuania	40.2	1.22
Singapore	10.1	1.08
Hong Kong	18.6	1.08

Source: United Nations

that the Jews find so pleasant but rather the notion of a covenantal life that proceeds uninterrupted through the generations." Still, it is remarkable to observe by how wide a margin the Israelis win the global-happiness sweepstakes. Israel is surrounded by neighbors willing to kill themselves in order to destroy it. "As much as you love life, we love death," Muslim clerics teach; the same formula is found in a Palestinian textbook for second-graders. Apart from the fact that the Arabs are among the least free, least educated, and (apart from the oil states) poorest peoples in the world, they also are the unhappiest, even in their wealthiest kingdoms. The contrast between Israeli happiness and Arab despondency is what makes peace an elusive goal in the region. It cannot be attributed to material conditions of life. Oil-rich Saudi Arabia ranks 171st on an international quality-of-life index, below Rwanda. Israel is tied with Singapore on this index, although it should be observed that Israel ranks a runaway first on my life-preference index, whereas Singapore comes in dead last.

Even less can we blame unhappiness on experience, for no nation in living memory has suffered more than the Jews, and none has a better excuse to be miserable. Arabs did not invent suicide attacks, but they have produced a population pool willing to die in order to inflict damage greater than any in history. One cannot help but conclude that Muslim clerics do not exaggerate when they express contempt for life. Israel's love of life, moreover, is more than an ethnic characteristic. Those who know Jewish life through the eccentric lens of Jewish American novelists such as Saul Bellow and Philip Roth, or through the films of Woody Allen, imagine the Jews to be an angst-ridden race of neurotics. Secular Jews in America are no more fertile than their Gentile peers, and are by all indications quite as miserable.

For one thing, Israelis are far more religious than American Jews.

Two-thirds of Israelis believe in God, although only a quarter observe their religion strictly. Even Israelis averse to religion evince a different kind of secularism than we find in the secular West. They speak the language of the Bible and undergo twelve years of Bible studies in state elementary and secondary schools. Faith in God's enduring love for a people that believes it was summoned out of a slave rabble for his purposes must be part of the explanation. The most religious Israelis make the most babies. Ultra-Orthodox families produce nine children on average. That should be no surprise, for people of faith in general are more fertile than secular people, as I have argued. Traditional and modern societies have radically different population profiles. In traditional society, women have little choice but to spend their lives pregnant. In the modern world, where fertility reflects choice rather than compulsion, the choice to raise children expresses love of life. The high birthrate in Arab countries still bound by tradition does not stand comparison to Israeli fertility, by far the highest in the modern world.

The faith of Israelis is unique. Jews sailed to Palestine as an act of faith, to build a state against enormous odds and in the face of hostile encirclement, joking, "You don't have to be crazy to be a Zionist, but it helps." In 1903, Theodor Herzl, the Zionist movement's secular founder, secured British support for a Jewish state in Uganda, but his movement shouted him down, for nothing short of the return to Zion of biblical prophecy would requite it. In place of a modern language the Jewish settlers revived Hebrew, a liturgical rather than a quotidian language since the fourth century BC, in a feat of linguistic volition without precedent. It may be that faith burns brighter in Israel because Israel was founded by a leap of faith. Two old Jewish jokes illustrate the Israeli frame of mind. Two elderly Jewish ladies are sitting on a park bench in St Petersburg, Florida.

"Mrs. Levy," asks the first, "what do you hear from your son Isaac in Detroit?" "It's just awful," Mrs. Levy replies. "His wife died a year ago and left him with two little girls. Now he's lost his job as an accountant with an auto-parts company, and his health insurance will lapse in a few weeks. With the real-estate market the way it is, he can't even sell his house. And the baby has come down with leukemia and needs expensive treatment. He's beside himself and doesn't know what to do. But does he write a beautiful Hebrew letter—it's a pleasure to read." There are layers to this joke, but the relevant one here is that bad news is softened if written in the language of the Bible, which to Jews always conveys hope.

The second joke involves the American businessman who emigrated to Israel shortly after its founding. On his arrival, he orders a telephone, and waits for weeks without a response. At length he applies in person to the telephone company and is shown into the office of an official who explains that there is a two-year waiting list and no way to jump the queue. "Do you mean there is no hope?" the American asks. "It is forbidden for a Jew to say there is no hope!" thunders the official. "No chance, maybe." Hope transcends probability.

If faith makes the Israelis happy, then why are the Arabs, whose observance of Islam seems so much stricter, so miserable? Islam offers its adherents not love—for Allah does not reveal Himself in love after the fashion of YHWH—but rather success. The Islamic world cannot endure without confidence in victory, that to "come to prayer" is the same thing as to "come to success." Humiliation—the perception that the ummah cannot reward those who submit to it—is beyond its capacity to endure. Islam, or "submission," does not understand faith—trust in a loving God even when His actions appear incomprehensible—in the manner of Jews and Christians. Because the whim of Allah controls every event from the orbit of

each electron to the outcome of battles, Muslims know only success or failure at each moment in time. The military, economic, and
cultural failures of Islamic societies are intolerable in Muslim eyes;
Jewish success is an abomination, for in the view of Muslims it is the
due of the faithful, to be coveted and seized from the usurpers at the
first opportunity. It is not too much of a stretch to assert that Israel's
love of life, its happiness in faith, is precisely the characteristic that
makes a regional peace impossible to achieve. The usurpation of the
happiness that Muslims believe is due to them is sufficient cause
to kill one's self in order to take happiness away from the Jewish
enemy. If Israel's opponents fail to ruin Israel's happiness, there is
at least a spark of hope that they may decide to choose happiness
for themselves.

Why are none of the Christian nations as happy as Israel? Few
of the European nations can be termed "Christian" at all. Poland,
the last European country with a high rate of attendance at Mass
(at about 45 percent), nonetheless shows a fertility rate of only 1.27,
one of Europe's lowest, and a relatively high suicide rate of 16 per
100,000 (versus nine per 100,000 in the United Kingdom). Europe's faith always wavered between adherence to Christianity as
a universal religion and ethnic idolatry under a Christian veneer.
European nationalism nudged Christianity to the margin during
the nineteenth century, and the disastrous world wars of the past
century left Europeans with confidence neither in Christianity nor
in their own nationhood. Only in pockets of the American population does one find birthrates comparable to Israel's—for example,
among evangelical Christians. There is no direct way to compare
the happiness of Israelis and American Christians, but the tumultu-
ous and protean character of American religion is not as congenial
to personal satisfaction. My suspicion is that Israel's happiness is

entirely unique. It is fashionable these days to speculate about the end of Israel, and Israel's strategic position presents scant cause for optimism. Israel's future depends on the Israelis. During two thousand years of exile, Jews remained Jews despite forceful and often violent efforts to make them into Christians or Muslims. One has to suppose that they did not abandon Judaism because they liked being Jewish. With utmost sincerity, the Jews prayed thrice daily: "It is our duty to praise the Master of all, to acclaim the greatness of the One who forms all creation, for God did not make us like the nations of other lands, and did not make us the same as other families of the Earth. God did not place us in the same situations as others, and our destiny is not the same as anyone else's."

How does it stand with the people Israel in the New Year 5770? As James Kugel, a Harvard scholar of the Hebrew Bible, explained in a lecture at my synagogue on Israel's Independence Day, for most of Jewish history *independence* was an alien idea. Except for a few decades of the Davidic kingdom, the Jewish commonwealth always paid tribute to the surrounding powers—Egypt, Assyria, Babylon, or Rome. Israel still faces an existential threat, but this should not obscure the fact that the position of the Jewish people today is at least as strong as ever before. Jews who have kept the faith in Israel as well as in the Diaspora have reason to look happily toward the new year. Israel's detractors, including defeatists on the American Jewish left, tell a tale of woe in support of one-sided Israeli concessions to Palestinian opponents whose main interest in gaining territory appears to be to fire more rockets at Israeli cities. In the absence of a permanent peace settlement, they say, Israelis will eventually abandon the country in despair, its economy will collapse under the weight of military expenditures, and the higher Arab birthrate will turn Israel into an apartheid island in a Muslim sea. But this gloomy view is wrong. Israeli fertility, at nearly three children per woman, is by far the highest in the industrial world. It has stabilized at a high level, moreover, while the fertility of its Muslim neighbors is in freefall.

Total Fertility, Israel and Selected Muslim Countries

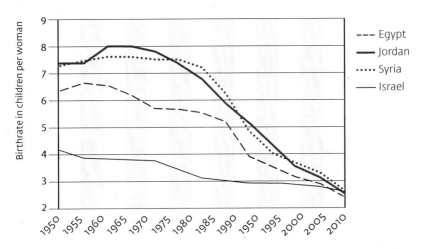

Source: United Nations

No data exist for West Bank demographics, for the Palestine Authority has invented more than a million "refugees" who do not exist, either because they never were born or because they have emigrated. It is a fair supposition that the West Bank birthrate also is in freefall. For poor countries, a sudden transition from ten-person to four-person families implies a coming social catastrophe in which a smaller base of young people will have to support a huge aging population. No nation in the world has survived this kind of demographic shock, and the prognosis for political stability in such countries is not good. Israel, by contrast, has the healthiest population pyramid in the industrial world.

Fears that immigration to Israel would dry up or even reverse, moreover, seem fanciful in light of the recently available 2008 data. Net immigration to Israel has recovered and is rising.

Israeli Immigration
Net Migrants Per 1.000 Population

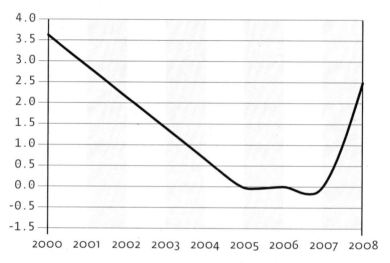

Source: Government of Israel

Israelis come to Israel, stay, and raise families because they love life. In fact, there is a statistically significant relationship between the two variables (among the industrial nations, the higher the fertility rate, the lower the suicide rate).

Israel lies in a region of its own. Only Greece has a lower suicide rate, but Greece also has a fertility rate of only 1.3. Why the Jews love life and hate death more than other peoples can be argued.

Goethe's devil said it best, perhaps, in his exchange with Faust, which I quoted earlier but will again here. What Faust wants is not the money, fame, and women that Mephistopheles proposes, and not even enlightenment, but rather life itself:

> What is apportioned to all humankind,
> Would I enjoy in my inmost self,
> Grasp the highest and lowest with my spirit,
> And bring their weal and woe into my own breast.

Mephistopheles responds to this with astonishment and contempt. Mere mortals, he tells Faust, cannot digest life:

> Believe me, who for millennia past
> Has chewed on this hard crust:
> From cradle to the grave
> No man ever has been able to digest this sourdough!
> Believe our kind: this whole
> Was made only for a God!
> He basks in light eternal.
> Us he brought down into darkness,
> While all you get is—day and night.

Life as such, with its messy birth, fears, uncertainties, and painful death, doesn't really appeal to human beings: "It was made only for a god," as Mephistopheles said. What makes life enjoyable is the sanctification of life, and the Jews, whose religion consists of bringing what is holy into the smallest acts of everyday life, seem to like life the best. The chorus in Sophocles' play *Oedipus at Colonus* agrees with Mephistopheles:

Not to be born at all
Is best, far best that can befall.
Next best, when born, with least delay
To trace the backward way.
For when youth passes with its giddy train,
Troubles on troubles follow, toils on toils,
Pain, pain for ever pain; and none escapes life's coils.
Envy, sedition, strife,
Carnage and war make up the tale of life.

To this, an old Jewish joke responds, "Perhaps it's better not to be born at all, but who has such luck? Not one in ten thousand."

Contrary to what Israel's detractors foreign as well as homegrown have claimed, time is on Israel's side. The population data suggest that its Muslim adversaries (to paraphrase Oscar Wilde) are going from infancy to senescence without passing through maturity. They are going directly from the rigid world of traditional society to the sex, drugs, and rock and roll that so appeal to the infertile young people of Iran. Israel's economy is a source of astonishment, a high-tech miracle that draws more private-equity investment than all of Europe. None of this can erase the fact that Israel is under existential threat, above all from Iran and its proxies in Lebanon and Gaza. But Israel has always been under existential threat. There were a couple of years, immediately after the late Egyptian leader Anwar Sadat made peace with Israel and while Iran and Iraq were at war with each other, in which the Jewish state could breathe more easily, but the threat never really disappeared. There is something about living on the land bridge between Europe, Africa, and Asia that creates insecurity. If the Israelis are the happiest country on earth, as the numbers indicate, it seems possible that they will do what is required to keep their country, despite the odds against them. I do not know whether they will succeed. If Israel fails, however, the rest of the world will lose a unique gauge of the human capacity for happiness as well as faith. I cannot conceive of a sadder event.

When the Jews say that God has sustained them for well over three millennia, they do not, strictly speaking, refer to any direct supernatural intervention—not, at least, after the destruction of the walls of Jericho around 2300 BCE. There are no miracles associated with the reign of King David or King Solomon; on the contrary, what makes David's story so credible is that in it, alone among all the chronicles of the early first millennium, supernatural events play no role whatsoever. The later miracles of the prophets Elijah and Elisha inspired faith but had no direct bearing on the battlefield. The miracle associated with the expulsion of the Seleucid king Antiochus Epiphanes in 164 BCE was not the military victory of the Maccabees—that was the work of human hands and iron weapons—but rather that a day's worth of sanctified oil lasted for eight during the rededication of the Temple at Jerusalem. God is not mentioned in the account of Jewish escape from genocide in the Book of Esther.

The miracle of Jewish survival is to be found in the love of life itself. That is not the dancing to bazouki music amid broken glass that one finds in the novels of Kazantzakis (Greek fertility at 1.3 is among the lowest in the world) but a deep and solemn joy that arises from cleaving to *ha-Kadosh baruch Hu*, as observant Jews refer to God in ordinary discourse: the Holy One, Blessed be He, the wholly Other, whose throne is hidden behind clouds and whose footstool is the world, who wears the universe like a suit of clothing and will replace it when it wears out—but who, with incomprehensible grace, concerns Himself with humankind, and in particular with Abraham and his descendants. The Jews have survived, first of all, because they wished to survive: What so often is called the "miracle of Jewish survival" arises from the Jewish sense of sanctity itself. Jewish demographics support this conclusion. Nonobservant Jews in the United States have the lowest fertility rate of any ethnic group, at around 1.1 children per woman, while Modern Orthodox Jews have between three and four children, and the ultra-Orthodox seven or more. Love of life (manifested in love of children) correlates not with Jewish ethnicity but with Jewish religion.

Worship yourself and you become the god that failed. That is the epitaph for most of the world's peoples, who fought for their place in the sun and now are dying slowly of their own disappointment. Satanic laughter accompanies them to their long sleep in the dust. "Life was made for a god!" the devil says, "and now that you know that your own self-worship involved a case of mistaken identity, why live?" More than ever, Franz Rosenzweig's formulation applies: The Jews, by their persistence through the millennia, stand surety for God's promise to the rest of humankind. And that is why Israel is so precious. The state of Israel may or may not be a light unto the nations; it may or may not be the cleverest, the most cultured, or the most humane of all nations. But the Jewish people in their national life are a unique, living repository of the hopes of all peoples. If the implacable grudge that the dying bear against the living succeeds in destroying this state, mankind's store of hope will be reduced by an irreplaceable margin.

Acknowledgments

René van Praag envisioned this book, and Diederik Boomsma, the editor of this volume, took on the Herculean labor of reviewing hundreds of essays published over the span of a decade and redacting them into a coherent narrative. I owe them an enormous debt of gratitude for their perspicacity and hard work. And I am grateful to Chris Rutenfrans, who as editorial page editor of *de Volkskrant* arranged the Dutch-language publication of some of my essays. Chris introduced my work to René van Praag and thus stood godfather to this book. Nicholas Frankovich proofread the manuscript expertly and made numerous improvements, and Rob Fellman executed a precise second proof.

To the former editor of *Asia Times Online*, Allen Quicke (1953–2010), and his successor, Anthony Allison, I owe the opportunity to develop the "Spengler" essays over the past decade. Joseph Bottum, then editor at *First Things* magazine, commissioned and edited several essays included in the present volume. Conversations and correspondence with friends too numerous to cite contributed to this book; it would be unfair not to mention Dr. Norman A. Bailey, Prof. Reuven Brenner, Prof. Gabrielle Brenner, Prof. Anna Geifman, Prof. Russell Hittinger, Prof. David Layman, Michael Ledeen, Herbert E. Meyer, Uwe von Parpart, Daniel Pipes, Prof. Carl Schachter (from whom I first learned about the dual nature of musical time), Rabbi Meir Soloveichik, George Weigel, and Prof. Michael Wyschogrod. Some of those I should wish to thank the most I cannot mention by name, for I know them as screen names at the *Asia Times Online* readers' forum. Many of them have professional backgrounds in fields that I address, and they have kept me on my toes and given me insights throughout.